Improving Assessment Through Student Involvement

Practical solutions for aiding learning in higher and further education

Nancy Falchikov

RoutledgeFalmer
Taylor & Francis Group

LONDON AND NEW YORK

First published 2005   CR/CW
by RoutledgeFalmer
2 Park Square, Milton Park, Abingdon, Oxon OX14 4RN

Simultaneously published in the USA and Canada
by RoutledgeFalmer
270 Madison Ave, New York, NY 10016

RoutledgeFalmer is an imprint of the Taylor & Francis Group

© 2005 Nancy Falchikov

The right of Nancy Falchikov to be identified as the Author of this
Work has been asserted by her in accordance with the Copyright,
Designs and Patents Act 1988

Typeset in Palatino by
Newgen Imaging Systems (P) Ltd, Chennai, India
Printed and bound in Great Britain by
MPG Books Ltd, Bodmin

British Library Cataloguing in Publication Data
A catalogue record for this book is available
from the British Library

Library of Congress Cataloging in Publication Data
Falchikov, Nancy, 1939–
    Improving assessment through student involvement: practical solutions
for learning in higher and further education / Nancy Falchikov.
        p. cm.
    Includes bibliographical references and index.
    1. College students – Rating of. 2. Educational tests and measurements.
3. Student participation in administration. I. Title.

LB2368.F35 2004   2004006775

ISBN 0–415–30820–8 (hbk)
ISBN 0–415–30821–6 (pbk)

Improving Assessment Through Student Involvement

The assessment of students is an activity central to the role of any professional in further and higher education, and is an area that is the subject of constant innovation and debate.

This book provides a scholarly account of the many facets of assessment, with a particular focus on student involvement. Peer and self-assessment are powerful assessment tools to add to the existing tutor-based methods of assessment and feedback, and this book is a comprehensive guide to the methods and issues involved.

Practical and accessible in style, yet grounded in research and rich in evidence-based material, *Improving Assessment Through Student Involvement* will be valued by all FE or HE professionals wanting to enhance both the effectiveness and quality of their assessment methods.

Nancy Falchikov is a respected authority on peer assessment, and worked for many years as a teacher and researcher in higher education. She has written widely on assessment matters, and is the author of *Learning Together: Peer Tutoring in Higher Education* (RoutledgeFalmer).

Contents

Preface

What this book is about

This book is about how students have been, are, and may be involved in assessment. As the title indicates, it is my belief that the process of assessment itself may be improved by student involvement, and that student learning may also benefit. In Chapter 1, we look at the seven pillars of assessment, on which the canopy of assessment rests. These pillars apply to all types of assessment, not merely those involving students. Seven questions are answered, relating to why how and what we assess, when we carry out assessments, who does the assessing and how well it is done. The final question, 'Whither?', asks what do we might do and where we might go next.

Chapter 2 poses the question, 'What's wrong with traditional assessment?' Some limitations of traditional assessment are considered, beginning with a review of reliability and bias in teacher and examiner marking. Not only is this issue important in its own right, it also has implications for testing the reliability or validity of self- or peer assessment. Typically, when students are involved in assessment, teacher marks are used as the standard against which student-generated marks are compared. Negative side effects of traditional assessment are discussed, including a brief exploration of the relationship between traditional assessment and academic dishonesty. The chapter concludes with a consideration of the role of the Internet in both facilitating and helping detect cheating, and advice to practitioners on this topic.

In Chapter 3, 'Changing definitions of assessment', conceptions are traced through three phases defined by Pearson *et al.* (2001); 'assessment as measurement', 'assessment as procedure' and 'assessment as enquiry'. In addition, I argue that we have already entered a fourth phase, 'assessment as quality control', which seems to be co-existing with other phases, particularly assessment as enquiry. I ask how it is that assessment as enquiry and assessment as quality control co-exist. What is the balance between them? How may we identify and preserve the best of both systems?

The question of why teachers involve students is discussed in some detail in Chapter 4, 'Why do teachers involve students in assessment?'. Reasons given by teachers who have published their own work are inspected, beginning with the 1950s. The chapter ends with a discussion of the benefits of involving students.

Chapter 5, 'How may students be involved in assessment?', is central to the theme of this book. In it, I review the ways in which students may be involved. Considerable space is allocated to peer and self-assessment, but collaborative assessment and feedback are also discussed. The chapter then goes on to look at the level of student involvement and closes with advice for practitioners.

In Chapter 6, 'Practical peer assessment and feedback: problems and solutions', possible answers to a number of frequently asked questions are presented. In this chapter, I also describe the development of peer assessment called 'Peer Feedback Marking' which, as the name implies, emphasizes feedback rather than marks.

Chapter 7, 'How well are students able to judge their own work?' and Chapter 8, 'How reliable or valid are student peer assessments?' describe the conduct and results of two meta-analytic studies: one dealing with self- and the other with peer assessment. The meta-analytic technique is described briefly, and outcomes of the two studies discussed. Each chapter ends with recommendations for conducting studies that wish to maximize the agreement between student and teacher marks.

Assessment in and by groups is the topic considered in Chapter 9, 'Assessment of groups by peers'. A number of studies are reviewed and the problems of peer assessment in groups discussed. Strategies for min-imizing or avoiding problems are discussed and, once again, the chapter ends with recommendations for practitioners.

In Chapter 10, 'Computer Assisted Assessment (CAA) and student involvement', I survey some recent developments in Computer Assisted Assessment (CAA), identifying a number of functions. Many of these functions involve students – some actively, some less so. Software now exists which acts to support the assessment process itself, for example, by facilitating the collection and management of marks. Web-based testing is also taking place. More interestingly, several examples of computer-based self- and peer assessment have been identified and these are described, along with other examples of computer support for, and encouragement of, student learning. Again, advice to practitioners brings the chapter to a close.

Chapter 11 summarizes the key findings and identifies areas for further research.

Who is this book for?

This book is for anyone in further or higher education who is concerned to improve the practice of assessment generally or to provide their students with as rich an educational experience as possible. As we have seen, it contains chapters on key issues, a critique of traditional practices and a survey of reasons why teachers choose to involve their students in assessment. It also provides a research-based overview of current practice of student involvement in assessment (self-, peer and collaborative assessment, assessment in groups and Computer Aided Assessment), and is, therefore, of interest to researchers in education as well as to practising

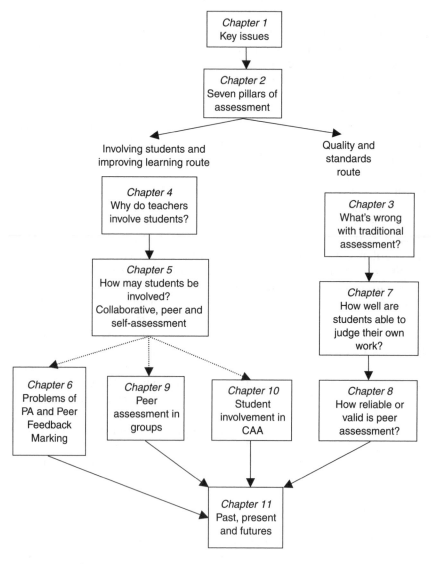

Figure 0.1 Structure of the book

teachers. The book also contains chapters which look at the reliability and validity of self- and peer assessments in both individual and group contexts. It is of particular relevance to staff developers and those teachers engaged in the quest not only for professional development, but also for formal professional qualifications in higher education.

How to read this book

Your particular needs are likely to determine how, exactly, you will read this book. It may be that you will choose to dip in and out as your needs dictate. There are, however, two main routes through it. All readers will probably wish to orient themselves by looking at the first two chapters. Then, those concerned with issues relating to assessment generally will tend to follow what I have called the 'Quality and standards route', while those interested in specific ways of involving students will follow the 'Involving students and improving learning route'.

The 'Quality' route contains Chapters 3, 7, 8 and 11. This route begins with a critique of traditional assessment and goes on to examine reliability and validity of self- and peer assessment.

The 'Involving students' route takes readers through Chapters 4, 5, 6, 9 and 10 before concluding with Chapter 11. After working through Chapters 4 and 5, readers following this route may wish to choose a particular path to follow. Those interested in peer assessment and its problems will wish to read Chapter 6, 'Problems of peer assessment and peer feedback marking (PFM)'. This chapter is of particular relevance to teachers and staff developers. Those who wish to learn more about peer assessment in groups and to deal with problems of how to differentiate between individual contributions when awarding marks, will choose Chapter 9, 'Peer assessment in groups'. Chapter 10, 'Computer Assisted Assessment (CAA) and student involvement' provides a third path. All these chapters contain practical advice for practitioners.

The structure of the book is summarized in Figure 0.1.

Acknowledgements

I wish to thank a number of people for help and support during the researching and writing of this book.

Thanks are due to the American Educational Research Association for their permission to reproduce the figures from *Review of Educational Research* (Volume 70, number 3, pages 305–6) in Chapter 8, and to Phil Davies for his screenshot in Chapter 10. Thank you, too, to Joanna Bull for permission to use extracts from the CAA Centre website materials, also in Chapter 10.

I am indebted to Mike Prosser at the University of Sydney for providing me with research facilities, and to other colleagues there for their welcome and stimulating discussions. Thanks are also due to David Boud and Judy Goldfinch with whom I worked on the two meta-analytic studies discussed. Thank you, Phoebe Fisher, for your illustration which we are, unfortunately, not able to include in the book. Thanks are also due to many other colleagues who have supplied me with copies of their own work or pointed out useful references: Dai Hounsell, Mark Lejk, Mary McCulloch, Fred Percival to name but four. Thank you Kim Addison for your practical support. George Brown once again provided encouragement and critical advice, as did Greg Michaelson, who has completed a double marathon of reading and critiquing. Thank you both. Finally, thank you Steve Jones for being a cat person.

Chapter 1

The seven pillars of assessment

This chapter considers the seven pillars on which the canopy of assessment in higher education rests. Careful attention to each of these pillars is necessary. The seven are

(1) Why assess?
(2) How to assess?
(3) What to assess?
(4) When to assess?
(5) Who assesses?
(6) How well do we assess?
(7) Whither? What next?

We shall now look at each.

1 Why assess?

This question deals not only with the purposes of assessment, but also the issue of who needs or uses the results. In 1987, Rowntree observed that the vast bulk of assessment literature is concerned with how to use assessment for purposes of grading and ranking. 'Only a minuscule proportion considers how to use it [assessment] to enhance the students' educational growth' (Rowntree, 1987: 10). In exploring the purposes of assessment, Rowntree identified six broad categories:

(i) Selection
(ii) Maintaining standards – or quality control

 (iii) Motivation of students
 (iv) Feedback to students
 (v)   Feedback to teachers
 (vi) Preparation for life

To what extent and in what ways do these purposes support student learning? It can be argued that selection and quality control benefit stakeholders other than students, though students need to be assured of the quality of the awards they achieve. Rowntree (1987: 22) talks of the 'constant prod from assessment' which encourages learning. Thus, the motivational purpose may be said to be more directly related to the needs of students than other purposes of assessment. However, Rowntree argued that motivational assessment may be seen as an instrument of coercion, a way of getting students to do something they wouldn't do otherwise. In this way, motivational assessment may also benefit the teacher rather than students. Thus, motivation has two faces. It encompasses both encouragement and coercion, the carrot and the big stick. Feedback is more obviously beneficial to students, and perceived as such by them. Preparation for life, on the other hand, clearly depends on the sort of life you wish to lead. Traditional interpretations of 'preparation' have focussed narrowly on employment and career advancement and have been predicated on competition. However, there are those, myself included, who see collaboration and sharing as more valuable life skills than excellence in struggle and competition, and assessment's role in preparing students for life seems to be changing. Birenbaum (1996), for example, stressed the function assessment has to help develop a self-regulated learner, capable of communicating and co-operating with others.

   These categories form a useful framework within which to consider assessment, but, as we have seen, emphases are changing. While Rowntree observed that little assessment literature was concerned with enhancing student growth, this small proportion is increasing rapidly, and, as we shall see in Chapter 4, many more teachers now wish to use assessment to achieve benefits for their students.

Purposes of assessment in the context of group work

Group working provides us with some additional purposes of assessment. This practice has become more widely used in recent years, and its assessment has often given rise to problems, most notably the difficulty of assigning individual grades for group efforts (e.g. Magin, 2001b). Although we shall return to discuss group work in the context of peer assessment in Chapter 9, we shall now consider how the purposes of assessment of group working may differ from those of learning alone. Webb (1995) considered theoretical and practical issues that need to be taken into account in the design, use and interpretation of assessments carried out in collaborative small groups. In her discussion of some of the reasons given to justify the use of group work, she noted that the most often cited reasons did not always coincide with the purposes of assessment. She identified four such purposes in the context of group work:

(1) to measure individual achievement (traditional purpose);
(2) to measure performance after learning in group setting;
(3) to measure group productivity and effectiveness;
(4) to measure students' abilities to work collaboratively.

Webb observed that these purposes sometimes represent competing goals of group work. For example, group productivity often competes with learning from group work. She also argued that the group processes may be different in the two contexts. 'Behavior that is conducive to producing a high-quality group product may not always be conducive to individual learning, and vice versa' (Webb, 1995: 241).

Formative and summative assessment

In answering the question, 'Why assess?', Biggs (1999) pointed to the important distinction between *formative* and *summative* functions. George and Cowan (1999: 1) described summative evaluation as consisting of judgements which, 'for the immediate future, form the basis of one or more decisions which stem from that judgement'. In summative assessment, students are graded at the end of a module, unit or course. Summative judgements are also used to accredit learners at the end of a programme. Nevo (1995) characterized these judgements as being for diagnostic and certification purposes. George and Cowan (1999: 1) also saw evaluation as formative 'when the intention is to identify scope and potential for improvement'. In formative assessment, results of assessment are used for feedback to teachers and students alike. Wiliam and Black (1996) identified *feedback* as a key component to formative assessment. They stressed the importance of Ramaprasad's (1983) conceptualization of feedback as 'information about the gap between the actual level and the reference level of a system parameter which is used to alter the gap in some way'. Thus, the authors reasoned that formative functions of assessment are validated in terms of their consequences. Hounsell (2003) provided an illuminating account of the tensions between our knowledge of the impact of formative feedback on learning and concerns about reduced opportunities for students to benefit from it.

Black and Wiliam (1998: 143) argued that formative assessment is at the heart of effective teaching and that self-assessment is *'an essential component of formative assessment'* (italics in original). Their review of research literature found evidence to support the assertion that formative assessment improves standards. In addition, many studies found that formative assessment helps low achievers more than other students.

Wiliam and Black (1996) characterized the relationship between formative and summative functions as a continuum. At the formative pole, assessments are evaluated by the extent to which they provide the basis for successful action and ignore problems of creating shared meanings. At the other, summative pole, shared meanings are important and 'undesirable consequences that arise are often judged by appeal to the need to create consistency of interpretation' (Wiliam and Black, 1996: 544). They concluded that significant tensions are created when the same assessments are required to serve both formative and summative functions. However, George and Cowan (1999: 17) saw the distinction between formative and summative evaluation as, 'a balance, which in the early stages of development will emphasise formative rather than summative evaluation; and which, in later stages, will dwell on the reverse balance'.

Who uses the results of assessment?

Dietel *et al.* (1991) identified four main groups of users of assessment: policymakers, administrators, teachers and students (and, during compulsory education, their parents). Each group uses assessment for a different purpose. The key purposes of assessment and areas of overlap between different stakeholders are summarized in Figure 1.1.

Answers to the question, 'Why assess?' may be grouped into two categories: summative and formative. In the former group are purposes such as selection and certification, as well as accountability and effectiveness monitoring. Purposes in the latter group are more student (and teacher) centred, including diagnosis, motivation, feedback and improving learning.

2 How to assess?

There are a number of conflicting modes of assessment. They vary from the informal to the formal. Assessment may be carried out quantitatively or qualitatively. It may take place at the end of sessions or modules or be spread throughout the academic year. It may focus on the product or process of learning. We shall look at a number of contrasting modes.

Quantitative vs qualitative

Biggs (1999) elaborated this distinction (see Table 1.1).

Quantitative approaches to assessment are concerned with measurement, while qualitative ones are not. The former types are analytic and give rise

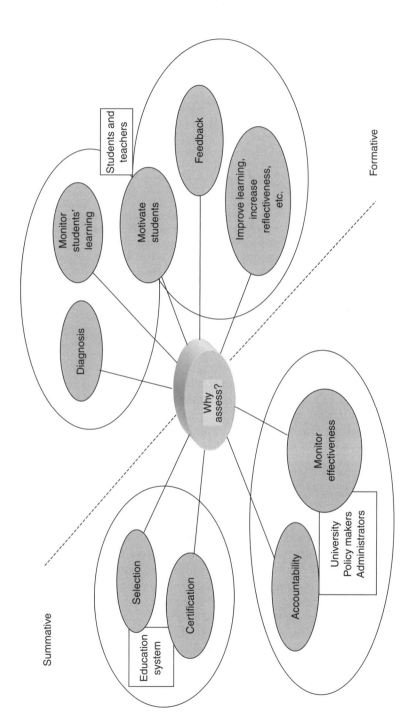

Summative

Students and teachers

Monitor students' learning

Diagnosis

Motivate students

Feedback

Improve learning, increase reflectiveness, etc.

Why assess?

Formative

Selection

Certification

Education system

Monitor effectiveness

Accountability

University
Policy makers
Administrators

Figure 1.1 Purposes of assessment

Table 1.1 Biggs (1999) quantitative and qualitative approaches to assessment

Quantitative assessment	Qualitative assessment
1 Learning performances are 'unitized'.	1 Learning is complexly structured, with new knowledge building on previous.
2 Assessment is analytic. Marks are allocated to units (sometimes arbitrarily). Units are correct or incorrect.	2 Assessment needs to reflect the complexity of learning structure and is holistic.
3 Units all 'worth' the same. Numbers of correct answers count rather than which are correct.	3 Assessment = grades not quantitative sums. The 'grade' is a descriptive statement which notes goodness of match between objectives and student achievement.
4 Individual performances may be compared.	4 Each student's assessment is independent of any other.

Source: Derived from Biggs (1999).

to numbers of 'correct' answers which determine the grade. In this sense they might better be regarded as grading or marking. Rowntree (1987: 10) observed that '. . . "grading" assumes that the teaching is essentially beyond reproach'. Qualitative approaches acknowledge the complexity of learning. They frequently relate to the process of learning, are criterion referenced and approach assessment by means of description and degree of match between objectives and student achievement.

Process vs product

What is assessed? Both products and processes of learning may be assessed. Products include traditional academic activities such as examinations and tests, coursework in the form of essays, lab reports, project reports and so on. Processes located within academic settings include class participation, group process analysis, interpersonal, communication or presentation skills development. Processes associated with professional practice include, on the medical side, clinical or dental procedures, practical surgical skills, anaesthesia skills, performance of residents and so on. Teacher performance is another example of a professional practice process. Assessment frequently relates to individual learners, but some of these (particularly processes) also occur in groups (see Hounsell *et al.*, 1996).

Continuous vs terminal assessment

Rowntree (1987) identified several other conflicting modes of assessment, including continuous vs terminal. Does the assessment take place regularly, or is it limited to the end of module or course? The contrast between coursework and examinations may also be related to this distinction, given that continuous assessment often takes the form of coursework and terminal assessment, the examination.

Internal vs external

Where does assessment take place? Is it carried out within the institution by teachers or students, or do individuals external to the institution have responsibility for assessment? Assessment of trainee teachers frequently involves classroom teachers, and, as we shall see later in the book, assessment may now take place in the workplace and involve employers and work supervisors more generally.

Convergent vs divergent

This distinction derives from Hudson (1967), who, in his psychological study of the English schoolboy, differentiated two types, the convergers and the divergers. The former, converger, was found to be better at standard intelligence tests than at open-ended tests, while the reverse was true of the diverger. Similarly, assessment can take these two forms. A convergent test is one which has correct or predictable answers, while a divergent test has many possible answers, relying on the creativity and interpretation of the testee.

Idiographic vs nomothetic

An *ideographic* methodology, such as that employed in ethnographic and action research, according to Uzzell (2000), captures the richness and complexity of a phenomenon, but risks basing conclusions on a small number of cases which may not represent the population as a whole. Assessments such as diary keeping, portfolio building, Records of Achievement (RoAs) and so on may be thought of as examples of ideographic methodologies. Another example is the in-depth interview. Hammond (2000) argued that such an approach may be of great value when the focus of interest is on dynamic processes within individuals. The ideographic approach is often contrasted with *nomothetic* methodology. In this, data are collected 'by some process of averaging' (Uzzell, 2000: 326) from a large number of people, and descriptive statistics such as means and standard deviations, calculated. Generalizations from such data are thought to have some degree of validity. An example of this type of methodology is a questionnaire survey.

Obtrusive vs unobtrusive

A final contrast distinguishes between assessment that is obtrusive and that which is not. Is assessment clearly signalled? Are learners aware that they are being assessed? Unobtrusive assessment, though undoubtedly useful in some circumstances, is ethically questionable, as informed consent is absent.

3 What to assess?

Here, we shall review foci of assessments, which can range from the traditional essay, laboratory report and examination to products and processes associated with newer, alternative assessments such as autonomous or 'authentic' assessments. We shall focus on traditional assessment in the next chapter, Chapter 2, and learn more about newer alternative assessments in Chapter 3. We shall now review some frequently used, and some not so frequently used, foci.

Case studies

A case study, according to Cohen *et al.* (2000: 181), 'provides a unique example of real people in real situations, enabling readers to understand ideas more clearly than simply presenting them with abstract theories or principles'. Case studies can also bring together theory and practice, establish cause and effect, and help readers recognize the powerful influence of the context on behaviour. Cohen *et al.* (2000: 182) argued that case studies encountered in the assessment literature can be clinical simulations or fictional accounts which are modelled on real life situations. Swanson *et al.* (1995) described the use of an example of the first type, Patient Management Problems (PMP) in the health professions. These are written clinical simulations designed to 'pose more realistic challenges to medical problem-solving skills' (Swanson *et al.*, 1995: 5). PMPs begin with a scenario which describes a patient situation. The examinee starts by seeking additional information and then initiates appropriate patient management activities, chosen from a series presented in the simulation. Feedback is then presented about the effects of actions on the 'patient'.

I have used examples of the second type in both psychology coursework and examination assessments. I prepared fictitious scenarios involving a dysfunctional family. Students were asked to choose any two members of the family who represent a different problem and answer a number of questions about each. They were required to analyse the family setting and identify factors which may have contributed to the situation, making use of developmental theory and research. Other questions probed stereotypes and required students to suggest helpful courses of action.

Assessing case studies

Case studies may be assessed in both traditional and more innovative ways, and for formative or summative purposes. In both examples cited previously, assessment was carried out by the teacher for summative purposes. Answers to my examination case study question were always interesting to mark, and usually achieved the aim of getting students to apply theory to practice. Marking case study answers shares many of the problems of essay marking. However, much may be achieved by open discussion and agreement between teachers and learners concerning the criteria by which work will be judged. Swanson *et al.* (1995: 8) noted that scoring 'rich and interesting' behaviour can be problematic, and that the variety of responses to this type of exercise makes developing scoring keys difficult. I echo their call for validation work of this type of assessment.

'Devolved assessment'

'Devolved' assessments are those conducted in 'real' settings, often by non-academics. Purcell (2001) provided an example of the use of devolved assessments in the context of competence-based learning of accounting technicians in areas where observations in the workplace, witness testimonies and simulations constitute the best sources of evidence. Further details are provided in Chapter 3. I have also used this type of assessment in a work-based module, 'Volunteering in the community', in which student volunteers contracted to spend a number of hours each week in an organization of their choice (Falchikov and MacLeod, 1996; MacLeod and Falchikov, 1997). Learning contracts were agreed and signed by each student, an academic and a representative from each organization. Student volunteers were supported by lectures and group activities delivered and organized by myself and a colleague dealing with theoretical aspects of working as part of a group, conflict, decision-making and other relevant topics.

Assessing 'devolved assessments'

In the volunteering module described above, assessment was carried out in a variety of ways, including some self- and peer assessment and assessment by the member of staff in the volunteer organization who had responsibility for the student. Our experience led us to conclude that work-place assessors were extremely generous, often failing to differentiate between students, even when two or three were in the same volunteer organization. However, we found good agreement between averaged peer and teacher ratings of oral presentations delivered in the classroom. Other examples of involvement of employers in assessment will be considered later in this chapter. Once again, assessment may be facilitated by the development and use of structures in which outcomes, sources of evidence and criteria are made explicit.

Exhibitions

Exhibitions may be live performances of artistic or technical skill or demonstrations of the products of learning (e.g. Nevo, 1995). They are classed as examples of alternative assessment by Birenbaum (1996) and Dierick and Dochy (2001) and included in a list of methods likely to facilitate self-evaluation and self-development by Klenowski (1995).

Assessing exhibitions

Little is to be found in the literature regarding assessment of exhibitions. However, in Nevo's (1995) examples, students were actively involved in the assessment process, being required to provide evidence of their ability to use knowledge. Nevo reported that the standards by which students are judged (presumably by teachers) must be stated in advance of the exhibitions. Klenowski (1995) discussed this form of assessment in the context of student self-assessment.

Interviews

'Interviews enable participants – be they interviewers or interviewees – to discuss their interpretations of the world in which they live, and to express how they regard situations from their own point of view' (Cohen *et al.*, 2000: 267). Interviews take a variety of forms, and are not always conducted face-to-face. For example, Woodfield and Earl-Novell (2002) reported research which used structured e-mail interviews.

Assessing interviews

Interviews are frequently used in the *study* of self- and peer assessment, usually in order to evaluate or assess either a person or a group, or to enable the gathering of data about some aspect of the process. However, there is scant information in the literature about how they are used as an assessment *method*. Similarly, I have found nothing about how interviews may be assessed.

Journals/reflective logs/diaries

Brown *et al.* (1997) argued that learning diaries, logs and journals are essentially the same, in that all are deemed to promote reflection and all are based on the assumption that reflection is beneficial to learning. Some authors, however, differentiate between these activities. For example, Freeman and Lewis (1998) see logs as being less personal than diaries, the former being a factual record of a learner's activities while diaries are a personal selection of events which can also include some reflection and analysis. Gibbs (1995) places journals between logs and diaries, in that they involve some reflection but are not as personal as a diary. We shall now look briefly at each variant, but consider their assessment together, at the end of the section.

Journals

Clandinin and Connelly (1994: 421) saw the purpose of journal writing as to provide a 'powerful way for individuals to give accounts of their experience', while Brown *et al.* (1997) 'unpacked' the concept of 'account', identifying four purposes of learning journals. They argued that this type of assessment tool provides students with opportunities to

- record their learning experiences;
- reflect on progress and problems;
- integrate theories, practice and different approaches;
- express feelings and mood states about their learning.

Logs

Brown *et al.* (1997: 196) described a learning log as 'a personal record of their [students'] experience which they can use to provide a self-report of their . . . learning'. Describing the use of learning logs in the assessment of problem-solving, Brown *et al.* (1997: 151) suggested that logs might include information concerning how problems had been solved, what false starts had been made, 'what loops in their reasoning occurred' and what approaches had been found to be helpful. Freeman and Lewis (1998: 254) stressed the importance of making marking criteria clear and explicit. They suggested, as a minimum, that students be told:

- what to record;
- how much detail to record;

- the number and range of items to include;
- the time period over which to record;
- the desired format;
- the type of analysis to be carried out prior to submission.

Diaries

Breakwell and Wood (2000: 294) stated that, 'any data collection strategy which entails getting respondents to provide information linked to a temporal framework is essentially a diary technique'. Diaries most usually involve written records, but can also include photographs, or, more recently multimedia. Diary entries may be specially elicited or spontaneously occurring records. In diaries, although information is usually temporally ordered, frequency of entries can vary, as can the degree of structure supplied or required. Diaries are described as an appropriate form of assessment where the learning is focusing on the processes of doing something rather than on the outcome. Diary writing, according to Ashcroft and Foreman-Peck (1994: 59) can be 'a way of building up students' confidence in their own thoughts and feelings, rather than taking on other people's in an uncritical fashion. It could be said therefore to encourage independent thinking'. These techniques are thought to have a number of advantages in that they are easy to use (though some guidance is still necessary) and they are cost effective. In addition, self-reporting is believed to engender self-revelation, and is, therefore, useful for collecting 'intimate' information. However, a number of disadvantages have also been identified. Respondents may under- or over-report events or behaviour depending on perceived disapproval or approval of others. Studies involving this type of assessment can suffer significant drop-out which increases the bias of the sample. In addition, students may be unwilling to participate or may lie. However, problems of unwilling participants, poor recruitment and drop-out can be helped by the formal requirement to keep a journal, diary or log as part of the assessment of a course.

Assessing logs, journals and diaries

As with many of the newer assessment methods, little is recorded in the literature about how logs, journals or diaries may be assessed. Boud and Knights (1994) asserted that setting an assignment which teachers believe will encourage reflection is not sufficient, as the intent of the student is a crucial determinant of what actually happens. Additionally, Brown *et al.* (1997) pointed out that no study had been done to ascertain whether the use of learning journals changes the style of learning. Based on my own experience of using the learning log method, assessment may be carried out in a number of ways. Teachers may mark the written record, or portions of it selected by students, as they would an essay, using the guidelines supplied as criteria against which to judge the work. Students may submit a self-assessment of all or part of the record. McNamara and Deane (1995: 21) argued that, in the self-assessment part of their implementation, criteria and 'means for assessment' are up to the student. Teacher marking is likely to be summative, whereas student assessment is more likely to be either totally formative or summative only in part. Given the personal nature of diaries, journals or logs, peer assessment is not a suitable method.

Learning contracts

A learning contract has been defined as simply 'an agreement between a student and a tutor about what and how a student will learn' (Ashcroft and Foreman-Peck, 1994: 62). In cases where learning contracts are used to assess learning on work placements, the employer is also usually included in the contract. The Maricopa Center for Learning and Instruction Faculty in Progress Program guidelines (Maricopa, FIPP, 2003–04) also make explicit the need for making clear what, exactly, is to be included to support claims that learning has occurred. The guidelines also specify that contracts should be based on personal or professional needs as well as on requirements of the programme. The contract should also include a timeline, including specific dates, months, or semesters indicating when the student plans to complete the activities. Further details are to be found on their website.

The Postgraduate Certificate in Teaching and Learning for lecturers, with which I am associated at Napier University, requires participants in the programme to design their own learning contract for the final module of the course, the Independent Professional Study element. The Napier scheme identifies important features of learning contracts. Learning contracts should

- be written;
- record a negotiated agreement;
- be used to assist the planning of learning;
- used to measure progress;
- put responsibility on the learner;
- give a title;
- indicate a rationale;
- indicate actions that will occur;
- outline how output/results will be presented;
- reveal the criteria for assessment (Earl *et al.*, 2003: 13).

Assessing learning contracts

There seems to be some confusion in the literature regarding what, exactly, is to be assessed in a learning contract. Is it the contract itself or the match between the learning objectives contained within the contract and the evidence supplied by learners? The Napier University Postgraduate Certificate procedures follow both paths. Tutors work with learners to construct a learning contract, which is then scrutinized by a panel of teachers. Learners are not allowed to proceed until the contract and the learning objectives it contains have been approved. Brown *et al.* (1997) addressed the issue of learning contract assessment in the context of self-assessment of work-based learning. They describe a process, similar to that used by Napier University, in which a contract of learning objectives is drawn up by tutor, mentor and student but which is then later used as a guide to assessment.

Negotiated reporting procedures

Serafini (2000) described negotiated reporting, in the context of compulsory education, as a form of self-assessment based on negotiated criteria which reflect the teacher's perspective, information from 'standards documents', and beliefs and values of the community. Students help create their own report cards using negotiated reporting. The Australian Northern Territory University's Faculty of Education, Health and Science (NTU, 2003) use a negotiated summary report in the assessment of pre-service teachers. The report is jointly prepared by pre-service teachers and their supervisors. Guidance is given on their website about both structure and content of the report.

Assessing negotiated reporting procedures

Little is to be found, so far, in the literature about either negotiated reporting procedures or their assessment. In the NTU (2003) example, we do not learn the use to which the negotiated report is put, neither are details of the assessment procedure made explicit.

Observations

Cohen *et al.* (2000) see observation as an attractive technique, because, when carrying it out, you are dealing with a real situation rather than artificial laboratory-based behaviour. However, most situations are complex and Simpson and Tuson (1995: 22) pointed out that,

> One of the most difficult decisions is choosing exactly who or what you are going to select as the observational focus of your study and putting strict boundaries around it so that your study is kept manageable in terms of scale.

Observations can be placed on a continuum from highly structured to unstructured. Cohen *et al.* (2000) (and, indeed, any good research manual) provide further details for interested readers of how observations may be made.

Simpson and Tuson (1995) reviewed some of the problems to which observational methods can give rise. As they pointed out, observing others at close quarters as they go about their normal business intrudes into people's personal lives and space, and raises certain ethical issues.

Observation is occasionally used as an assessment strategy in higher education. For example, in Radnor and Shaw's (1995) 'reconciliation model' of assessment, assessment is integrative and formative, no specific instruments are used, and teachers form judgements through observation and students' responses to set tasks. Similarly, the AAHE (2001a) described a project to be guided by Alverno College faculty, based on the 'student assessment as learning' principle. Integral to this process is the observation and judgement of each student's performance on the basis of explicit criteria. Swanson *et al.* (1995) reported that observations of students in the workplace, along with witness testimonies and simulations, can provide good sources of evidence of learning, and can constitute 'devolved assessments', as we saw above.

Assessing observations

Observation as assessment involves several problems. For example, McMartin *et al.* (2000) noted its time-consuming nature. Unstructured observations, where no criteria are made explicit and where checklists are not used, are particularly problematic. Structured observations, with operationalized behaviours and explicit criteria, are preferable. There is some information to be found on the Internet relating to the assessment of the observational technique. One of the more useful contributions came from the Center for Applied Research and Educational Improvement at the University of Minnesota (CAREI, 2003). In this, details of an assignment using observational techniques is described in some detail. Learners are provided with task information, hints on how to proceed and a rubric for assessing the final product. It is not clear from the information provided whether assessment of the product is carried out by teacher or student, though the tone of the report suggests the former option.

Oral presentations

Oral presentations seem to feature more and more in higher education, and much has been written about their assessment. In oral presentations, students, working alone or in small groups, typically research a topic and present their work to their peers. Several overviews of alternative or new assessments refer to oral presentations as a widely used vehicle (e.g. McDowell, 1995; Birenbaum, 1996; McDowell and Sambell, 1999; Dierick and Dochy, 2001). Reports of individual studies are numerous (e.g. Carter and Neal, 1995). In particular, Magin and colleagues have been involved in studies of assessment of oral presentations at the University of New South Wales for a number of years (e.g. Magin and Reizes, 1995; Magin and Helmore, 1999, 2001; Magin *et al.*, 2001).

Assessing oral presentations

Oral presentations are often associated with self- or peer assessment (e.g. Price and Cutler, 1995; Roach, 1999). I have used oral presentations with a variety of students at a variety of levels and for a variety of purposes over a number of years (e.g. Falchikov, 1995a)' I find that involving students in the assessment of presentations is extremely beneficial. At its most basic, having to provide feedback to a peer requires concentration, which, in itself makes for more active engagement than simply listening. This is as true for teachers as for students. Other skills may be developed, not least of all the skills of analysis and application of criteria. Tact, too, may be encouraged when having to critique a peer's presentation.

Portfolios

Birenbaum argued that the most quoted definition of 'portfolio' is that provided by Arter and Spandel (1992) who described it as a 'purposeful collection of student work that tells the story of the student's efforts, progress, or achievement in (a) given area(s)' (Birenbaum, 1996: 8). Portfolios must include not only the guidelines for selection of items, but must involve students in the selection of portfolio content. They must also contain the criteria for judging merit and evidence of self-reflection on the part of the student. Hall (1992) defines a professional development portfolio for teachers and lecturers as 'collection of material, made by a professional, that records, and reflects on, key events and processes in that professional's career' (Hall, 1992: 81, in Challis, 1999: 370).

D'Aoust (1992) identified three types of portfolio:

- Exemplary folio – best/most representative examples
- Process folio – examples of the developmental process
- Combined folio – 2 sub-folios incorporating exemplary and process elements

Challis (1999) argued that it is difficult to describe a 'typical' portfolio, given the very personal nature of this form of assessment. She noted that some portfolios, such as those used simply to record a range of activity, can be relatively unstructured. However, when portfolios are to be used as part of a formal assessment, some structure is desirable.

As we shall see in Chapter 10, Chang (2001: 144) developed and described a web-based learning portfolio (WBLP) system designed to help students produce learning portfolios quickly and easily.

Challis (1999: 370) listed the benefits arising from the use of portfolio-based learning:

- it recognizes and encourages the autonomous and reflective learning that is an integral part of professional education and development;
- it is based on the real experience of the learner, and so enables the consolidation of the connection between theory and practice;
- it allows a range of learning styles to be used according to the preferences of the learner;
- it enables assessment within a framework of transparent and declared criteria and learning objectives;
- it can accommodate evidence of learning from a range of different contexts;
- it provides a process for both formative and summative assessment, based on either personally derived or externally governed learning objectives;
- it provides a model for lifelong learning and continuing professional development.

Keith (1996: 180) also argued that, when used formatively, portfolios become 'a tool for learning as well as measurement'.

Portfolio-based learning seems to be widely used in the professions. Challis (1999) and Ben-David (2000) reported examples from the medical profession. Challis has also reported examples of portfolio use with pre-registration house officers, in general practice training, with specialist registrars, for continuing professional development and in nursing education. Young (1999) referred to portfolio use in the Health Sciences. Several examples come from teacher education (e.g. Halsall, 1995; Young, 1999; Gosling, 2000). Portfolios are also used in the teaching of English as a Second Language (ESL) (e.g. McNamara and Deane, 1995). Ashcroft and Foreman-Peck (1994) discuss the use of portfolios in the context of British National Vocational Qualifications (NVQs).

Assessing portfolios

However beneficial a portfolio may be to the user, its assessment may be problematic. Challis (1999: 375) argued that the 'highly individual nature of each portfolio means that their assessment can present as many challenges as the building of the portfolio itself'. Challis sees self-assessment as a necessary component, but argued that assessment external to the student is also necessary. Ben-David (2000) saw understanding of the criteria involved as crucial in producing agreement between assessors.

Challis (1999) provided guidelines for developing an assessment framework for portfolios. She argued that

- assessment should be carried out within a criterion-referenced framework;
- criteria (benchmarks or standards) should be explicit;
- criteria should link to specific learning outcomes/objectives;
- evidence of learning should be accompanied by explanatory reflective statement;
- evidence must be authentic (relate to learner), appropriate to demonstrate learning claimed (valid) and of sufficient recency for assessor to infer that learning is still current.

Furthermore, Challis (1999: 370) pointed out that when portfolios are formally assessed, we should remember that a portfolio remains the 'practical and intellectual property of the person who develops it'.

Birenbaum (1996: 11) elaborated a rubric for judging a portfolio as a whole, based on a four point scale. This is summarized in Table 1.2.

Records of achievement and profiles

According to Ashcroft and Foreman-Peck (1994: 63), records of achievement (ROAs, sometimes called profiles) are 'systematic attempts to involve students in recording, reviewing, and evaluating their academic and personal progress and development throughout their college careers'. ROAs have potential to provide a fuller picture of a learner than a set of examination marks. Various forms of profiling and pupil records have been used in compulsory education for some time (e.g. Broadfoot, 1986) and also in further education (e.g. Mansell, 1986). The UK's Department for Education and Skills (Dfes, 2003) has a National record of achievement website which, in theory at least, provides information for adult learners,

Table 1.2 Birenbaum's rubric for judging a portfolio

4 points	3 points	2 points	1 point
Entries carefully chosen to give picture of a reflective learner, what learner knows and can do and of progress. Entries bear relationship to each other and to a central organizing theme. Rationale for choices clearly stated and reflects well grounded self-assessment. Student aware of audience's perspectives.	Evidence of thought regarding choice of entries. Each justified and reflected upon. More and less effective entries compared. Student aware of own learning process. Some evidence of reflection. BUT Portfolio lacks a central purpose, and entries do not create a coherent picture. Insufficient evidence of awareness of audience perspectives.	Some evidence of intentional selection. Some evidence of reflection. BUT Reasons for selection shallow (e.g. 'I liked it'). Portfolio lacks organizing theme/central purpose. Not enough evidence to build picture of student as a learner.	Portfolio is haphazard collection. No evidence of intentional selection of entries. No comparisons between entries or organization according to central theme. No picture of student as reflective learner suggested.

employers, higher education students and jobseekers, as well as for personnel in compulsory education. My computer has crashed on each occasion I attempted to access the site, so, reader be warned.

Assessing ROAs and profiles

The personal nature of an ROA firmly places it in the formative assessment camp. While learners may receive guidance on the compilation of an ROA, the record is theirs and useful primarily as an aid to curriculum vita preparation and job applications.

Self- and peer assessment/evaluation

Ashcroft and Foreman-Peck (1994) include self- and peer assessment as methods of assessment, though these may be better thought of as processes which may be applied to a variety of methods rather than methods in their own right. These forms of student involvement in assessment occur in a multitude of situations (including many) and will be discussed in detail in Chapters 5, 'How may students be involved in assessment?', 6, 'Peer assessment and feedback', 7, 'How well are students able to judge their own work?', 8, 'How reliable or valid are student peer assessments?' and 9, 'Assessment of groups by peers'.

Simulations and games

Megarry (1978) argued that, while the notion that play and games have beneficial effects on learning has a distinguished pedigree dating back to Plato, it was not until the 1960s that publications about games and simulations entered the research literature. While simulations and games are often linked, the two types of activity differ in important ways. Simulations are 'exercises that involve an on-going representation of some aspect(s) of a real situation of some sort' which often involve role-play on the part of participants, while games are 'exercises which involve competition and have set rules' (Ellington *et al.*, 1993: 114). Of course, simulations and games may be combined to produce simulation games which possess some characteristics of both.

The use of simulations and games in assessment is widely reported in higher education (e.g. Gibbs, 1995; Birenbaum, 1996; Dierick and Dochy, 2001). This trend seems particularly marked in the assessment of medical and paramedical students. For example, as we saw earlier, Swanson *et al.* (1995) described the use of computer-based clinical simulations in health professional education. Similarly, Ben-David (2000: 472) described some recent innovations in assessment in medical education which also included 'objective structured clinical examinations' or the OSCE, along with the portfolio and 'hi-tech' simulations.

The benefits of simulations and games as an educational device are often referred to. For example, it has been argued that such activities present realistic scenarios to students (e.g. Swanson *et al.*, 1995) or that they make the learning situation democratic. Ellington *et al.* (1981) reported claims that games and simulations can be used to achieve objectives from Bloom's (1965) cognitive and affective domains. Unfortunately, as Percival (1978) argued, many such claims do not seem to be supported by evidence. Cohen *et al.* (2000) also expressed concern about the lack of information about the effectiveness of simulation methods, particularly given their growing use in classrooms. Some disadvantages of simulations have also been identified. For example, Swanson *et al.* (1995) noted that, no matter how realistic a performance-based assessment is, a simulation is still a simulation, and examinees do not behave in the same way they would in real life. Megarry (1978: 196) argued that the belief that gaming is 'democratic' is an illusion, in that 'most activities in education and training classrooms are imposed by the authority of the teacher'.

Assessing simulations and games

Self- and peer assessments of simulations and games seem common, in spite of the obvious difficulties associated with 'marking' complex behaviour. For example, Lennon (1995) used both self- and peer assessment of performance with a group of second year physiotherapy students during practical simulations. However, she concluded that the main aim of her study was not achieved, as students were found to be inaccurate self or peer assessors. Nonetheless, questionnaire data led her to assert that the learning objectives *had* been achieved and that the educational benefits of self- and peer assessment had been confirmed. Kwan and Leung (1996) described their use of peer assessment of a simulation training exercise in the department of Hotel and Tourism Management at Hong Kong Polytechnic University. The authors found some degree of agreement between tutor and peer marks, but deemed it to be less than reported in previous studies, suggesting that students were 'playing safe' and using a restricted range of marks compared with teachers. McDowell (1995: 305) reported the use of professional practice simulation with self- and peer assessment by final year students studying a 'technical subject'. However, her interest was in the unintended side effects of innovative assessment rather than its reliability or validity.

Work-based learning

Brown *et al.* (1997: 192) defined work-based learning as 'a special form of experiential learning in which students can develop, as part of their course, a range of social skills, academic and technical knowledge and expertise in the workplace'. They identified four broad-based categories:

- specific vocational training (e.g. in medicine, nursing or engineering);
- structured work experience (formal and systematic);
- semi-structured work experience (informal learning);
- random work experience (deliberate or opportunistic).

Work-based learning is particularly associated with sandwich placements, but by no means limited to such experiences.

Assessing work-based learning

Marshall and Mill (1993) listed three general principles relating to the assessment of work-based learning:

(1) assessment should be collaborative;
(2) assessment should be constructive and responsive to learners' needs;
(3) conditions necessary for good assessment must be prioritized in terms of time and resource allocation.

These conditions included

(i) having clear learning outcomes;
(ii) credit which reflects quality of learning (i.e. assessment must be fair);
(iii) a policy relating to the nature of evidence;
(iv) mechanisms to support collaboration between learners, teachers and employers;
(v) professional development for academic staff;
(vi) evaluation mechanisms.

Unfortunately, the authors did not provide evidence relating to the effectiveness of their advice. However, proponents of work-based learning claim that it confers benefits to learners. Bucklow (1993) explored issues of quality relating to assessing workplace learning, and concluded that, as students, academic staff and employers might be looking for different outcomes, the assessment process should be sensitive to these different viewpoints.

Brown *et al.* (1997: 194) concluded that, although it may be seen as a potentially useful adjunct to more traditional forms of learning, work-based learning 'is probably an inadequate replacement for deep active learning in an academic context'.

Summary

We can see that there are marked differences between the assessment methods, particularly in terms of their frequency of use and what we know about their effectiveness. These differences are summarized in Table 1.3.

4 When to assess?

Summative assessments may take place on a regular and frequent basis or be restricted to ends of modules, years or programmes (the 'terminal assessments'), as we saw earlier. In an ideal world, formative assessments occur regularly. As we shall see, the 'when' of assessment is typically related to the 'how', in that different types of assignment are used in terminal and continuous assessments. Comparing terminal and continuous assessments, coursework is typically marked by a teacher known to the students, while it is not uncommon, even in universities, for examinations to be marked by people who do not know individual candidates. Large classes and recent moves towards 'blind' marking assure this impersonal practice. I should, perhaps, point out that I am not hostile to 'blind' marking – far from it. The adverse effects of marker bias are too well known and established to be ignored. Other differences between terminal assessments and coursework are equally obvious to practitioners. Exams

Table 1.3 Summary: foci of assessment

What is assessed	Assessment method	How effective?	Examples (reviews and practice)
Case studies	Traditional (by teacher) or alternative (students may be involved) Formative and/or summative	Some evidence of integration of theory with practice Personal experience supports their usefulness	Cohen *et al.* (2000) Falchikov (see above) Swanson *et al.* (1995)
'Devolved assessment'	Alternative (self-, peer and employer assessments) Formative and/or summative	Good teacher/peer agreement found Employers tended not to differentiate between students and seemed over-generous.	Falchikov and MacLeod (1996) MacLeod and Falchikov (1997) Purcell (2001)
Exhibitions	Alternative (students involved) Self-assessment Formative and/or summative	Some evidence of benefits (students provided evidence to support evaluations) Little other evidence found	Birenbaum (1996) Dierick and Dochy (2001) Klenowski (1995) Nevo (1995)
Interviews	Alternative?	No hard evidence found	Cohen *et al.* (2000) Woodfield and Earl-Novell (2002)
Journals/ logs/diaries	Alternative (students involved in selection of contents + some self-assessment) and traditional Formative and/or summative	Proponents claim benefits, but little hard evidence found Personal experience supports their usefulness	Ashcroft and Foreman-Peck (1994) Boud and Knights (1994) Breakwell and Wood (2000) Brown *et al.* (1997) Clandinin and Connelly (1994)

(Table 1.3 continued)

Table 1.3 Continued

What is assessed	Assessment method	How effective?	Examples (reviews and practice)
Learning contracts	Alternative (agreement between student and tutor/employer) and traditional (depending on what is assessed) Self-assessment Formative and/or summative	Little hard evidence found Personal experience supports their usefulness	Ashcroft and Foreman-Peck (1994) Brown et al. (1997) Earl et al. (2003) Maricopa FIPP (2003–4)
Negotiated reporting	Alternative (evaluation negotiated between learner and teacher/supervisor) Self-assessment Formative and/or summative	No hard evidence found	NTU (2003) Serafini (2000)
Observations	Predominantly traditional Summative and/or formative	No hard evidence found	AAHE (2001a) CAREI (2003) Cohen et al. (2000) McMartin et al. (2000) Radnor and Shaw (1995) Rowntree (1987) Simpson and Tuson (1995) Swanson et al. (1995)

Freeman and Lewis (1998)
Gibbs (1995)
McNamara and Deane (1995)

Method	Description	Findings	References
Oral presentations	Alternative and traditional Peer and self-assessment Summative and/or formative	Generally found to be effective and beneficial to students. Stimulates active engagement, use of analytic skills, application of criteria, tact and diplomacy	Birenbaum (1996) Carter and Neal (1995) Dierick and Dochy (2001) Falchikov (1995a) Magin and Helmore (1999, 2001) Magin and Reizes (1995) Magin et al. (2001) McDowell (1995) McDowell and Sambell (1999) Price and Cutler (1995) Roach (1999)
Portfolios	Alternative and traditional Students involved in selection of contents Self-assessment Product assessed traditionally (by teacher) Formative and/or summative Many production guidelines available	Proponents claim benefits, but little hard evidence found	Arter and Spandel (1992) Ashcroft and Foreman-Peck (1994) Ben-David (2000) Birenbaum (1996) Challis (1999) Chang (2001) D'Aoust (1992) Gosling (2000) Halsall (1995) Keith (1996) McNamara and Deane (1995) Young (1999)
ROAs/ profiles	Formative	No hard evidence found	Ashcroft and Foreman-Peck (1994) Dfes (2003) Mansell (1986)

(Table 1.3 continued)

Table 1.3 Continued

What is assessed	Assessment method	How effective?	Examples (reviews and practice)
Simulations and games	Alternative Formative?	Proponents claim benefits, but little hard evidence	Ben-David (2000) Birenbaum (1996) Dierick and Dochy (2001) Ellington *et al.* (1993) Gibbs (1995) Kwan and Leung (1996) Lennon (1995) McDowell (1995) Megarry (1978) Percival (1978) Swanson *et al.* (1995)
Work-based learning	Alternative and traditional Employer involvement and some self-assessment Formative and/or summative	Proponents claim benefits, but little hard evidence.	Brown *et al.* (1997) Bucklow (1993) Marshall and Mill (1993)

tend to be exclusively summative in nature, while coursework can more readily accommodate a formative component (though it does not always avail itself of this opportunity). Feedback is generally available relating to coursework, but less frequently for exams. In higher education, examination results are generally made available quite soon after they have been sat. Ideally, coursework is returned within living memory of its completion.

5 Who does the assessing?

This section identifies what some have called the 'sources' of assessment or the people or things that actually do the assessing. We shall discuss five key players:

- Tutor
- Self
- Peer
- Computer
- Employer

In some senses, this is a well-travelled territory. *Tutor assessment* needs no explanation, and increasingly, this may also be said of self- and peer assessment. However, here are some definitions. *Self-assessment* refers to 'the involvement of learners in making judgements about their own learning, particularly about their achievements and the outcomes of their learning' (Boud and Falchikov, 1989: 529). Self-assessment is formative, in that it has beneficial effects on learning, but may also be summative, 'either in the sense of learners deciding that they have learned as much as they wished to do in a given area, or . . . it may contribute to the grades awarded to students' (Boud and Falchikov, 1989: 529).

In *peer assessment*, students use criteria and apply standards to the work of their peers in order to judge that work. It, like self-assessment, is formative for the assessor, but may also be summative.

Employer assessment and *computer assessment* may need a little more introduction. The use of computers to support student involvement in assessment will be discussed in Chapter 10. Employers are beginning to feature at several stages in assessment. Views of employers about desirable attributes of the graduates they will employ have been sought for some time. These opinions are often equated with the needs of society, though this link may be questioned. The potential for mismatch between employer and educator aims is even greater. For example, employers would not necessarily welcome graduates openly analytical and critical of the structures of which they will become a part, though they may welcome critical analysis once graduates have 'bought in' to the organization. It is important to note that, in spite of pressures to bring the two together, the purposes of education as seen by educators and employers are not identical.

As we saw earlier, employers are often involved in student assessment in cases of work-based learning. An example of the involvement of employers in university-based student assessment is provided by Goldfinch *et al.* (1999) who described a pilot study of employer involvement in the development and assessment of group working skills. A development of this work was reported by Laybourn *et al.* (2001).

6 How well do we assess?

This question raises issues such as reliability and validity, equity and bias, cheating, quality and standards. We shall look at each in turn.

Reliability

Davis and Rose (2000: 48) define reliability as 'the consistency or stability of any experimental effect'. Cohen *et al.* (2000: 117) add that reliability operates, 'over time, over instruments and over groups of respondents'. In the context of assessment this means that marks awarded by one person should resemble those awarded by another, or, indeed, that marks we award one day will be the same as, or very similar to, those awarded to the same piece of work on another occasion. We need to consider all aspects of assessment in order to gauge its reliability: methodology, measuring instruments used and those responsible for the assessment, teachers or students.

Three types of reliability are usually identified: reliability as stability, as equivalence and as internal consistency.

Reliability as stability

We need to be sure that our measuring instrument will yield very similar results if we were to repeat the measurement with the same group. This is sometimes known as test–retest reliability. Similarly, we need to be sure that our instrument will produce roughly similar measures if used with similar groups of students. Of course, very often we are seeking evidence of change which we attempt to find by conducting pre- and post-tests (e.g. Cheng and Warren, 1997).

Reliability as equivalence

This type of reliability includes use of equivalent or alternative forms of an instrument. It also entails inter-rater reliability.

Reliability as internal consistency

Reliability as internal consistency is concerned with a test or instrument as a whole and whether measurements made using some parts of a test resemble those made using other parts. Internal consistency is calculated by splitting the test in two, calculating scores for each half and inspecting the correlation between them.

Unfortunately, we too frequently find that we do not manage to achieve high standards of reliability of assessment, as will be discussed in Chapter 2 (e.g. Newstead and Dennis, 1994). However, we should do all within our power to achieve a reliable outcome. Without reliability, our marks and remarks can be meaningless and misleading. However, we might also reflect on Nevo's (1995: 100) assertion that consistency 'may be crucial for the trivial, but misleading for the insightful'.

Validity

Simply put, an instrument can claim to be valid if it measures what it sets out to measure. Thus, to be valid, an assessment procedure must measure what it claims to measure. However, Cohen *et al.* (2000: 105) argued that recent conceptualizations of validity are broader, and that, in quantitative data, 'validity might be addressed through the honesty, depth, richness and scope of the data achieved'. According to Nevo (1995: 97), validity refers to the 'substance' of the measurement. Perhaps, as assessment becomes more than measurement, we need to take this broader view, even though it leads us into further difficulties of how we might judge concepts such as honesty and richness.

Less contentious is the view that there are several kinds of validity:

- Face validity
- Content validity
- External validity
- Internal validity
- Predictive validity
- Construct validity

Face validity is the requirement for an instrument or test item to appear to have relevance to the task in hand. In order to demonstrate *content valid-ity*, 'the instrument must show that it fairly and comprehensively covers the domain or items that it purports to cover' (Cohen *et al.*, 2000: 109). Here, the relevance to assessment is particularly marked. Any attempt at assessment must relate to all stated learning outcomes. *External validity*, according to Cohen *et al.* (2000: 107) refers to the degree to which results can be generalized to a wider population, while *internal validity* 'seeks to demonstrate that the explanation of a particular event, issue or set of data which a piece of research provides can actually be sustained by the data'. *Predictive validity*, according to Hammond (2000), asks whether the results of a test predict future behaviour. In the context of assessment, this kind of validity is of particular interest to employers.

In the context of assessment, particularly in cases where data are rich and complex (e.g. when assessing case studies, logs or portfolios), validity depends on making explicit the details and aims of the exercise. In quantitative data, Cohen *et al.* argued that validity depends on sampling, appropriate instrumentation and statistical treatments. Thus, we must turn to our assessment methods to ensure that they do, in fact, measure what we believe them to do. Is a timed examination a true measure of the totality of a student's learning? Of course it cannot be, but most of us would not make such a claim.

We shall return to consider reliability and validity in the context of student involvement in assessment in Chapter 7, 'How well are students able to judge their own work?,' and Chapter 8, 'How reliable or valid are student peer assessments?'

Equity and bias

It can be argued that equity and bias are part of the larger picture of reliability, in that biases threaten reliability. However, biases seem to have a life of their own, too. *Bias* may be defined as the distortion of a result by a neglected factor (*Concise Oxford Dictionary*, 1976). In assessment, bias may be caused by gender, ethnicity, age, previous experiences, or, as we shall see in Chapter 9, by deliberate acts to advantage one's friends or benefit one's self. As I have argued in the context of gender bias, 'any assessment procedure which is affected by the sex of the marker is invalidated to the extent that marker bias is found to exist' (Falchikov and Magin, 1997: 387). This statement applies equally to other kinds of bias. *Equity* may be seen as absence of bias, or 'fairness' (*Concise Oxford Dictionary*, 1976). Fairness is something we strive for in our assessment procedures. These issues, too, will be discussed later in the book, particularly in Chapter 9 ('Assessment of groups by peers').

Cheating

Cheating requires that one person manipulate a situation so as to gain personal advantage by deceiving others. Cheating can take many forms, from plagiarism to invention of data, or to buying ready-made assignments from the Internet. It seems likely that many attempts at cheating go undetected, but concerns about cheating and plagiarism are increasingly being aired. We shall return to this important issue in Chapter 2, 'What's wrong with traditional assessment?'

Quality and standards

Although maintenance and improvement of quality and standards are of prime importance to assessment, we shall delay discussion of them until later in the book. In Chapter 3, we shall consider the paradigm of 'assessment as quality control' and discuss some recent moves which emphasize accountability and standards. Other chapters will also address issues of quality: Chapter 7, 'How well are students able to judge their own work?' and Chapter 8, 'How reliable or valid are student peer assessments?'

7 Whither? What do we do or where do we go next?

It may seem strange to regard the future as a pillar of current practice. However, at any time, we need to be aware of what works in our own practice and what current research tells us about best practice across the sector. We also need to use what we have learned to plan improved procedures in the future if we wish to provide our students with the best learning experiences we can. Our students are the future and the planning of their education is in our hands. However, in order not to pre-judge the issue, we shall delay consideration of the details of this final question until the end of the book (Chapter 11).

We shall now move on to look at what is wrong with traditional assessment and consider why many people now seek alternatives to it.

Chapter 2

What's wrong with traditional assessment?

In this chapter, I shall argue that students are intimately involved in traditional assessment, though in a very different way from their involvement in more innovative schemes. It is well known and frequently quoted that assessment 'drives' learning. We shall traverse some of the routes that learners take, and look at some of the obstacles they find on their way. We shall also attempt to answer the questions:

> What's wrong with traditional assessment methods? They've worked well up until now and why change them?

Let us look at each of a number of issues relating to traditional assessment.

Limitations of assessment as measurement

Serafini (2000), in analysing assessment practices, conceptualized traditional assessment as 'assessment as measurement'. This is characterized by use of a limited number of assessment strategies and techniques. It relies heavily on traditional unseen examinations and essay-type continuous assessments or multiple-choice questions. It has been argued that over reliance on a single technique can have adverse effects, as many aspects of learning are not measured by any one assessment method. For example, as Elton and Johnson (2002: 7) noted, 'traditional assessment practices, consisting pre-eminently of the assessment of essay and problem type final examinations and similarly constructed coursework, cannot adequately test for imponderables like independent critical thinking, creativity, etc. and this is particularly so for time limited examinations'. Similarly, traditional methods may not be good at laying the foundations for lifetime learning or preparation for work.

In the assessment as measurement paradigm, argued Serafini (2000: 2), 'objectivity, standardization and reliability take priority over concerns of teacher and student involvement'. Valid assessment requires that we measure what we set out to measure, but, too often, as Race (2002: 2) maintained, we measure what we are able to measure: 'ghosts of the manifestation of the achievement of learning outcomes by students'. Reliability of assessment may be tested by multiple or by double blind marking, but few of us have time to achieve more than some double marking at best. In addition, Race argued that agreements between markers do not give cause for great confidence that our marking is reliable, as multiple marking causes regression to the mean. O'Donovan *et al.* (2000) also reported a growing concern over reliability and standards in UK higher education, noting the increased proportion of 'good' degree results (upper 2nd and 1st class) awarded in recent years, at a time of rapid expansion and severe cuts in higher education.

Burke (1969) identified a major problem with one aspect of traditional assessment, in that use of the A-B-C-D-F grading system is often deeply antagonistic to the goals of education. Birenbaum (1996: 5) noted that other negative consequences of the assessment as measurement model include inflated test scores and 'test pollution', teaching to the test or, in extreme cases, teaching the test.

The traditional examination

Rowntree pointed out that most of the features of traditional examinations, such as their unseen nature and the presence of an invigilator with a policing role, do not apply to coursework, even when the tasks involved are very similar. However, although students are given the same task, they usually have a choice of questions and it would be very unusual for students to enter an examination room without having consulted past papers to get an idea of what was required of them. Indeed, many teachers now give time to helping students improve their exam techniques. In addition, examinations are held relatively infrequently and there is usually a time lag between completion and receiving results, though this now often characterizes coursework as well.

The traditional exam is often criticized, but has been seen as having some advantages. Miller and Parlett (1974: 5,6), in their classic monograph, argued that it

- helps students 'bring things together';
- is 'short and sharp';
- is a straightforward test of 'what they have at their fingertips'.

However, the examination system has disadvantages, not least of all the marking of essay type questions which has been found to be unreliable.

Such disadvantages may be intensified in very large classes. Miller and Parlett found that, for students, being a member of a very large group was experienced as impersonal and the assessment seen as bureaucratic. Students preferred knowing who was to examine them. According to Miller and Parlett (1974), examinations may also involve other, often ignored sources of unreliability. For example, one exam paper is chosen from many possible others. In addition, combining marks from different papers is a cause of concern for many teachers (e.g. Crooks *et al.*, 1996).

Reliability and bias in teacher and examiner marking

What is 'fair'?

Few, if any of us, will not have experienced at some time, a sense that some grade awarded to us was unfair. It is reasonable to suppose that the root cause of such feeling of unfairness is the perception that marking is not reliable. In fact, Ashcroft and Foreman-Peck (1994) reported that lack of reliability associated with assessment is a very common source of student discontent. In the past, the power relations inherent in traditional assessment militated against any action on the part of the student to question unfair grading or to redress any possible wrongs. It can be argued that, in the current climate of UK higher education, things seem to be changing, but there is ample evidence that lack of consistency in teacher marking and teacher bias persist in spite of efforts to eradicate them (e.g. Newstead and Dennis, 1994).

Elton and Johnson (2002) noted that the two most common aspects of reliability are marker reliability and paper reliability. Marker reliability (inter-rater reliability) requires that two markers award the same mark for a given assignment, while paper reliability requires that a given student perform equally on two supposedly equivalent papers. Elton and Johnson (2002) noted that, while marker reliability has come under scrutiny, research on paper reliability is rare. However, they discussed the results of one such study by McVey (1976, cited by Elton and Johnson, 2002) which compared student performance on two papers and found that the best and worst students performed similarly on both. However, the rank ordering of the middle group of students differed in the two conditions, suggesting that some performed well and others badly on questions which were supposed to be of equivalent difficulty. Elton and Johnson (2002: 9) also asserted that the problem of paper reliability affects all except the best designed multiple-choice tests, 'although these obviously do well on marker reliability'.

Miller and Parlett (1974: 45) argued that, in examiner marking, 'there is often a curious mixture of bureaucratic and personalized assessment in operation, accompanied by indecision about what is fair'. The authors distinguished two conceptions of fairness which may go some way toward accounting for the indecision: striving after objectivity which discounts any previous knowledge of the student and fairness *due* to knowledge of students and their circumstances. Thus, it seems that we cannot escape some degree of unfairness.

Power relations in assessment

Experiences of fairness may also be seen to stem from the power relations inherent in traditional assessment. Students typically have little or no say in the setting of assignments, let alone in the marking of them. Too often, particularly in the recent past, teachers act alone, with no check nor balance in place to prevent abuse of their role. This situation readily gives rise to problems relating to marker reliability and student discontent.

Studies of marker reliability

The history of the investigation of marker reliability is a long one. For example, Edgeworth (cited by Rowntree, 1987) conducted a very early study of inter-rater reliability in 1889, when a number of examiners produced percentage marks for a piece of Latin prose which varied from 45 to 100 per cent. Rowntree also noted similar findings from the early and middle parts of the twentieth century. A striking example of unreliability was reported by Wood (1921, also cited by Rowntree, 1987), in which a model answer prepared by one examiner was mistakenly graded by another, who deemed it a failure.

There have been many studies of reliability of teacher assessments, from Hartog and Rhodes' examination of examinations (1936) to more recent investigations of reliability of Tutor Marked Assignments (TMAs) in the British Open University (e.g. Byrne, 1980) or Newstead and Dennis' (1994) study of reliability of external and internal marking of psychology examinations. All attest to the unreliability of marking written work. In his survey of literature relating to the reliability of examinations, Cox (1967: 296) identified three types of error which may be involved in marking: differences in the standard of marking employed by different markers, differences in the dispersion of marks awarded by them and 'random error' which accounts for 'all differences not included in the other two'. More recently, Laming (1990: 243) argued that, in addition to this random component, marks 'may also depend on idiosyncrasies of the individual examiners'. As we shall see later (particularly in Chapter 9), these biases are also found in student peer assessments. Thus, weaknesses in the traditional system do not prove the superiority of newer methods.

Bias in traditional marking

Newstead and Dennis (1994) argued that several different kinds of bias might operate in terms of gender or racial background. Of course, where differences exist, any valid assessment outcomes should reflect them. In some cases bias may be deliberate, in others unconscious. In studies of bias, the markers are typically the focus of attention. Different markers bring different understandings to the task of assessing students. For example, Cox (1967) illustrated that, even when teachers shared an understanding of the criteria to be used in assessment, it was possible for individuals to place greater or lesser value on any criterion, and, thus, evaluate a piece of work differently. Marking in the absence of explicit and well-understood criteria may give rise to additional variation. Furthermore, Montgomery (1986: 21) argued that, 'the act of assessment is influenced simultaneously by the characteristics of at least two individuals – the ratee and the rater'. Rowntree (1987) holds these 'prejudicial aspects of assessment' to account for many of the adverse side effects of traditional assessment.

Negative side effects of traditional assessment

While marker unreliability may be regarded as the most significant adverse effect of traditional assessment, other negative effects can also arise. Rowntree (1987) attributed malign effects to situations where the *rewards are extrinsic*, as is the case in much traditional assessment. Too many students are encouraged, 'to regard learning and education instrumentally rather than expressively . . . Students come to want "the certificate" more than (and, if necessary, instead of) the learning supposedly signified by that certificate' (Rowntree, 1987: 45). This attitude is encouraged by educational philosophies in which students are seen as consumers and education as the market.

Rowntree also argued that the *competitive aspects of assessment*, such as grading on the curve, can give rise to adverse effects. Even when no formal 'curve' exists, there may be an unstated expectation on the part of the teacher that only a few will excel, that the majority will do moderately and that a very few will do poorly or fail.

There are other questions we might ask and issues we might explore.

Does traditional assessment produce passive consumers with poor motivation?

Ramsden (1997) noted that students' interest and approach to studying are strongly related to experiences of teaching and assessment, and that lack of interest or poor motivation can be seen to arise 'from a context', rather than being a fixed attribute of an individual. This does not mean that traditional assessment techniques are necessarily responsible for poor motivation or passive learning or that newer methods are uniformly successful in motivating active learning. However, as Broadfoot (1979, summarized by Boud, 1995a: 16) argued, given that 'the essentially interactive basis of all learning is not reflected in the almost entirely one-sided nature of assessment', it seems that some students may become alienated by the non-participative assessment processes they have experienced. Alienation too readily translates into lack of motivation. Boud (1995a) argued that effective learning requires that learners be able to influence their own learning, rather than waiting for others to do it for them. Learners typically have little or no control over traditional assessment processes which force them to be passive consumers of what is thrown at them.

Playing the game, cracking the code and the hidden curriculum

Miller and Parlett (1974) argued that a key concept in student approaches to assessment is the 'hidden curriculum' (Snyder, 1971), in which, '. . . the student has to decide which pieces of work can be "selectively neglected" out of the mass of set work; or which particular method of doing problems will get him the highest marks' (Miller and Parlett, 1974: 51).

Cowan (1988: 193) acknowledged the importance of the hidden curriculum in his report of the changes entailed in his introduction of student self-assessment. He firmly linked the hidden curriculum to traditional assessment. 'The old authoritarian strategies, which had served me well when I controlled assessment (and hence the hidden curriculum), were rendered totally inappropriate'.

Morgan and O'Reilly (1999) argued that assessment is viewed as a game by both teachers and students, and that success is too often seen as the capacity to play the game and 'crack the code'. Three broad types of playing the system were identified by Miller and Parlett (1974): 'cue-deafness', 'cue-consciousness' and 'cue-seeking', differentiated by the degree to which students seek out and use 'clues' from within the educational setting to maximize performance. However, Miller and Parlett (1974: 49) argued that, across all categories, the students were 'resolutely instrumental'. They noted that even cue-seekers were sometimes forced to sacrifice intrinsic interest for extrinsic reward when faced with the 'artificial' situation of *the examination game*.

Miller and Parlett (1974) also noted other differences between the three groups, some of which relate to the form of assessment. For example, cue-seekers tended to choose subjects with flexible assessment procedures such as those where more than one type of exam contributes to final assessment, or where there are no compulsory questions in a traditional exam. In 'seen' examinations, Miller and Parlett reported that cue-seekers attempted to find out which theoretical arguments might be favoured by teachers and wrote these out in advance to perfect them. Cue-conscious students used a different strategy. They revised the given topic very thoroughly, but didn't write out answers in advance. The cue-deaf group were initially heartened by the idea of a 'seen' exam, but soon became depressed, arguing that standards would improve generally since everybody knew the questions. Miller and Parlett (1974) concluded that cue-seekers are experts at playing the examination game, using exam techniques to maximize performance. Such students view assessment as highly artificial and revise very selectively and in depth. Performance of their cue-conscious peers, however, is based on a mixture of hard work and luck. The cue-conscious also revise selectively but more widely than cue-seekers and in less depth. Cue-deaf students, believing that hard work pays off, revise everything.

Although we may regard the phenomenon of cheating as a current problem, Miller and Parlett (1974) noted it as an unwelcome addition to the hidden curriculum. They reported several references by teachers to the belief that essay swapping was occurring within their own university, and in other universities where, they claimed, it is already 'part of the "hidden curriculum" ' (Miller and Parlett, 1974: 103). More recently, Norton *et al.* (2001: 270) suggested that students are 'picking up on hidden messages that operate in higher education' and are learning how to be strategic. They equated such behaviour to Miller and Parlett's (1974) 'cue seeking'. Norton *et al.* (2001: 271) noted the 'rules of the game' of essay writing and tactics used by students to help them gain better marks. Those in which the students engaged in most frequently included the following:

- Choose the easiest title to give you a good chance of getting a high mark (listed by 79 per cent of the group).
- Try to include information not covered in the lectures/obscure references (79 per cent).
- Use up-to-date/interesting references/lots of references/contradictory references in your essay (75 per cent).
- Play the role of a good student (55 per cent).
- Use big words/technical terms/jargon to impress your lecturer (49 per cent).

This might indicate that students were employing several useful strategies. However, further investigations found no correlation between rule use and final essay grade, which suggested to the authors that using 'rules of the game' was not a very effective tactic.

Does traditional assessment have adverse effects on student approaches to learning?

Students are often aware of the implications of grading on the curve, and this knowledge can have a malign influence on their learning. By way of illustration, Vandome *et al.* (1973, cited by Rowntree, 1987: 56) reasoned that students, ' . . . feel they will gain through the poor performance of others and suffer by imparting their own knowledge to fellow students. In this way, a potentially rich source of knowledge – communication of ideas among students – tends to be stifled'. When competitive rather than co-operative behaviour is encouraged, there may be other adverse consequences, such as hiding scarce resources such as journals, books or papers within libraries for personal use or the illegal borrowing of books. We shall explore these types of behaviour further in the section on academic dishonesty.

Dochy *et al.* (1999) asserted that, in general, traditional measuring instruments do not seem to assess higher order cognitive skills. Similarly, Mooney *et al.* (1998) argued that multiple choice questions assess only recall and recognition, and promote a surface approach to studying. They argued that even knowledge recalled at the time of testing may be lost as a result of the surface approach taken. This view is widely shared (e.g. Wolf *et al.*, 1991; Swanson *et al.*, 1995; Scouller, 1998; Davies, 2000b). However, some (e.g. Tamir, 1996) argue that multiple-choice questions may be constructed so as to minimize some of the disadvantages of this assessment method. Boud (1990, 1995a,b) observed that, in traditional assessment, teachers often assess that which is easy to assess (factual material) rather than that which we hope to develop in our students (interpretation and criticism).

Are students stressed by traditional assessment?

Miller and Parlett (1974) reported that about a third of their sample of final year students experienced 'fair' to 'moderate' anxiety when facing end of session examinations, while nearly a quarter were regarded as belonging to a 'high' anxiety group. Similarly, Elias (1989) found 'debilitating school stress' linked with competition, evaluation and test-based accountability. Academic problems have been found to be the primary cause of psychological distress in students at the University of Cambridge, UK (Surtees *et al.*, 2000). Furthermore, research by Kang *et al.* (1996) found examinations to be a salient cause of stress-related altered immune response in adolescent subjects.

However, some students also experience coursework stress throughout the year. Indeed, Archer and Lamnin (1985) and Sarros and Densten (1989) found that students identified the size and number of assignments as major stressors. This might suggest that alternative assessment, with its greater emphasis on coursework and continuous assessment, may be more stressful for some students than more traditional methods. However, examinations were also high on Sarros and Densten's list of student stressors.

Ramsden (1997) reported that when students perceive a learning situation to be threatening (whether or not it actually is) they are more likely to adopt a mechanical, rote learning approach to tasks. He also noted that research findings show that overloading syllabuses, as well as inappropriate assessment questions or techniques, may force students into taking 'reproductive approaches' (Ramsden, 1997: 204). There also appears to be a link between stress and academic dishonesty.

The relationship between traditional assessment and academic dishonesty

Kibler (1993) reported some evidence for an association between anxiety or tenseness and cheating behaviour. Similarly, Caruana *et al.* (2000) identified student stress as second most important situational factor affecting academic dishonesty. First was pressure to obtain good grades. We have seen earlier that traditional assessment can give rise to stress in students. Thus, it may be that traditional assessment procedures, with the limited opportunities they provide for students to influence the process or its outcomes, and their emphasis on grades, act to encourage academic dishonesty. However, other influences may also be in evidence, as we shall see later. For example, both teachers (e.g. Davies, 2000b) and students (Caruana *et al.*, 2000) report that students are under great pressure to produce high quality coursework.

However, before we continue this discussion, it might be useful to attempt to clarify what, exactly, is meant by 'academic dishonesty'. What are the temptations to Kloss's (1996: 3) 'ethically impaired undergraduate'? Academic dishonesty has been described as 'intentional participation in deceptive practices regarding one's academic work or the work of another' (Gaberson, 1997: 1). Academic dishonesty can encompass a variety of behaviours which can vary from inadequate paraphrasing (e.g. Roig, 1999) to purchase of specially written assignments through the Internet (e.g. Gibelman *et al.*, 1999). Most of us are likely to agree that use of Internet 'paper mills' (e.g. Pemberton, 1992), impersonating another person (e.g. Rowntree, 1987) or placing a programmable calculator in the toilet and using it to facilitate cheating in an examination (e.g. Harpp and Hogan, 1998) are dishonest behaviours. However, some behaviours, such as plagiarism, are complex, and there is some degree of overlap between categories.

Cheating

McDowell and Brown (2001: 3) defined cheating as 'gaining an unfair advantage or breaking rules in assessment'. Norton *et al.* (2001) described the following as 'cheating behaviours' in which their students had engaged:

- presenting a false bibliography (39 per cent);
- Avoiding putting simple/basic textbooks in the bibliography even though you have used them (28 per cent);
- putting a theorist's name against your own point/criticism/comment to make it look erudite (16 per cent);
- inventing studies/research/articles to include in the essay (14 per cent);
- changing dates of old research to make it look like up to date research (5 per cent).

Results of the survey by Norton *et al.* (2001) showed that use of 'rules of the game' and cheating behaviours occurred widely and were correlated positively.

Plagiarism

Gaberson (1997: 1) defined plagiarism as 'the use of published or unpublished work or specific ideas of another person without giving proper credit to that person'. Plagiarism can take many forms. Walker (1998) conceptualized it as a continuum, varying from 'sham paraphrasing' (material copied verbatim, source acknowledged, but represented as paraphrased) to 'purloining' (assignment copied from another assignment or paper without knowledge of the author). However, Walker made no mention of copying with consent or of buying/acquiring material from the Internet, both of which involve presenting the work of others as your own. He also attempted to differentiate between a minor infringement and a major one, defining a 'minor infringement' as less than 50 per cent of assignment plagiarized and a 'major infringement' as more than 50 per cent.

Gibelman *et al.* (1999) listed the following examples of plagiarism:

- direct copying of another's work without citation;
- failure to use quotation marks;
- omitting citations;
- combining the work of two authors without reference to either;
- carelessness in preparing reference lists;
- representing ideas or work of another as one's own;
- failure to secure permission for use of figures, tables or illustrations, whether published or not.

Clearly, some of these are more serious than others.

McDowell and Brown (2001: 2) argued that it is often difficult to prove that plagiarism has been committed intentionally, 'which is surely at the heart of culpability'.

What are the causes of, or reasons for, cheating?

Ashworth *et al.* (1997) suggested that current concerns about an increase in the prevalence of cheating may be well founded, and argued that fears may be fuelled by factors such as those listed here:

- the move towards mass participation in higher education in the UK;
- a decline in the tutor–student ratio;
- a reduction in class contact time;
- minimal personal contact between student and teacher;
- new approaches to course delivery stressing collaborative learning.

To this list could be added increased use of distance learning, the rise in popularity of e-learning and moves to establish virtual universities and the like. Ashworth *et al.* (1997: 188) also suggested that the rapidly expanding number and variety of electronic information sources (e.g. full text CD-ROM databases, electronic journals, Internet) may present 'clear opportunities for malpractice'.

Ashworth *et al.* also reported results of their small-scale study which indicated that Master's level students suggested two main reasons why cheating occurs:

(1) It is a conscious choice motivated by idleness, rebellion, lack of interest, the potential gain and probability of not being discovered.
(2) It constitutes a non-habitual strategy for coping with demands of work and pressure to succeed.

These reasons for cheating relate closely to two theories of cheating: the generality vs specificity theory (Burton, 1963, in Hardin and Bader, 1999) and the planned vs spontaneous theory (Genereaux and McLeod, 1995, in Hardin and Bader, 1999). The first theory addresses the question, 'Do people act in a consistent way irrespective of the situation or do they tailor their actions to the situation?' and the second, the question, 'Is cheating planned or does it result from taking advantage of favourable circumstances?'

Deckert (1993) discussed some of the difficulties associated with applying Western notions of plagiarism in contexts where scholarly traditions differ from Western ones. Deckert (1993: 132) differentiated between the Western tradition which 'honors a person's divergent thinking through that individual's arbitration and participation in ongoing academic exchange' and the Chinese tradition which emphasizes 'close allegiance to a few acknowledged authorities with resulting convergence of perspective'. He reported the results of an investigation which supported the view that students were not familiar with Western concepts of plagiarism, and that they had poor ability to recognize it. He concluded that Chinese students tended to overuse source material 'through an innocent and ingrained habit of giving back information exactly as they find it' (Deckert, 1993: 133).

What type of assessment attracts cheating?

There is some evidence that cheating is present during both coursework assessment (e.g. Newstead *et al.*, 1996) and examinations (e.g. Tankersley, 1997). Cheating occurs, too, when term papers are assigned. For example, Goode (1999) noted that the creator of the 'School sucks' website, which provides free term papers, reports 80,000 hits per day, on average. Paper mills 'service' the need to produce essays and other traditional forms of assessment. Tankersley (1997) also reported cheating in clinical laboratory work. Thus, it might be argued that traditional types of assessment attract higher rates of cheating than newer forms.

Factors which have been identified as facilitating or excusing cheating are shown in Table 2.1. The central, small column indicates whether each factor is likely to occur when assessment takes the traditional or a newer form. Explanations and justifications for decisions are included in the right hand column. A comparison of 'T' and 'N' totals provides a rough measure of whether dishonest behaviour is more associated with traditional than with newer assessment.

The number of 'T' ratings, indicating a greater likelihood for cheating to occur when assessment takes a traditional form, outnumber 'N' ratings, which might suggest that dishonest behaviour is more likely to be associated with traditional assessment than with newer types. Thus, the argument that traditional assessment encourages cheating is supported.

Who is it that cheats?

Cheating has certainly been shown to vary according to individual factors. Table 2.2 shows some of the effects of different personality types on cheating behaviour. However, Kerkvliet and Sigmund (1999) identified the following variables as *not* having an influence on cheating:

- the student's expected grade in the class;
- whether or not student was studying at a liberal arts college;

Table 2.1 Factors which have been identified as facilitating or excusing cheating: traditional and new assessment contexts

Factor	T/N/both?	Notes/commentary
Alienation from university due to lack of contact with staff/Anomie/Social alienation (Ashworth *et al.*, 1997; Walker, 1998; Pullen *et al.*, 2000)	N	Those with social forms of alienation exhibit higher levels of cheating than others (Caruana *et al.*, 2000). 'Anomie' is taken to indicate a poorly ordered condition in a society (Srole, 1956).
Belief that no-one is hurt by cheating/'no real harm is done' (Hardin and Bader, 1999; McLaughlin, 2001)	Both	McLaughlin (2001: 58) speculated whether those stealing electronically held information from the Internet assume that the authors do not care what happens to them and believe that their theft is 'unreal' and that 'no real harm is done'. Here, the relationship (if any) between cheating and assessment type is unclear.
Careless note taking, revising and proof reading (Wilhoit, 1994)	Both	These may occur even when students know the rule.
Collaborative and group learning/difficulty in differentiating between acceptable collaboration and plagiarism/collusion (Wilhoit, 1994; Ashworth *et al.*, 1997; Walker, 1998)	N	Newstead *et al.* (1996) also found that the desire to help a friend was the most frequently cited reason for abetting plagiarism.
Competition for grades/jobs/places in graduate school etc. (Roig and Bellow, 1994; Wilhoit, 1994; Walker, 1998; Goode, 1999; Caruana *et al.*, 2000; Pullen *et al.*, 2000)	N	McDowell and Brown (2001: 1) argued that, in the UK, getting a top grade was not 'of compelling importance to many undergraduates' in the past, as a lower second class degree was not seen as a disadvantage in either the employment market or a future career. Nowadays, 'the assessment stakes' are higher, and cheating is thought to be a more likely occurrence.

Cultural values which define cheating differently from Western cultures (Deckert, 1993; Walker, 1998; Pullen et al., 2000)	Both	Deckert (1993: 142) recommended that results of his study be used as a 'point of departure' to help teachers encourage students with a non-Western background to make the transition to a different standard. Walker (1998) suggested supplying students whose first language is not English with samples of work.
Culture in which students are unwilling/unable to police themselves (Glick, 2001)	T	Students lack power in traditional assessment contexts. For example, McDowell and Brown (2001: 7) argued that students 'may feel powerless within their course, particularly in relation to assessment. They may feel victims of an arbitrary system with no sense that they can take positive steps to improve their performance'. This may lead to cheating in order to get by.
Distance learning (Kennedy et al., 2000)	?	While distance learning characterizes much current HE, further investigation of the role of assessment is required.
'Hands off' approach by teachers (Walker, 1998)	Both	Involving staff and students in developing 'honesty policies' for institutions may help promote awareness. Teachers might also run workshops. Roig and Bellow (1994: 3) predicted that, as teachers are required to promote 'academic integrity', they would be likely to hold more condemnatory attitudes toward cheating.
'Hidden curriculum which delivers negative messages' (Glick, 2001: 251)	T	Cowan (1988: 193) described the hidden curriculum as a feature of 'old authoritarian strategies'.
Honor system in place (Mathews, 1999) e.g. University of Denver (2000) Honor code statement, including the Honor Code Pledge which students are required to sign. http://www.du.edu/honorcode/statement.htm	Both	Cole and McCabe (1996) sought an answer to the question of why honour codes appeared to act as a deterrent to cheating. Honour codes typically include requirements for reporting and non-toleration of cheating. Behaviour of students from institutions with and without honour

(Table 2.1 continued)

Table 2.1 Continued

Factor	T/N/both?	Notes/commentary
		codes was compared, and 'although students at honour code schools show a greater willingness to report a student cheater they do not know, all students display an overwhelming unwillingness to report a friend' (Cole and McCabe, 1996: 72). Goode (1999) reported some success with 'honor codes' in combating cheating in high school.
Ignorance/confusion (Walker, 1998; Straw, 2000)	T	It may be argued that new assessment is characterized by more transparency (and the potential to dissipate ignorance and confusion) than traditional assessment.
Incorrect instruction (Wilhoit, 1994)	Both	Wilhoit noted some scepticism regarding this factor, but also advised reviewing quality of our teaching.
Institutional tolerance of cheating (Glick, 2001)	T	Glick (2001: 251) stressed the importance of creating 'a pervasive institutional culture of integrity'.
Lack of commitment (Roig and Bellow, 1994)	Both	This factor was identified by Haines et al. (1986, quoted by Roig and Bellow, 1994) along with immaturity as the two key factors in cheating.
Lack of time/poor time management/procrastination (Wilhoit, 1994; Walker, 1998)	Both?	This may be a feature of modern HE in which students need to work in order to pay fees. The relationship to assessment type is unclear, however.
Large classes (Ashworth et al., 1997; Pullen et al., 2000)	Both?	This is a feature of modern HE in which there is greater participation than in earlier times. The relationship to assessment type is again unclear.
Low chance of being caught (Caruana et al., 2000)	Both	In traditional assessment, there may have been low awareness of cheating as a problem and lack of policing. In new assessment, large classes may aid lack of detection.

Factor		Explanation
Membership of sorority/fraternity (Storch and Storch, 2002)	Both	Results of a study by Storch and Storch (2002) revealed not only higher rates of self-reported academic dishonesty among fraternity and sorority members compared to non-members, but also a positive relationship between the degree of involvement in fraternity or sorority sponsored activities and academic dishonesty. Kloss (1996: 3) noted the existence of 'fraternity files', use of which can constitute cheating.
Negative/poor or absent role models (Gaberson, 1997; Glick, 2001)	Both	Gaberson (1997) noted that those whose dishonest behaviour has gone unnoticed or unpunished may become role models.
Number of tests given in a class prior to survey (the greater the number, the higher the probability of cheating, Kerkvliet and Sigmund, 1999)	T?	Tests are an assessment tool used in traditional assessment. However, over testing may apply to any assessment context.
Number of test proctors per student (the greater the number, the lower the probability of cheating) (Kerkvliet and Sigmund, 1999)	T	Proctors or invigilators are required in traditional assessment contexts.
Number of versions of a test available to teachers (the more versions, the lower the probability of cheating) (Kerkvliet and Sigmund, 1999)	T	Tests are a traditional assessment tool.
Overemphasis on grades and competition (Glick, 2001)	T	This characterizes traditional assessment as measurement (cf. Radnor and Shaw, 1995; Birenbaum and Dochy, 1996; Serafini, 2000).
Parental expectations (Davis, 1992)	Both	This factor is more relevant to compulsory education contexts than to HE.
(Desire to) pass examinations (Davis, 1992)	T	Examinations are a keystone of traditional assessment.

(Table 2.1 continued)

Table 2.1 Continued

Factor	T/N/both?	Notes/commentary
Peer pressure (Davis, 1992; Walker, 1998)	Both	Davis argued that 'heavy duty cheaters' are motivated by external factors.
Perceptions of unfairness in tests/grading (Walker, 1998)	T	It has frequently been argued that, in new assessment contexts, students have more power and control (e.g. Angelo and Cross, 1993; Anderson and Freiberg, 1995; Birenbaum and Dochy 1996) and many perceive new assessment as fairer than traditional assessment (e.g. Burnett and Cavaye, 1980; Fry, 1990; Falchikov, 1995a; Ewers and Searby, 1997).
Reluctance of academic staff to report offenders (Caruana et al., 2000)	Both	Some teachers take a 'hands off' approach to their work (Walker, 1998), while others fear the lengthy process of investigation and possible litigation that reporting cheating would entail (Hardin and Bader, 1999).
Size of credit load (students with larger loads have greater probability of cheating) (Kerkvliet and Sigmund, 1999)	Both?	It may be argued that, in modular systems, students have higher workloads than before. However, this is a feature of modern HE and the relationship to assessment type is unclear.
Stress (Caruana et al., 2000)	Both	While a link between traditional assessment and stress has been suggested (Miller and Parlett, 1974; Rowntree, 1987), students are subject to stressors (e.g. financial; personal) whatever the assessment regime.

Unwillingness of students to expose peers (Caruana et al., 2000)	T/ Both?	There is some evidence that students are willing to expose peers in current climate (e.g. Davies, 2000b).
Warning reminders (when students not given additional verbal reminders before exam, cheating not discouraged) (Kerkvliet and Sigmund, 1999)	T	Examinations are a traditional assessment tool.
Weak sanctions (Caruana et al., 2000)	T	New assessment, to a greater extent than traditional, is characterized by greater transparency, including explicit institutional guidelines on sanctions. McDowell and Brown (2001) noted that institutions are becoming more accountable and concerned with validity of awards.

Key
T = effect more likely to be associated with traditional assessment.
N = effect more likely to be associated with new assessment.

Table 2.2 Individual differences and academic dishonesty

Individual difference	Effect on cheating behaviour
Ability of student	Newstead *et al.* (1996) found cheating to be more common in less able students than more able ones.
Academic discipline	Newstead *et al.* (1996) found cheating more common in science and technology students than in students from other disciplines. Pullen *et al.* (2000) found more examples of student use of cheat sheets (with facts, formulae, concepts and definitions) in the area of business than would have been expected from proportion of classes offered. Mathematics produced significantly fewer cases of cheat sheet use.
Age of student	Newstead *et al.* (1996) found higher rates of cheating in younger students compared with more mature ones.
Average weekly consumption of alcohol	The more alcohol consumed, the greater the probability of cheating (Kerkvliet and Sigmund, 1999).
Desire to be expelled	In a personal account of one student's cheating in medical school, Leavitt (1995) suggested that the student might have cheated in order to be expelled and saved from a career of which he was frightened.
Gender	The predominant view is that women are less likely to cheat than men. e.g. Hardin and Bader (1999), Caruana *et al.* (2000) in the USA; Newstead *et al.* (1996) in the UK. However, Goode (1999) and Kerkvliet and Sigmund (1999) argued that women now appear to cheat as much as men. Mathews (1999) found no gender differences in *attitudes* to cheating.
Grade Point Average (GPA)	Higher GPAs have been found to be associated with a lower probability of cheating (Kerkvliet and Sigmund, 1999) than lower ones. However, Goode (1999: 18) reported that it is now the 'best students' who cheat, whereas, in the past, cheating was more associated with less academically able students.
Immaturity *	Ashworth *et al.* (1997) identified maturity and self-respect as an inhibition to cheating. * Also referred to as inadequately developed belief systems; lack of 'internal resources' (Syder and Shore, 2001: 212); 'impaired or stalled moral development' (Gaberson, 1997: 3). See also Roig and Bellow (1994); Ashworth *et al.* (1997); Walker (1998).

(Table 2.2 continued)

Table 2.2 Continued

Individual difference	Effect on cheating behaviour
Laziness	Wilhoit (1994) found lazy students had taken a conscious decision to cheat. See also Newstead *et al.* (1996); Walker (1998).
Personality type	People with type A personalities are less prone to academic dishonesty than others (Caruana *et al.*, 2000).
Tendency to procrastinate	Those who procrastinate have higher levels than those who do not (Caruana *et al.*, 2000).
Religiosity	Storch and Storch (2001: 548) found 'High nonorganisational and intrinsic religiosity' was associated with lower rates of academic dishonesty than other groups.
Year of study	The further along a course of study, the more likely a student is to cheat (Kerkvliet and Sigmund, 1999; Kennedy *et al.*, 2000). Kennedy *et al.* (2000) found that more graduates than senior students believed it is easier to cheat in distance learning classes.

- spatial separation of students during exams;
- use of multiple choice questions.

It should be noted that some caution needs to be exercised in interpreting Tables 2.1 and 2.2, as many studies supplying these data were carried out in the USA, and, as Caruana *et al.* (2000) suggested, it may be unwise to generalize findings to other countries.

How prevalent is cheating?

Cheating cannot be said to be a modern occurrence. For example, Frey (2001) reported that, in imperial China, test administrators were required to search students for crib sheets, and that the punishment for those found cheating was death. Similarly, McLaughlin (2001) argued that taking the words or ideas of another person is not a new phenomenon, but that the problem has been magnified by the Internet. Surveys suggest high levels of cheating in higher education in a variety of countries (e.g. Desruisseaux, 1999): in Russia (Poltorak, 1995); the UK (e.g. Newstead *et al.*, 1996); the USA (e.g. Kerkvliet and Sigmund, 1999); Japan (Diekhoff *et al.*, 1999); Poland (Lupton *et al.*, 2000). Cheating also seems to occur in other countries such as South Africa (the Transkei), though levels in this country were reported to be much lower than those in the USA (Mwamwenda and Monyooe, 2000).

However, there appears to be some feeling that cheating has become more prevalent in recent years (e.g. Davis, 1992; Ashworth *et al.*, 1997; Storch and Storch, 2002). Caruana *et al.* (2000) noted that, in 1992, 60–70 per cent of an American student sample reported to have engaged in cheating. Hardin and Bader (1999) reported results of surveys of academic dishonesty by students in 1999 in which up to 80 per cent self-reported one or more incidents of cheating. The difficulties associated with detection and proof were cited as reasons for the increase compared with previous figures. 'Students know that a professor who sets out to punish a cheater will be faced with a lengthy process of administrative procedures and possible litigation' (Hardin and Bader, 1999: 229–41). However, Ashworth *et al.* (1997) suggested that increasing demands for accountability in current higher education may have drawn the attention of educators to cheating and plagiarism. Similarly, McDowell and Brown (2001) argued that the current belief that cheating is more prevalent now than in previous times may not be well founded, given that cheating is not a well-documented phenomenon. They also suggested that we are now more aware of the problem than previous generations of teachers may have been. It should also be noted that the research by Caruana *et al.* (2000) established that some studies of cheating do not find an increase in rates over the years.

The role of the Internet in facilitating and detecting cheating

Gibelman *et al.* (1999) argued that the Internet not only plays an important part in facilitating professional development, it also makes cheating easy. These researchers noted several forms of cheating that are facilitated by the Internet:

- cutting and pasting from the Internet and passing off the work as one's own;
- sharing answers by electronic mail;
- stealing information from another's computer screen or e-mail system.

Paper mills

'Paper mills' are websites devoted to the supply of completed essays and other written assignments. Many include warnings to users, 'hypocritical disclaimers' (Kloss, 1996: 3) about plagiarism and statements to the effect that the essays are provided as guidance to purchasers only. However, their main use is universally understood to be otherwise.

Gibelman *et al.* (1999) conducted a quasi-experiment to investigate 'paper mill' cheating in the context of social work education. Gibelman's team asked students help them locate suitable websites and chose one identified by students as suitable for their purposes. They reported that the site 'had every appearance of legitimacy', being 'bright, bold and well-designed' (Gibelman *et al.*, 1999: 3). Additionally, it carried a caveat stating that plagiarism was illegal and that papers purchased were to suggest approaches to authors. Two options were available: 'off the shelf' and written to order. The researchers bought one of each sort, noting uncomfortable feelings of being engaged in an illegal activity while so doing. However, in most other respects they reported that it was 'not dissimilar to ordering socks from a mail-order catalogue' (Gibelman *et al.*, 1999: 4). After purchases had been completed, the authors were contacted by the vendor offering bargains, including a free paper for every ten purchased – 'a sort of frequent plagiariser plan' (Gibelman *et al.*, 1999: 4). The two papers, along with another genuine paper written by a student, were sent to a small sample of experienced professors throughout the USA for grading. Eleven responded, which represented 73 per cent of the sample. Gibelman *et al.* (1999) noted a very wide range of grades awarded to the papers and no consistent pattern among markers. However, the genuine paper received the highest mean and median score, the customized paper the next highest and the 'off the shelf' version scored lowest marks. The authors noted that you get what you pay for. They also concluded that plagiarism involving the use of paper mills was likely to go undetected.

Technological detection of plagiarism

Kennedy *et al.* (2000) argued that, even as the Internet has facilitated cheating, it has also provided us with the means to combat this problem. In the UK, the JISC (2002) electronic plagiarism detection project has reviewed electronic attempts to solve the problem of plagiarism. The outcomes of the project are technical reviews of free-text plagiarism and source code plagiarism, a report of a pilot study of free-text detection software in five UK institutions and a good practice guide to plagiarism prevention. The team concluded that, while technology can help in this respect, it cannot replace human expertise, and that the best approach was to target processes and procedures. Joy and Luck (1999) whose aptly named system, SHERLOCK, is designed to discover plagiarism at Warwick University, UK, also expressed the view that it is always possible for plagiarism to go undetected, irrespective of the sophistication of the detection software.

There are many websites devoted to plagiarism and its deterrence. A simple search using your favourite search engine will locate examples. Ten of the many resources gleaned from the Internet are listed in the Appendix.

Advice to practitioners: strategies for preventing cheating

A variety of strategies for combating plagiarism and cheating have been suggested. See Table 2.3. It should be noted, however, that Kerkvliet and Sigmund (1999: 331) registered some regret concerning the absence of *research to test the effectiveness of measures* taken to discourage cheating. They argued that, lacking empirical guidance, teachers 'almost haphazardly use different deterrent techniques to counter the plethora of cheating methods students have invented'. Their own research found that multiple-choice questions, used by some to discourage cheating, do not seem to be effective. Separating out students during examinations does not seem to work as a deterrent either. Kerkvliet and Sigmund suggested that the devices used by those who cheat are personal and capable of operating at any proximity, and, thus, hard to detect and eradicate.

Table 2.3 Advice to practitioners: some strategies for combating plagiarism and cheating

Action (1) Develop a climate which encourages academic honesty

- Enforce disciplinary sanctions against those who cheat/respond in accordance with the severity of error/apply policy consistently (Capano, 1991; Wilhoit, 1994; Gaberson, 1997).
- Halt marketing of term papers over the Internet (remove order blanks/advertisements, etc.) (Capano, 1991).
- Make rules and penalties clear (McDowell and Brown, 2001; Vernon *et al.*, 2001).
- Offer written guidelines on plagiarism/academic integrity/collaboration (Wilhoit, 1994; Cole and McCabe, 1996).
- Provide proper proof reading guidelines (Wilhoit, 1994).
- Provide workshops, organize reviews, provide guidance on processes of adjudication, etc. for teachers (administrators) (Cole and McCabe, 1996).

Action (2) Implement procedures which discourage cheating

- Adjust seating in examination halls (Cole and McCabe, 1996).
- Grade other demonstrations of learning (e.g. presentations) as well as written papers (Gibelman *et al.*, 1999).
- Instruct students to copy the first page of Web referenced works, in case site disappears (Vernon *et al.*, 2001).
- Introduce progress checks (Straw, 2000).
- Require oral reports and ask questions (Vernon *et al.*, 2001).
- Require outlines/ several drafts of essays to be submitted (Wilhoit, 1994; Cole and McCabe, 1996; Drogemuller, 1997; Gibelman *et al.*, 1999).
- Require students to submit original references/photocopies of documented material (Wilhoit, 1994; Drogemuller, 1997).
- Require up-to-date bibliographies and reference lists (Vernon *et al.*, 2001).
- Use a teacher rather than a graduate teaching assistant to invigilate testing (Kerkvliet and Sigmund, 1999).
- Watch students write (Vernon *et al.*, 2001).

(Table 2.3 continued)

Table 2.3 Continued

'Heroics by individual whistle blowers hardly make a dent. It is a problem of cultural change requiring renewed commitment to a larger educational community' (Alschuler and Blimling, 1995).

Action (3) Use teaching strategies and student activities which help combat cheating and plagiarism

- Ask students to prepare essay questions (Gibelman *et al.*, 1999).
- Assign frequent small papers (Straw, 2000).
- Define/discuss plagiarism thoroughly (Wilhoit, 1994; Vernon *et al.*, 2001).
- Discuss hypothetical causes (Wilhoit, 1994).
- Get students to revise plagiarized passages (Wilhoit, 1994).
- Introduce collaborative test taking (enables monitoring of potential cheating) (Muir and Tracy, 1999).
- Involve students in drawing up policy regarding cheating (e.g. Columbia College Student Council proposal, 2002).
- Let students know that you know about the 'paper mill' websites and demonstrate your skills at cutting and pasting from a website into a text file (Vernon *et al.*, 2001).
- Organize student led initiatives e.g. taking responsibility for explaining to faculty the role they must play in encouraging academic integrity (Cole and McCabe, 1996).
- Organize student peer education on academic integrity (Cole and McCabe, 1996).
- Take students to an online paper repository and analyse a weak paper (Vernon *et al.*, 2001).
- Teach proper use of Web resources (Vernon *et al.*, 2001).
- Teach moral decision-making skills (Gaberson, 1997).
- Teach students how to paraphrase (cf. Roig, 1999, whose work suggested that plagiarism by college students may be due, in part, to their inability to process difficult materials).
- Teach students how to reference/review conventions for quoting and documenting material (Wilhoit, 1994; Drogemuller, 1997; Straw, 2000).
- Use peer groups to comment on drafts (Vernon *et al.*, 2001).

Action (4) Design assessment instruments that make cheating difficult

- Change topic regularly (Drogemuller, 1997; Straw, 2000).
- Design assignments so as to give specific parameters (Drogemuller, 1997).
- Do not recycle exam papers or questions (Cole and McCabe, 1996; Gibelman *et al.*, 1999).
- Make the work product based (Drogemuller, 1997).
- Provide 'targeted non generic instructions for papers' (Vernon *et al.*, 2001: 194).
- Randomize questions in computer aided assessment (CAA, 1999).
- Set more specific assignments/exam questions rather than the usual open-ended ones (Gibelman *et al.*, 1999).
- Try to make the assignment interesting and relevant (Drogemuller, 1997).

Detection strategies

Vernon *et al.* (2001) suggest three approaches to the detection of plagiarism: direct investigation by search, use of a detection service and analysis by means of plagiarism detecting software, e.g.

- JISC (2002)
- PREVENTION (2003)

Using peer assessment to combat plagiarism

Davies (2000b: 347) observed that the increasing availability of electronic based sources of material give tutors little time to identify and locate source references, and that 'this issue of plagiarism could fast become a major obstacle in ensuring quality of assessment'. He then described his computerized system of peer assessment, the Computerized Assessment with Plagiarism (CAP) system, developed to combat plagiarism.

The eight steps involved in the CAP process are shown in Table 2.4.

In step 4, in which the CAP is used for peer assessment of reports, students are instructed to follow up at least eight of the ten references included in each report and compare the report with the browser page simultaneously displayed on the screen. Students are then asked to submit comments and report any Web plagiarism they had detected. Students are required to perform this process on at least ten reports from the database. Finally, Davies asked each student to complete a questionnaire once the process had been completed.

Davies speculated whether the exercise had succeeded in eradicating plagiarism, and concluded that some instances of plagiarism remained. For example, many students persisted in their belief that pasting a small paragraph was acceptable, in spite of guidance received which made it clear that this was *not* the case. Moreover, while 20 per cent of students identified plagiarism to some extent, only 10 per cent admitted to this. However, students reported that the process had had a dramatic, though not necessarily positive, effect on their referencing skills. Davies (2000b: 351) reported one student as saying, 'I cut and pasted, but didn't include the reference so I couldn't get caught'. Over 90 per cent reported having enjoyed the exercise, which they saw as a challenge. They appeared to enjoy catching out peers in plagiarism. Davies rated the use of the CAP as a success, believing it to have benefited learning. We shall return to the peer assessment aspect of this work later in the book.

Table 2.4 Components of the Computerized Assessment with Plagiarism (CAP) process (Davies, 2000b)

(1) Students are instructed to develop a report using the WWW as the main source of information.
(2) Reports are submitted via e-mail. The tutor creates a database of reports.
(3) Students complete multiple-choice test 1.
(4) The CAP is used for peer assessment of reports.
(5) Students complete multiple-choice test 2.
(6) Feedback and marks are given to students.
(7) Students supply feedback to tutors concerning mark allocation.
(8) Further marks are allocated to students for their use of the CAP system.

Cheating and distance learning

Distance learning may be seen to present additional opportunities for cheating. Carnevale (1999) described some tactics available to teachers to prevent cheating on distance learning courses:

- make an unexpected phone call to discuss work or enquire about sources;
- make regular phone calls to discuss progress;
- use an 'exam cam' (A47), a small camera fixed to a student's computer which sends images of the student taking a test or discussing issues;
- use proctors to observe students taking tests and examinations (Carnevale suggests enlisting Army personnel or priests in this role);
- require students to write a 500-word essay at the beginning of every semester to act as a 'fingerprint of writing style' (A48);
- get to know students better through discussion and other online inter-action;
- employ a 'ringer' or 'pigeon';
- use search engines to locate sources of suspect text.

Summary

Thus, we can now begin to frame answers to the questions with which we began this chapter, 'What's wrong with traditional assessment methods? They've worked well up until now and why change them?' Traditional assessment has been found wanting. There is little other than custom and familiarity to suggest that traditional methods have worked 'well'. They have been found to be unreliable and biased. There is some evidence to suggest traditional assessment methods produce passive learners and have the power to reduce motivation. Traditional assessment has also been found to be associated with lower level cognitive activities and reproducing or surface approaches to studying. In contrast, there is a growing body of evidence to suggest that more innovative approaches to assessment, such as self-, peer or collaborative assessment, encourage students to use deeper approaches to studying than traditional assessment. For example, Cowan (1988) noted that his students began to use more of a questioning approach after having experienced self-assessment. Lennon (1995) chose to introduce self- and peer assessment explicitly to foster deeper approaches to studying. Other examples are emerging (e.g. McDowell and Sambell, 1999; Safoutin *et al.*, 2000). Leon (2001) reported that research confirms that the more coursework students complete, the better they do in terms of the depth of their learning. This might suggest that modern assessment practices involving continuous assessment, and emphasizing coursework, are more beneficial to students than traditional practices which emphasize end of year examinations.

Finally, traditional assessment has the power to distress students and there is an uncomfortable relationship between it and various forms of cheating and academic dishonesty. How many more reasons do we need to encourage us to try something different?

Appendix: Internet resources to help combat plagiarism

Cut-and-Paste Plagiarism – http://alexia.lis.uiuc.edu/~janicke/plagiary.htm
Preventing, detecting and tracking online plagiarism.
Antiplagiarism Strategies – http://www.virtualsalt.com/antiplag.htm
Ideas to use in preventing and detecting plagiarism.
Plagiarism and the Web – http://www.wiu.edu/users/mfbhl/wiu/plagiarism.htm
Bruce Leland's list of methods for combating plagiarism in the classroom.
Plagiarism and Anti-Plagiarism – http://newark.rutgers.edu/~ehrlich/plagiarism598.html
Guide for teachers and faculty discussing some issues and responses to the problem.
Electronic Plagiarism Seminar – http://www.lemoyne.edu/library/plagiarism.htm
Tips for preventing and identifying plagiarism, including scientific fraud. Lists of plagiarism detection software sites and term paper mills. Bibliography and webography.
Plagiarism Q&A – http://www.ehhs.cmich.edu/~mspears/plagiarism.html
Resources for students and teachers regarding avoiding and detecting plagiarism.
Plagiarism and How to Avoid It – http://ec.hku.hk/plagiarism/introduction.htm
Techniques, listing references, self-tests and worksheets from David Gardner of the University of Hong Kong.
Avoiding Plagiarism – http://www.rio.maricopa.edu/distance_learning/tutorials/study/plagiarism.shtml
Examples and practice exercises from Rio Salado College.
Centre for Interactive Systems Engineering – http://cise.sbu.ac.uk/
Research centre at South Bank University, UK, with interests in plagiarism prevention and detection techniques.
Combating Cybercheating – Resources for Teachers – http://www.epcc.edu/vvlib/cheat.htm
Links to discussions of plagiarism and techniques to combat it. (All accessed 10.02.04)

Chapter 3

Changing definitions of assessment

Until recently, books on assessment were likely to be about, or contain chapters on, techniques and assessment tools such as essays, multiple choice questions, true/false items, matching items and so on. Very often, information on test construction and scoring would be included. Some texts featured extensive references to formal and national testing. Many stressed reliability and validity of test items. It was extremely unlikely that now familiar terms such as 'portfolios', 'posters', 'competence' or 'reflection' would feature in such books. Until recent years, portfolios were limited to the realm of artists, and performance assessment was not much heard of outside the dance studio. Our experience of posters was of displays erected on billboards to advertise goods and services. Reflection was what one strove for in good window cleaning. Certainly, few books mentioned the students whose learning was the subject of assessment. The student's primary role was that of test taker. Most such books featured examples of what Serafini (2000) called 'assessment as measurement'.

Serafini (2000) saw 'assessment as measurement' as the first of three paradigms of assessment. It was followed, historically, by 'assessment as procedure' and 'assessment as enquiry'. Serafini argued that differences between the three paradigms were underpinned by the shift from a positivist to a constructive perspective of knowledge. Serafini was not alone in suggesting and describing changes in our conceptions of assessment. Earlier, Klenowski (1995) had argued that a paradigm shift had taken place in the early nineties regarding methods for evaluation of student achievement and performance. Birenbaum and Dochy (1996: xiii) described this shift as being from the 'culture of testing' to a 'culture of assessment'.

Radnor and Shaw (1995) suggested some triggers for the recent changes. They argued that, during the 1980s, in the UK, pressure was developing for increased integration of assessment with teaching. While they were writing about compulsory and further education, their arguments have some resonance for higher education. They identified key events in this development as being the launch of the Technical and Vocational Education Initiative (TVEI) by the UK government in 1983 and its focus on skills, increased emphasis on reliability and validity, and growing concern with accountability and the use of testing and examinations as performance indicators. Radnor and Shaw (1995: 126) also noted that these developments were taking place during a 'period of distrust of teachers'. Here we see the beginnings of a number of features now familiar in higher education: the move toward more learner centred education, the challenge of performance assessment, concern with comparability and increased external accountability.

Work by Pearson *et al.* (2001) suggests the need to add a fourth paradigm to the three suggested by Serafini (2000). Thus, 'assessment as quality control' will be considered as a successor to 'assessment as measurement', 'assessment as procedure' and 'assessment as enquiry'. We shall start by looking more closely at the first of these.

Assessment as measurement

As we saw in Chapter 2, traditional assessment as measurement is primarily associated with norm-referenced standardized testing where objectivity, standardization and reliability take priority over other concerns, including teacher and student involvement. Birenbaum (1996) described this traditional approach to instruction and assessment in terms of the empty vessel conception of the learner. Like Serafini, she saw it as involving the testing of basic skills, measurement and the use of psychometric models. She argued that this approach to assessment is based on a behaviouristic theory of learning.

Edwards and Knight (1995: 12) argued that the familiarity of the traditional system can blind us to a number of important features. These features are shown in Table 3.1. Traditional assessment as measurement has negative consequences, as discussed in Chapter 2.

Assessment as procedure

In the second of Serafini's categories, 'assessment as procedure', the primary focus is, unsurprisingly, on assessment *procedures* rather than the underlying *purposes* of assessment. Serafini argued that this paradigm differs from the previous one in that the procedures involve qualitative data collection methods. However, in other respects, assessment as procedure seems to share characteristics with its predecessor, assessment as measurement. Daly used the term 'methodolatry', 'an overemphasis on the correct method of doing things, rather than on the purposes for doing those

Table 3.1 Characteristics of traditional 'assessment as measurement'

Characteristics	Source
Authoritative	Radnor and Shaw (1995)
Can give rise to negative feelings which can persist	Edwards and Knight (1995) Boud (1995a)
Decontextualized knowledge, unrelated to student experience, examined	Dochy (2001)
Distant – process hidden from students (e.g. criteria not made clear)	Dochy (2001) Edwards and Knight (1995) Radnor and Shaw (1995)
External focus	Radnor and Shaw (1995)
Instruction and testing seen as separate activities/methods do not always reflect aims	Dochy (2001) Edwards and Knight (1995)
Learners 'disempowered'/can avoid taking responsibility for own learning	Edwards and Knight (1995)
Methods hard to implement in rapidly expanding HE system	Edwards and Knight (1995)
Methods not scientifically based/ do not represent 'a gold standard', rather 'depend entirely upon a community of discourse, upon the shared understanding of academics in a field, developed through years of experience'	Edwards and Knight (1995: 12)
Moderated ex-post facto	Radnor and Shaw (1995)
Narrow range of methods used	Edwards and Knight (1995)
Propostitional rather than procedural knowledge assessed	Edwards and Knight (1995)
Supplies delayed feedback	Radnor and Shaw (1995)
Testing involves:	Biggs (1999)

- measurement of performance along a scale;
- adherence to mathematical and statistical conditions (e.g. scores normally distributed);
- stability over time of characteristics to be measured;
- valid test results when used for selection purposes;
- tests that differentiate between students, spreading scores;
- testing be done under standardised conditions.

Characteristics	Source
Tests basic skills and ignores higher order cognitive skills	Birenbaum (1996) Dochy (2001)
Tests (pencil and paper type) usually administered in class	Dochy (2001)
Uses psychometric models	Birenbaum (1996)

things (cited by Serafini, 2000: 2–3), to describe the focus on procedures that characterizes assessment as procedure.

Assessment as enquiry

Birenbaum (1996: 7) listed a number of characteristics of a new 'culture' of assessment, corresponding to Serafini's third paradigm of assessment as enquiry:

- a meta-cognitive component is included;
- a psychometric-quantitative approach is challenged by a contextual-qualitative approach;
- it is characterized by constructivism;
- single scores become profiles and quantification becomes portrayal.

Birenbaum and Dochy (1996) also saw the culture of assessment as emphasizing integration of assessment with instruction, assessment of processes rather than products and the evaluation of individual progress relative to each individual's starting point.

Serafini (2000) argued that, in assessment as enquiry, students become involved in the process through a wide variety of alternative assessment devices and methods. He also observed that the shift towards enquiry-based assessment often requires that teachers change their perceptions of their role.

There are several variations in naming this paradigm. In addition to Serafini's (2000) 'assessment as enquiry', we can add Allal and Ducrey's (2000) 'dynamic assessment movement', Reynolds and Trehan's (2000) 'participative assessment' and Radnor and Shaw's (1995) 'reconciliation model'. Birenbaum (1996) noted a 'new era in assessment', but did not name it, other than as 'the culture of assessment' (Birenbaum and Dochy, 1996) to differentiate it from the 'culture of measurement'. Other themes also emerge within this category: authentic assessment, autonomous assessment, competence-based assessment, performance assessment, and, more recently, sustainable assessment. It might also be appropriate to explore the Alverno College (2001, 2003) 'assessment as learning' para-digm and Angelo's (1999: 1) 'transformative assessment-as-culture-change model' here, too. We shall return to a brief discussion of these models later.

Before looking in greater detail at some varieties of 'assessment as enquiry', we need to introduce another important factor, accountability, which, it has been argued, plays a key role in some current conceptions of assessment.

Assessment and accountability

Pearson *et al.* (2001: 175) argued that, '[a]ssessment and accountability are two of the most powerful, most controversial, and – no matter how honourable the intentions of those who encourage them as tools of reform – most damaging policy initiatives on the American educational landscape'. They acknowledged the need for institutions and teachers to be accountable for student performance, but argued that some action is required to ensure that assessment and accountability give rise to productive outcomes. They asserted that accountability takes two forms: an external model with externally imposed criteria and an internal one in which schools and teachers hold themselves accountable. They identified three phases of development. We shall look briefly at each.

Pearson's phase 1. Pearson *et al.* (2001) argued that phase 1 extended from approximately the 1920s to the late 1980s. During this period, the authors contend that external accountability made 'consistent but incremental gains in influence, largely supported by technical advances in testing' (Pearson *et al.*, 2001: 175). Assessment began to be seen as 'science', and standardized, large-scale tests were developed. They noted that, during this period, external agencies became more and more involved in matters traditionally reserved for local educational agencies.

Pearson's phase 2. Pearson *et al.* (2001: 176) described the second phase as being concerned with 'corralling the negative effects such as assessment seemed to be having on curriculum and instruction'. They noted concerns about the harmful effects assessment, particularly MCQ testing, seemed to be having on student development. These concerns led to the development of *internal accountability* on the part of educators, according to Pearson *et al.* (2001). Educators began to support 'performance assessment', using terms such as authentic, alternative and situated (everything that did not characterize MCQs). According to Pearson *et al.*, these professional developments were accompanied by a national push for standards by policymakers. Moreover, the authors argued that these two movements provided opportunities for educators to promote 'coherence and alignment' (Pearson *et al.*, 2001: 176) among the key elements of education (curriculum, teaching, assessment, professional development and learning).

Pearson's phase 3. The current phase in the development of our conceptions of assessment, argued Pearson *et al.* (2001: 177), is one of 'hyperaccountability' and a growing acceptance of external influence. This phase corresponds to our fourth paradigm, 'assessment as quality control'.

Assessment as quality control

A return to standardized testing has taken place in compulsory education (Pearson *et al.*, 2001). In higher education in the UK, much central funding is now linked to research and successful pursuit of external funding to support such activities. The baleful influence of the Research

Assessment Exercise (RAE) is widely debated (e.g. Prestwich, 2001). Organizations such as the Quality Assurance Agency for Higher Education (QAA, 2000) not only provide guidelines, but also exert pressure on teachers and teaching. Progression rates in universities and colleges in the UK are now explicitly linked to student maintenance funding. Standardized testing is also now being debated for higher education. For example, Irwin (1996) reported that the then president of the British Psychological Society, Stephen Newstead, had called for nationally set examinations as a means of addressing major discrepancies between university exam results. National examinations, argued Newstead, would ensure comparability between disciplines and represent a move toward standardization of British degrees. Newstead's conclusions were based on his research which indicated clear inconsistencies between disciplines, as well as gender bias in marking, and cheating on the part of students taking the examinations (Newstead and Dennis 1990). Newstead argued that examination results were increasingly being used as measures of teaching quality and of lecturers' performance which puts 'different pressures on them'. He argued that teachers might be tempted to ensure that students do well. He also noted that institutions differ in the proportion of good results achieved in ways that are 'hard to explain in terms of intakes', and that the number of first class degrees awarded in UK institutions had increased by 50 per cent since 1980. Irwin (1996: 1) also reported that Newstead had called for marking schemes which he rated as contentious, 'because they remove the discretion of the examiner'.

A synthesis of views

A model of the development of conceptions of assessment which summarizes and synthesizes these views is shown in Table 3.2. In the final phase, assessment as quality control, both teachers and students seem to be losing some influence over what is assessed and when and how the assessment takes place. As Boud (2000: 156) has argued recently, 'accountability and portrayal of accomplishments is clearly important, but in the process of giving attention to certification we have pushed into the background a concern for learning and the necessary assessment processes which need to accompany it'. This phase presently co-exists with assessment as enquiry. In fact, the two models of assessment may be more closely related than many would wish to acknowledge. For example, Gipps (1995) observed that, while the use of performance assessment is part of a move away from highly standardized procedures, a major function of the national assessment programme has proved to be accountability and comparability, features of what we have termed 'assessment as quality control'.

Table 3.2 Summary: paradigms of assessment and their characteristics

Paradigm	Characteristics	Underlying philosophies	Student role	Reported activities undertaken by students
Assessment as measurement	Assessment as 'science' Authoritative Basic skills/knowledge tested Certification function Decontextualized knowledge examined External accountability Feedback (official reports) delayed Instruction and testing separate Moderated ex-post facto Narrow range methods Norm referenced with national norms Negative consequences 'Objective' Propositional knowledge assessed Quantification Reliability and validity Single scores Tasks unrelated to real life Test instruments constructed and used Tests administered in class Testing process hidden, methods opaque Terminal product assessed	Positivist Empty vessel theory of learning Behaviouristic theory of learning Psychometric methods	Able to avoid taking responsibility for own learning Learners 'disempowered' Students absent from consideration except as testees	Testing
Assessment as procedure	Procedures assessed Qualitative data collected Results reported to external bodies	As above	As above	Testing, but involving wider variety of methods and qualitative data

(Table 3.2 continued)

Table 3.2 Continued

Paradigm	Characteristics	Underlying philosophies	Student role	Reported activities undertaken by students
Assessment as enquiry	Change in teacher role required Contextual-qualitative Elements of teaching integrated with assessment Formative function Individual student progress monitored Inquiry emphasized Internal accountability Meaningful tasks Meta-cognitive component Moderation and partnership Performance assessment Portrayal not qualification Positive assessment emphasized Processes often assessed Profiles not single scores	Cognitive learning theory Constructivist theory of knowledge Multi-dimensional nature of intelligence Social interactionist	Actively engaged learners Partnership and dialogue with teachers Students practice reflection Students share responsibility Students have varying amounts of control	Wide variety e.g. Authentic performance tasks Criteria generation Exhibitions Group projects Interviews Journals Learning response logs Negotiated reporting Observations Oral presentations Peer assessment/evaluation Portfolios Simulations Self-assessment/evaluation Student-led conferences
Assessment as quality control	Calls for standardized testing in HE Growing acceptance of external influence Hyperaccountability Negative consequences Standardized testing in compulsory education	?	Constrained Pressurized Reduced control	Assessment factories Cheating Plagiarism

Can we conclude that the golden age of assessment as enquiry is fast passing? Are government agencies managing to turn back the clock? Has the wheel come full circle? Maybe, before considering an answer, we should take a critical look at all phases, including assessment as enquiry. Maybe there was no golden age at all, just variations in the lighting.

Problems associated with the four paradigms

Problems of the first phases, assessment as measurement and process, have been identified as involving inflation of test scores, test pollution such as teaching to the test, or, in extreme cases, teaching the test (Birenbaum, 1996). Problems of marker reliability and bias occur along with negative side effects such as poor motivation, stress, passivity and cheating. Major problems do not seem to characterize the third phase, assessment as enquiry, if we are to believe much that is written in the literature. This does not mean, however, that it is a system without flaws. As we shall see later on in this chapter and in future chapters, many activities and assessment tasks that fall under this umbrella have more than their fair share of problems.

I would like to predict that anyone who has used peer assessment regularly, because of its many benefits, will also have encountered problems. It will come as no surprise to learn that many students dislike having to mark their peers, particularly if they are friends (e.g. Fineman, 1981; Falchikov, 1995a; Jordan, 1999). One of Fineman's (1981: 89) students was reported as expressing the view that, 'Friendships and tensions within the group affected my marks, however hard I tried to be honest. In many cases I overcompensated and was over-generous'. Some students also question their own competence when required to carry out self- or peer assessments. We shall return to discuss these issues further in Chapter 9.

John Cowan (1988) writes honestly, but cheerfully, about the many problems he encountered when first using self-assessment. He reported that the first term appeared to be a disaster. Students didn't know where or how to start. He recounted his trying too hard to be non-prescriptive and felt his lack of knowledge about how to facilitate fully autonomous learning or self-assessment.

Self- and peer assessment are not alone among new assessments in attracting problems. For example, a number of problems associated with the use of portfolios in compulsory education settings have been identified (e.g. Birenbaum, 1996; Dierick and Dochy, 2001). Relationships between portfolio scores and similar assessments have been found to be weak, which casts some doubt on their reliability and validity. However, we should not be too ready to throw out the proverbial baby just because we can't immediately see a way to clean the water. Many innovations are worth the effort of a second and third modification. Any innovation requires careful preparation and ongoing fine tuning at least (e.g. Jordan, 1999; Lejk, 1999a,b). Sometimes more dramatic changes are called for.

The current move to assessment as quality control also seems to have negative consequences. Ongoing debates in the UK on the topic of grade inflation, whether in the context of secondary and high school or college and university, indicate a return to a concern with inflated scores on the part of educators. Attracting even more debate is the question of cheating or plagiarism which we discussed in Chapter 2. Suffice it to say that plagiarism seems to be a worldwide phenomenon which is seen to be growing in prevalence, in parallel with the growth in the extent and acceptance of external accountability in further and higher education.

Variations within the category of assessment as enquiry

As we saw previously, our modern understanding of assessment involves a number of conceptualizations, all of which, to some degree, involve students as active participants in the process. Such formulations include the following:

- 'assessment as learning' or transformative assessment (AAHE Assessment Forum 1997; Alverno College 2001);
- 'authentic assessment' (e.g. Torrance, 1995a);
- autonomous assessment (e.g. Brown and Glasner, 1999);
- competence-based assessment;
- performance assessment;
- sustainable assessment (Boud, 2000).

In addition to many of these conceptualizations, Birenbaum (1996) listed other new terms currently in use to describe assessment. These include direct assessment, constructive assessment, incidental assessment, informal assessment, balanced assessment, curriculum-embedded assessment and curriculum-based assessment. She speculated whether this profusion of terms represents a richness or confusion. As several literature searches have failed to supply much information relating to these, we might conclude that the latter view is supported.

It should be noted that, while these categories are treated as separate entities by many writers and practitioners, there appears to be considerable overlap between them. For example, Torrance (1995a) interpreted 'performance assessment' as equivalent to 'authentic assessment'. Similarly, Ben-David (2000: 474) advocated assessment methodologies which focus on creating authentic environments which involve 'integrated' performance. Likewise, Pearson *et al.* (2001) discussed the development of performance assessment using terms such as 'authentic', 'alternative' and 'situated'.

We shall now look briefly at each of the main assessment categories.

Assessment as learning

Alverno College philosophy

Alverno College faculty (2003: 1) see 'assessment as learning' as a 'multi-dimensional process of judging the individual in action' whose aim is to create 'learning that lasts'. Teachers have it in their power to create conditions that enable learners to integrate 'domains of growth' (Mentkowski *et al.*, 2000: 216): reasoning, performance, self-reflection and development. For learning to be integrative and lasting, the educational system must be coherent, connecting teaching, learning and assessment. In 'assessment as learning', two key features are identified:

(1) Teachers and other trained assessors observe and judge a student's performance based on explicit criteria.
(2) Diagnostic feedback combined with reflective self-assessment by each student, helps to create a continuous process that improves learning and integrates it with assessment.

The Alverno College website (Alverno College, 2003) provides information about both their ability based curriculum and their philosophy of 'assessment as learning', as well as material describing their 'Diagnostic Digital Portfolio (DDP)'. This web-based portfolio, 'enables each Alverno student – anyplace, anytime – to follow her learning progress throughout her years of study'. It also 'helps the student process the feedback she receives from faculty, external assessors and peers. It also enables her to look for patterns in her academic work so she can take more control of her own development and become a more autonomous learner'.

The American Association for Higher Education guidelines

The AAHE Assessment Forum Guide (2001b), based on the Alverno premise, contains the principles of good practice for assessing students. These are listed as follows:

(1) Assessment for student learning begins with educational values.
(2) Assessment is most effective when it reflects an understanding of learning as multidimensional, integrated, and revealed in performance over time.
(3) Assessment works best when the programs it seeks to improve have clear, explicitly stated purposes.
(4) Assessment requires attention to outcomes but also and equally to experiences that lead to those.
(5) Assessment works best when it is ongoing not episodic.

(6) Assessment fosters wider improvement when representatives from across the educational community are involved.
(7) Assessment makes a difference when it begins with issues of use and illuminates questions that people really care about.
(8) Assessment is most likely to lead to improvement when it is part of a larger set of conditions that promote change.
(9) Through assessment, educators meet responsibilities to students and to the public.

Angelo's transformative model and guidelines

Angelo (1999: 1) advocated a 'transformative assessment-as-culture-change model' and supplied research-based guidelines for effective assessment practice. Assessment practices should help students develop skills, dispositions and knowledge needed to carry out the following:

(1) Engage actively – intellectually and emotionally – in their academic work.
(2) Set and maintain realistically high, personally meaningful expectations and goals.
(3) Provide, receive, and make use of regular, timely, specific feedback.
(4) Become explicitly aware of their values, beliefs, preconceptions, and prior learning, and be willing to unlearn when necessary.
(5) Work in ways that recognize (and stretch) their present learning styles or preferences and levels of development.
(6) Seek and find connections to and real-world applications of what they're learning.
(7) Understand and value the criteria, standards, and methods by which they are assessed and evaluated.
(8) Work regularly and productively with academic staff.
(9) Work regularly and productively with other students.
(10) Invest as much engaged time and high-quality effort as possible in academic work.

Authentic assessment

Newmann and Archbald argued that assessment should focus on the achievement of authentic learning outcomes, drawn from a cognitive theory of learning and performance. Authentic achievement is that in which outcomes measured represent 'appropriate, meaningful, significant and worthwhile forms of human accomplishment' (Newmann and Archbald, 1992: 71). Nevo (1995: 94) argued that, in alternative assessment, students are evaluated on the basis of their 'active performance in using knowledge in a creative way to solve worthy problems'. These problems must be authentic representations of real-life problems and assessment must be 'receptive to various innovative methods of evaluation', different from traditional paper and pencil tests and exams. Interaction between assessor and those being assessed is encouraged. According to Nevo, alternative assessment requires that assessors be trained. Two assessment methods identified are portfolios and exhibitions. Both emphasize the importance of the student's participation in the evaluation process.

Pangaro (2000) argued that, over the next few decades, assessment in the context of medical education may, to a greater and greater extent, emphasize authentic methods which focus on real doctor–patient interactions rather than simulated ones. He stressed the desirability of consistent evaluation of students 'in their natural habitat' (Pangaro, 2000: 478). Dierick and Dochy (2001) outlined some recent developments in the field of learning and instruction, also noting that real life contexts are now increasingly seen as important.

Examples of authentic assessment

Authentic assessment appears to be increasingly used in further and higher education. For example, Segers (1996) described the assessment procedures operating in a problem-based program at the Maastricht School of Economics and Business Administration. Assessment involves solving of authentic real life problems and is, thus, contextualized.

Activities used in authentic assessment

- Authentic (real-life) tasks (Klenowski, 1995; Birenbaum, 1996; Segers, 1996; Dierick and Dochy, 2001)
- Exhibitions (Klenowski, 1995; Nevo, 1995; Birenbaum, 1996; Dierick and Dochy, 2001)
- Group activities (Birenbaum, 1996; Dierick and Dochy, 2001)
- Interviews (Birenbaum, 1996; Dierick and Dochy, 2001)
- Journals (Birenbaum, 1996; Dierick and Dochy, 2001)
- Observations (Birenbaum, 1996; Dierick and Dochy, 2001)
- Oral presentations (individual or group) (Klenowski, 1995; Birenbaum, 1996; Dierick and Dochy, 2001)
- Overall tests (Dierick and Dochy, 2001)
- Performances (Klenowski, 1995)
- Portfolios (Birenbaum, 1996; Serafini, 2000; Dierick and Dochy, 2001)
- Practical activities (Klenowski, 1995)
- Research projects (Klenowski, 1995)
- Scientific experiments (Klenowski, 1995)

- Self-, peer and co-assessment (Birenbaum, 1996; Dierick and Dochy, 2001)
- Simulation exercises (Dierick and Dochy, 2001).

The research literature contains many examples of reports of assessment which include these activities. My own work, for example, has involved my students in all of the activities listed. However, I have not used the term 'authentic' to describe the type of assessment being carried out. Of course, this does not mean that the activities were not authentic. Dierick and Dochy (2001) have argued that students rate assignments such as projects, group exercises, portfolios and peer assessment as meaningful because they are authentic. Thus, the use of authentic assessment may be far more widespread than appears at first glance.

Perhaps more surprisingly, Klenowski (1995) argued that essay examinations can constitute authentic assessment (not that they always do). Dierick and Dochy (2001) also listed take-away exams in this category. Much will depend on what it is that constitutes the examination. Similarly, Torrance (1995b) noted that a test is not a unitary concept. Sometimes it consists of multiple-choice questions, while at others times it can consist of 'authentic' tasks.

Autonomous assessment

Brown and Glasner (1999) identified issues of power and control as central to the concept of autonomous assessment. They argued that broadening the base of who does the assessing to include the students themselves presents both a response and a challenge. Brew (1999) argued that students are increasingly exercising control over their study, and are now questioning authority at all levels. Brew also discussed control issues in the context of assessment, describing a typology of self- and peer assessment practices, derived from the three 'knowledge interests' outlined by Habermas (1987): technical, communicative and emancipatory knowledge. She argued that the ability to assess oneself and one's peers in each of these three areas is essential for the development of autonomous independent professional judgement. When self- or peer assessment has an emancipatory component, meta-level skills such as critical reflection may be developed through teaching strategies which encourage this practice, she argued. We shall return to discuss Brew's typology and identify examples of current practice which fall into the category of authentic assessment further in Chapter 5.

Halsall (1995) identified the following as attributes of autonomous learning:

- diagnosing one's own learning needs;
- formulating own learning objectives;

- identifying resources necessary to allow achievement;
- taking initiative in use of these;
- assessing one's own progress and achievements;
- identifying and providing evidence as to these.

Halsall also stressed the importance of self-assessment and student involvement.

Examples of autonomous assessment

Self-, peer and collaborative assessments are regarded as being examples of autonomous assessment. Such methods are widely used worldwide, as the rest of the book will illustrate. Autonomous assessment may be achieved in other ways, too. For example, Halsall (1995) described the development and use of learning contracts on a competence-based PGCE (Post Graduate Certificate in Education) course at Manchester Metropolitan University. He argued that one of the main reasons for using learning contracts was 'to use negotiated, formative assessment and its concomitant demands for professional deliberation to develop the skills of autonomous learning' (Halsall, 1995: 106).

As with authentic assessment, the attributes of autonomous assessment may be in evidence in the absence of the label.

Activities used in autonomous assessment

- Learning contracts (Halsall, 1995)
- Negotiated assessment (Halsall, 1995)
- Portfolios (Challis, 1999)
- Reflection (Halsall, 1995)
- Self- and peer assessment (Stefani, 1998; Brew, 1999; Brown and Glasner, 1999).

Competence-based assessment

Ben-David used Miller's (1990) pyramid of competence in her discussion of assessment methodologies which focused on creating authentic environments, particularly in the later stages of undergraduate education (Ben-David, 2000: 474). Miller's (1990) pyramid is illustrated in Figure 3.1.

Ben-David stressed 'integrated' over 'discrete' performance, where 'integrated performance' is defined as 'readiness for the next phase'. At the base, a learner 'knows' something, while at the next level up, she 'knows how' to do it. The third level involves being able to 'show how' something may be done and the final, top level involves being able to 'do'.

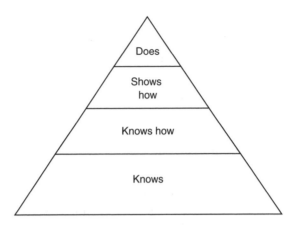

Figure 3.1 Miller's pyramid of competence

Problems with competence-based assessment

Winter (1995) described the use of a set of general assessment criteria in a competence-based degree in social work (the Accreditation and Support for Specified Expertise and Training – ASSET programme). The ASSET programme was developed within a partnership between Anglia Polytechnic University and the Ford Motor company in response to difficulties associated with assessment related to the NCVQ programme. Winter (1995) summarized criticisms of the NCVQ model. These included

(1) lists of specific requirements are behaviourist and atomistic;
(2) the system is reductionist rather than holistic;
(3) the system does not encourage initiative and responsibility;
(4) lists cannot encompass complex concepts such as maturity, critical thinking, group work or complex skills in general;
(5) the model is atheoretical and lacking in intellectual rigour.

Purcell (2001) responded to some of these criticisms, identifying what she labelled as 'misconceptions' about competence-based assessment. Among these misunderstandings are views that such assessments

- rely on assessment of performance in the workplace;
- are appropriate only at vocational or technical level (and, therefore, not suitable at higher or professional levels);
- are concerned with practical skills and not with understanding;
- do not prepare learners for further development.

Purcell (2001) argued that these beliefs do not apply to all competence-based assessments and reported a case study which used a model developed by the Association of Accounting Technicians (AAT) which challenged some misconceptions. The AAT model, rated as suitable for application to the assessment of higher or professional qualifications, integrated assessment of skills, performance, knowledge and understanding.

Theoretical underpinnings

Edwards and Knight (1995: 14) asserted that competence-based assessment takes the following perspectives into account:

- philosophical bases;
- psychological bases;
- sociological 'ramifications' (i.e. social purposes served by assessment of competency and its impact on relationships between and within groups of peers, tutors and mentors);
- practical issues such as expense and demands on staff time.

However, Edwards and Knight (1995: 11) asserted that assessment of competence is 'riddled with contradictions, problems and flaws'. They argued that, because of this, many shy away from it and continue with the familiar, tried and tested traditional system. In addition, Cumming and Maxwell (1999: 183) argued that competence-based assessment has 'no apparent underlying theory', and that its aims have not been sustained in practice. They recommend a return to fundamental principles. Thus, further discussion on this topic is both necessary and inevitable. It is to be hoped that continuing research and development activities will shed further light on this question.

Examples of assessment of competences

The higher and further education research literature contains many examples of the assessment of competencies in practice. For example, ten Cate and De Haes (2000) described the assessment of medical students' communication skills and attitudes at the University of Amsterdam. They noted that, in practice, patient care is concerned only with actual behaviour, 'behaviour-in-daily-practice' (ten Cate and De Haes, 2000: 40). This, they argued, corresponds with the top level of Miller's pyramid of competence. Carter and Neal (1995) described the assessment of competencies within an industrially based MSc in engineering project management, developed jointly by the engineering department at Lancaster University and the training department of Smiths Industries Aerospace and Defence Ltd. Edwards and Knight (1995: 23) discussed the NCVQ approach to the assessment of competencies in FE and ways of incorporating competencies into degree profiles. They also debated the value of Records of Achievement (ROAs) and increased collaboration between higher education and professional groups such as those involved in social work training or engineering.

Activities used in competence assessment

- Case studies (e.g. Purcell, 2001)
- Collaboration between higher education and professional groups (e.g. Edwards and Knight, 1995)
- Communication skills development (e.g. ten Cate and De Haes, 2000)
- 'Devolved' assessments (including observations in the workplace, witness testimonies and simulations, involving employers in assessment) (e.g. Tait and Godfrey, 1998; Purcell, 2001)
- 'Integrated performance' (e.g. Ben-David, 2000)
- Performance (e.g. Purcell, 2001)
- Records of Achievement (e.g. Edwards and Knight, 1995)
- Skills development (e.g. Purcell, 2001)

Research and development into competence assessment

Some research into the assessment of competence has been undertaken. For example, van der Vleuten *et al.* (2000) reviewed research findings relating to the assessment of clinical competence during the clerkship phase of the undergraduate medical training programme. They considered reliability, validity, the effect of competence assessments on the training programme and learning behaviour, acceptability and costs. Information gained during this exercise was used to select assessment methods to evaluate student performance. The authors argued that reliability may be compromised in two main ways. First of all, competence measurement is situation-specific, and second, assessors may be prone to subjective judgements. The authors recommend multiple assessors as a means of minimizing subjectivity of judgement. Van der Vleuten *et al.* (2000: 593) argued that generic skills associated with competence in the context of clinical performance are 'virtually non-existent'. Similarly, they reported that definition of constituent attributes of competence has been found to be problematic, as individual competencies are not independent of each other. As with reliability, the authors recommend that greater validity may be achieved by the use of variety: in this case a variety of test methods.

Sensi *et al.* (2000) investigated the effects of different scoring methods on the results of clinical competence assessments. Participants in their study were final year medical students using 'Procuste', a programme of multimedia computer-based simulated cases which required learners to choose diagnostic and therapeutic options according to a cost/benefit analysis. Three scoring methods were compared: one using weighted and unweighted items, another with unweighted items only, and a method including a single-item analysis. The first method was used as a reference. Results of the analysis found the first method generated 'a more realistic pass/fail rate compared with the two other methods' (Sensi *et al.*, 2000: 601) and showed a better correlation with curriculum scores.

Performance assessment

Cumming and Maxwell (1999) argued that performance assessment must be contextualized, holistic and integrated. Similarly, Pearson *et al.* (2001: 176) argued that developments such as performance assessment provided opportunities for educators to promote 'coherence and alignment' among the key elements of education (curriculum, teaching, assessment, professional development and learning). Ben-David (1999) reported calls for national examinations and performance assessment which emphasized complex higher order knowledge and skills in the setting in which they naturally occur. She argued that the expectations of several groups needed to be considered: faculty, students, future employers and professional or certifying bodies. Ben-David asserted that performance assessment implies explicit criteria, feedback and self-assessment.

Ben-David (1999: 24) also provided examples of activities to be undertaken by faculty in order to implement assessment programs in outcome-based education. These included the requirement to carryout the following:

- outline philosophy and assessment premises;
- define relationship between faculty and students;
- establish outcome behaviour principles;
- select methods by which outcome behaviours are defined, for example critical incident techniques;
- develop assessment criteria;
- establish an assessment 'taskforce' to co-ordinate development of assessment materials;
- work towards establishing an 'assessment oriented faculty';
- design systematic assessment program;
- indicate the flow of assessment information, lines of communication, etc.

Ben-David stressed the need to ensure that students are included and informed. 'In an outcomes-based program often students may feel they are over tested and under informed'.

Examples of performance assessment

Few examples of performance assessment based within higher education have been found. McMartin *et al.* (2000: 111) described the implementation of the scenario assignment, 'a qualitative performance assessment tool designed to assess students' knowledge of engineering practices, team-work and problem solving'. The authors claimed that it is less time-consuming than observation, design assignments or portfolio building. The tool requires students to respond to an open-ended problem descrip-tion as though they were project manager whose job it is to prepare a team to solve the problem. Reliability of the tool, which was found to be generally high, was based on the level of inter-rater agreement between two trained readers who had practised and developed a common understanding of the scoring criteria. The authors included the detailed analytic rubric for scoring scenarios in the appendix to their paper.

Activities suggested as suitable for use in performance assessment

- Assessing core abilities repeatedly over time to measure growth (e.g. Ben-David, 1999)
- Developing and using explicit assessment criteria (Ben-David, 1999; AAHE, 2001a,b)
- Portfolio development (e.g. Broadfoot, 1995)
- Remediating deficiencies (e.g. Ben-David, 1999)
- Use of contextualized, holistic and integrated activities (e.g. Cumming and Maxwell, 1999)
- Use of critical incident techniques (e.g. Ben-David, 1999)
- Use of scenario assignments (e.g. McMartin *et al.*, 2000)
- Use of self-assessment (e.g. Clarke and Stephens, 1996)
- Writing exercises (structured) (e.g. Stiggins, 1987).

Sustainable assessment

'Sustainable assessment encompasses the knowledge, skills and predis-positions required to support lifelong learning activities. If assessment tasks within courses at any level act to undermine lifelong learning, then they cannot be regarded as making a contribution to sustainable assess-ment' (Boud, 2000: 151). Boud (2002) suggested that, in order for students to become effective lifelong learners, they need to be prepared to under-take assessment of the tasks they face throughout their lives in both for-mal and informal settings. In this respect, sustainable assessment may be said to resemble authentic assessment. Boud uses characteristics of effective formative assessment identified by recent research to illustrate features of sustainable assessment. He stresses the importance of feedback, arguing that students should be encouraged to seek feedback from a variety of sources within their environment to enable them to undertake subsequent learning more effectively. Such feedback might come from peers, from other practitioners, or from written and other sources.

Boud's 'sustainable assessment' must be regarded as being very closely associated with that of Mentkowski and associates' (2000: 216) 'learning that lasts', which, they argued, is 'integrative; experiential; self-aware and self-reflective; self-assessed and self-regarding; developmental and individual; transitional and transformative; active and interactive, independent and collaborative; situated and transferable; deep and expansive, purposeful and responsible'.

Boud (2000) identified features that assessment tasks should promote if they are to be regarded as part of sustainable assessment:

(1) confidence that new learning tasks *can* be mastered;
(2) exploration of criteria and standards which apply to any given learning task;
(3) active engagement with learning tasks with a view to testing understanding and application of criteria and standards;
(4) development of devices for self-monitoring and judging progression towards goals;
(5) practice in discernment to identify critical aspects of problems and issues;
(6) access to learning peers and others with expertise to reflect on challenges and gain support for renewed efforts;
(7) use of feedback to influence new ways of engaging with the learning task;
(8) care in the use of language to avoid creating premature closure on ongoing learning.

As Boud has argued elsewhere, the use of value-laden, judgmental words, 'final vocabulary' (Rorty, 1989) is to be avoided, as it may damage self-esteem and inhibit learning (Boud, 1995a). In spite of the links between sustainable assessment and the Alverno College conception of learning that lasts (Mentkowski and associates, 2000) which stresses the importance of self-assessment, Boud (2002) sees sustainable assessment as distinct from self-assessment. Although he states that they share practices in common, he also maintains that many examples of self-assessment are not adequate for sustainable assessment purposes, and 'it is quite possible to promote many aspects of sustainable assessment without engaging in self-assessment per se' (Boud, 2002).

Examples of sustainable assessment

Boud (2002) suggested that a good example of sustainable assessment from his own practice is the use of a self-assessment schedule (Boud, 1992) in combination with group generated criteria. Boud also indicated that it is also possible to find examples that work in small advanced classes and in seminars, though examples of use in very large classes are harder to locate.

Activities used in sustainable assessment

Boud (2002) has maintained that sustainable assessment cannot be opera-tionalized in a straightforward way, arguing that what is sustainable activity in one situation or for one student may not be so in other situations or for other individuals. Sustainable assessment cannot exist independ-ently of the environment of learning. In terms of the activities used in similar types of assessment and listed in Table 3.3, he stated that,

> any or all of them could be conducted in a way which is more or less sus-tainable. It is not so much the class of activity, but the way in which any of them is conducted. I see sustainability as a purpose of assessment, not a method or approach. While traditional unseen examinations are the least likely to be able to be effectively revised with the goal of sustain-ability in mind, even they could be tweaked a bit in that direction!
>
> (Boud, 2002)

Summary of methods and activities used in assessment as enquiry

Methods and activities used in the six varieties of assessment as enquiry are shown in Table 3.3. An undifferentiated formulation, 'Alternative' assessment, is also included.

Similarities and differences between varieties of assessment as enquiry

As we can see in summary Table 3.3, several varieties of assessment as enquiry share a number of attributes. For example, the greatest overlap is in self-, peer and co-assessment which feature in five of the six varieties. The generating of explicit criteria features in four varieties, as do per-formances and observations. No variety has fewer than two attributes, largely due to the very wide variety of activities associated with sustain-able assessment. Of course, it is entirely possible that greater overlap is present, but not made explicit in the literature.

Key differences between traditional and alternative assessments

As we have seen earlier, while varieties of alternative assessments may share some characteristics, they all differ from traditional assessment in

Table 3.3 Summary of activities associated with different forms of assessment as enquiry

Variety of assessment	Activities																											
	Authentic tasks	Case studies	Criteria explicit/generated	Communication exercises	'Devolved' assessment	Exhibitions	Group activities	Integrated performance	Interviews	Journals	Learning contracts	Learning response log	Negotiated reporting	Observations	Oral presentations I&G	Overall tests	Performances	Portfolios	Practical activities	Problem solving	Records of Achievement	Research projects	Scientific experiments	Self-, peer and co-assessment	Simulations	Student-led conferences	Essay exams[a]	Take-away exams[a]
Alternative (undiffer'd)?	×		×			×	×		×	×		×	×	×	×	×	×	×	×	×		×		×	×	×		
Authentic	×					×	×		×	×				×	×	×	×	×	×			×	×	×			×	×
Autonomous				×							×											×	×	×				
Competence-based		×			×			×													×							
Performance assessment			×											×			×							×				
Sustainable	×	×	×	×	×	×	×	×	×	×		×	×	×	×	×	×	×	×	×	×	×	×	×		×	×	×

Notes

a It has been argued that these activities can constitute authentic or sustainable assessment (Dierick and Dochy, 2001; Boud, 2002). However, this is clearly not always the case, as much depends on the content of the examinations and the arrangements for completing them.

I & G = Individual and group.

Table 3.4 Characteristics of traditional and alternative assessments summarized

Traditional assessments	Alternative assessments
Propositional knowledge likely to be assessed	Procedural knowledge assessed
Narrow range of methods used	Wide range of methods used
Methods do not always reflect curriculum aims	Methods try to reflect curriculum aims
Assessment separated from teaching and learning	Assessment integrated with teaching and learning
Assessment methods opaque e.g. criteria not made clear	Methods aim for transparency. Criteria explicit
Learners lack power	Learners have degrees of power
Learners can avoid taking responsibility for own learning	Learners encouraged to take responsibility for learning
Reliability and validity a major concern	Reliability and validity a concern
Methods not scientifically based	Some methods based on, or derived from, theory
Methods hard to implement in a rapidly expanding HE system	Use of some varieties stimulated by expansion
Often gives rise to negative feelings which can persist over years	Negative feelings generally transitory
Has negative consequences	Few negative consequences reported so far

several important ways. Most important of these differences is the role of the student and the amount of power ceded to learners by teachers. However, Birenbaum (1996) argued that alternative and traditional assessments can be seen as complementary not contradictory. What is important, she argued, is to match assessment techniques with purposes.

Characteristics of traditional and alternative assessments are shown in Table 3.4.

Irrespective of one's philosophical point of view and assessment preference, traditional assessment seems to have rather more negative characteristics than its alternative counterpart. In the next chapter we shall look at the reasons why teachers decide not to use traditional assessment, choosing rather to involve their students in newer forms of assessment. We shall also trace the changing patterns of reasons over the past fifty or so years.

Chapter 4

Why do teachers involve students in assessment?

Themes from the 1950s to 1980s

The second half of the twentieth century saw new interest in involving students in assessment. We shall inspect each decade in turn, starting with the 1950s, as this point marked the publication of the earliest examples of self- or peer assessment I have been able to locate.

In *the 1950s*, lecturers began to involve students in assessment. However, they did not appear to be concerned with either formative or summative aspects of the process. What appeared to motivate most teachers who published their work were statistical issues relating to reliability or validity of ratings. They were also concerned with issues of performance and selection. However, even then, one researcher at least (Kubany, 1957) valued the student perspective and began to analyse the process of involving students in assessment. The few studies reported in the 1950s fall into two main categories: 'Measurement' and 'Investigating the process'.

Studies involving students in assessment continued to be concerned with methodological issues into *the 1960s*. In this decade we also see early signs of interest in problems associated with traditional assessment, and in group dynamics and their effects on assessment. There are also continuing tentative investigations into the processes of involving students in assessment. Studies in this decade may be grouped into three categories: 'Measurement', 'Addressing problems of assessment' and 'Investigating the process'.

The theme of using innovations in assessment to address problems in the educational system continued into *the 1970s*. For example, Korman and Stubblefield (1971: 670) observed that 'many students become overly involved in grade getting, often to the detriment of more fundamental educational values'. However, other themes emerged, including a 'modern' reason for involving students. The *benefits* of student involvement began to be made explicit, and were seen as grounds for involving students in assessment (e.g. Friesen and Dunning, 1973). Towards the end of the decade, pressures in the educational context similar to those being experienced in the present day were cited as the rationale for the introduction of peer assessment. Such changes included increased demands on staff time and energy, a proliferation of learning objectives and widely differing abilities of students in relation to handling increased responsibilities. Lawrence and Branch (1974, referred to in Lawrence and Branch, 1978: 12) also described their students as 'co-producers rather than consumers' of the educational programme. This may be an early indication of teachers beginning to question their power, perhaps. Studies conducted in the 1970s may be grouped into four main categories: 'Measurement', 'Investigating the process', 'Addressing problems' and 'Benefits'. In addition there are early indications of two further proto-categories: 'Pressure' and 'Teachers beginning to question their power'.

The benefits of student involvement in assessment in the context of professional education, first cited as the spur to innovation by researchers in *the 1970s*, characterized a number of studies in *the 1980s*. The benefits of student involvement in assessment were also recognized more widely. It should be noted, however, that in some cases, justification for the implementation of a scheme was made post hoc. Another feature of student involvement in assessment in the 1980s was the recognition that communication skills are important in a variety of professions, and that students are well placed to carry out assessments of these skills. Moreland *et al.* (1981) began to put self- and peer assessment under the microscope. Other studies followed, several of which addressed problems with traditional assessment. Added to this variety of reasons for carrying out peer and self-assessment, occasional researchers still wished to study reliability or validity of student marking. Also during this decade, there appeared to be more examples of staff beginning to question the power imbalance between themselves and students. Towards the end of the decade, employment requirements were cited as a reason for introducing a peer assessment scheme in the context of team work (Earl, 1986).

The reasons for involving students in assessment throughout the 1980s fall into seven categories: 'Benefits'; 'Investigating processes'; 'Addressing problems of assessment'; 'Measurement'; 'Assessing and developing professional and communication skills'; 'Transferring power' and 'Pressure'.

Main themes and numbers of studies located between the 1950s and 1980s are shown in Table 4.1.

In the 1990s, many examples of assessment studies which involve students are in evidence. We shall look at this decade in some detail.

Table 4.1 Summary: themes of the 1950s to 1980s

Decade	Main themes	No. of studies
1950s	Measurement and performance	3
1960s	Tentative investigations of processes and problems	8
1970s	Further investigations: methodologies and individual differences	15
1980s	Benefits, professional education and communication skills	14

The 1990s: benefits and pressures

This decade produced many more papers about aspects of student involvement in assessment than any decade which preceded it. In fact, entries in the 1990s exceeded the total of entries from previous decades: 1995, a UK Research Assessment Exercise year, was a particularly rich year for publications on the topic. However, although I searched thoroughly for papers, the rate of production and breadth of coverage exceeded my ability to keep up (I am put in mind of the difficulties of ever finishing painting the Forth rail bridge), and the corpus discussed is certainly incomplete. However, I hope and believe that the studies summarized are a reasonable representation of the whole corpus.

Two key themes emerge in the 1990s: benefits and pressures. The benefits of involving students in assessment are widely reported throughout this decade. However, teachers report being under pressure from at least two main sources: increasing class sizes and their associated assessment burden, and external and internal organizations that are making other demands. Dochy and McDowell (1997) reviewed developments in the learning society which might be seen to act as current pressures on teachers. They listed these as

(1) the information age which is characterized by 'an infinite, dynamic and changing mass of information' (Dochy and McDowell, 1997: 280);
(2) the use of the Internet, multimedia and educational technology;
(3) the changing labour market and the needs of employers for immediately employable graduates;
(4) the student as consumer;
(5) lifelong learning;
(6) the move away from testing towards assessment (which we discussed in the previous chapter);
(7) new roles for teachers in new learning environments;

(8) the move towards assessing skills and competencies;
(9) the use of co-, self- and peer assessment;
(10) different functions of assessment with many now arguing that assessment practices may be used to improve instruction;
(11) standard setting and the use of profiles.

We see the effects of these pressures within the corpus of assessment studies that involve students reported in the 1990s.

Many rationales are familiar from previous decades, but an important 'flavour' to this decade, particularly at the beginning, is that of autonomous learners and lifelong learning. For example, Williams (1992: 46) cited the 'goal of developing more autonomous learners with self responsibility for continuing education throughout life' as a reason for involving students in assessment. The objective of saving the teacher's time occurs explicitly in the 1990s, though it had been hinted at in previous decades. Some studies simply build on previous work, giving no rationale for the study being reported. Yet other studies rely on the assumed knowledge of the reader. A common theme in some studies involving self- and peer assessment appears to be a growing desire to increase participation of students in the learning process and to development a less teacher-centred education.

A number of studies (e.g. Mathews, 1994) discuss benefits of involving students in assessment in the context of group work. We shall return to discuss this topic more fully in Chapter 9. A very few studies give no clear rationale for their implementation (e.g. Hahlo, 1997).

I grouped reasons for involving students in assessment in the 1990s into eleven categories:

(1) Benefits, improving student learning and development
(2) Facilitating acquisition and development of skills
(3) Pressure from external and internal bodies
(4) Addressing problems of assessment
(5) Measuring reliability or validity
(6) Investigating the process
(7) Developing communication skills
(8) Transferring power
(9) Providing feedback
(10) Saving teachers' time and reducing their workload
(11) Dissemination and application

Many studies fall into more than one category. For example, Goldfinch and Raeside (1990) listed four reasons for involving their students in assessment:

(1) to help fulfil Napier University's mission statement and provide students with experience necessary for their careers (Pressure);
(2) to develop personal qualities such as responsibility and enterprise (Benefits);
(3) to help students work as part of a team (Pressure? Benefits?);
(4) to help address the problem of the difficulty of differentiating between group members (Problems).

Details and examples of the categories of reasons for involving students in assessment in the 1990s are shown in Table 4.2(1)–(11), beginning with the most frequently mentioned. A key to abbreviations used in Tables 4.2 and 4.3 is to be found in Table 4.4.

Benefits, improving student learning and development

A wide variety of benefits are identified in many studies. Studies were generally rated as fully or partially successful, but benefits not always investigated systematically, and formal evaluation is generally absent.

Facilitating acquisition and development of skills

As with the previous category, the literature is rich in variety here, too. A wide range of skill development areas are to be found in the reasons given for involving students in assessment. Some are specific, others more general. Samples of studies are shown in Table 4.2(2).

Pressure from external and internal bodies

This category deals explicitly with some of the pressures identified by Dochy and McDowell (1997). Pressure from external or internal bodies to introduce innovative methods of assessment may be imposed or self-enforced. An influential national movement, in terms of higher education assessment practice in the UK, was the Enterprise in Higher Education initiative which is mentioned explicitly by a number of teachers and researchers (e.g. Stefani, 1994) or more obliquely (e.g. Fry, 1990). The Royal Society for Arts Capability programme was similarly influential in the UK. More recently, the Quality Assurance Agency for Higher Education (QAA) and Teaching Quality Assessment (TQA) initiative have exerted pressure on higher education in the UK. Samples of studies are shown in Table 4.2(3).

Table 4.2 Themes and features of the 1990s

Features/methods/motivation	Outcomes	Studies	Areas of implementation
(1) Benefits			
(a) Multiple benefits (e.g. higher order cognitive skills, increased autonomy, increased participation)			
Peer marking to aid learning; encourage working outside class	Advantages identified	Fry (1990)	1st yr tutorial problems mechanical engineering
To help students improve awareness and understanding of subject and thus encourage evaluation skills and aid preparation for final yr. project`	Students rated scheme positively.	Edwards and Sutton (1991)	SA by 1st yr Management Information Systems course students
Objective to enhance learning potential	Objective achieved	Stefani (1992)	Biochemical practical work
Improving learning, sharpen critical abilities, increase autonomy	Self reports suggested improvements; see Chapter 6	Falchikov (1994, 1995a,b)	1st yr. soc. sci. oral presentations and 3rd yr students developmental psychology/ oral presentations
Improve learning and investigate effects of practice	PA improved in second semester, but author concluded that students were not good assessors	Freeman (1995)	1st and 2nd yr engineering undergraduates and diploma students/peer contribution to activities
To improve self-learning by learning how to judge the quality of one's own work and that of others	Students not 'overwhelmingly enthusiastic' but leaning towards acceptance. Authors advocate use of P & SA, groups and computer-based feedback to maintain quality	Oldfield and MacAlpine (1995: 129)	Oral presentations final yr business/marketing
Peers to provide feedback prior to essay submission and improve understanding and achievement	Student self-reports suggested exercise was beneficial; see Chapter 6	Falchikov (1996a)	Essays 4th yr Biological Sciences

Aim	Findings	Reference	Context
To identify and evaluate benefits of PA as perceived by students	Results 'very encouraging'. Student self reports endorse benefits	Orsmond et al. (1996)	1st yr biology undergraduate posters
To sharpen students' critical faculties and encourage students to contribute to critical discussion	Teachers valued increased student involvement; students perceived scheme fair	Ewers and Searby (1997)	Musical composition
To encourage higher order cognitive abilities	Majority of students rated selves as capable of SA of LOCs, less so for HOCs	Zoller and Ben-Chaim (1997)	SA by biology majors, HOCs questions
(b) Autonomy/independent learning			
S & PA to encourage students to take responsibility for own learning	Outcomes achieved (more marked in 3rd year). See below	Price and Cutler (1995)	Variety of products/activities (3 yrs geography);
Increase autonomy	See above and Chapter 6	Falchikov (1994, 1995a,b)	1st yr. soc. sci. oral presentations and 3rd yr. students developmental psychology/ oral presentations
SA activities to establish goals for future independent learning	Activities found to complement traditional evaluation techniques. Students have 'greater voice'	McNamara and Deane (1995)	University ESL students
P & SA for increased independence	Opportunities provided	Beaman (1998)	Adult learners
(c) Fostering deep approach			
S & PA to help foster deeper approach to learning by encouraging students to apply theory to practice	Modest to low correlations between teacher and peers, but questionnaire data suggested confirmed benefits. See below	Lennon (1995)	2nd year health science physiotherapy undergraduates; practical simulation
(d) Developing reflection			
To help students develop into reflective practitioners	Educational benefits deemed to outweigh risks (agreement between PA and teacher marks moderate only)	Kwan and Leung (1996)	3rd yr hotel and tourism management training exercise

(Table 4.2 continued)

Table 4.2 Continued

Features/methods/motivation	Outcomes	Studies	Areas of implementation
To investigate whether students understand reflection and critical evaluation	Portfolios beneficial	Askham (1997)	2nd yr HND Advanced investment
Role of portfolios in aiding reflection	Portfolios = 'true union of assessment and learning'	Woodward (1998: 421)	Bachelor of Teaching course
(e) Anxiety reduction			
To reduce maths and test anxiety	Achieved, plus improvement in statistics achievement.	Bangert (1995)	Performance-based assessments of maths graduate students
(f) General investigations of learning and assessment			
Investigation of SA	Problems due to 'mismatch' between student understanding of criteria and teacher expectations, but 90% students rated experience as aiding learning.	Trevitt and Pettigrove (1995)	3rd year fire science and forestry undergraduates/test
Study of learning, including SA	SA associated with improved performance	Hassmén et al. (1996)	Students from introductory psychology course
(g) Investigating beneficial effects on learning			
	Study rated successful; advantages reported by students and teachers	Ngu et al. (1995)	Essay marking, Master's level computing science and engineering students using 'peers' (computer-assisted PA scheme)

(2) Facilitating acquisition and development of skills
(a) Improving S & PA skills

Enabling students gain experience of using assessment criteria to judge performance	Students used more restricted range than tutors and some criteria rated more consistently than others.	Lennon (1995)	2nd yr Physiotherapy
Developing S & PA skills	Authors concluded staff assessment had little advantage over PA	Butcher *et al.* (1995)	1st yr Biosciences; PA of poster presentations
Encouraging growth in S & PA skills	PA rated as beneficial	Oldfield and MacAlpine (1995)	1st and 2nd yr BEng and 2nd yr HD
Examining students' awareness of own strengths and weaknesses	Poor match between T and student ratings	Penny and Grover (1996)	Final yr students of Education
Preparation for S & PA	Students remained unconvinced, fearing lack of objectivity	Greenan *et al.* (1997)	Group and written report presentations
Helping students develop SA abilities	Revised exercise deemed successful in developing confidence in SA (no evidence supplied)	MacAlpine (1999)	Electrical engineering
Making students aware of assessment criteria	Scheme generally well received, but weaker students least positive about it	Taras (1999)	Social and international studies

(b) Transferable skills

To develop range transferable skills (ability to work in team, design experiments, retrieve information, analyse data, communicate effectively orally and in writing)	P & SA offer reliable and valid alternative/complementary assessment strategies. See above	Butcher *et al.* (1995)	1st yr students of Biosciences; PA of poster presentations
Skills of autonomous learning	Students were required to provide evidence of achievement	Halsall (1995)	Competence-based PGCE
Musical performance and report writing	Authors thought PA helped students in terms of future performance. See Chapter 5	Hunter and Russ (1996)	PA of 2nd yr musical performance

(Table 4.2 continued)

Table 4.2 Continued

Features/methods/motivation	Outcomes	Studies	Areas of implementation
Lifelong learning skills (and helping faculty gain insights into self-directed learning)	The authors concluded that practice is required	Sullivan et al. (1999)	S & PA of PBL in context 3rd yr surgical clerkship
Skills to become competent resource based learners (self-judgement and networking skills)	Students reported finding exercise difficult but valuable in improving self-judgement and providing opportunity to see alternative approaches	MacDonald et al. (1999)	Electronic formative peer review
(c) Improving/acquiring computer/programming skills			
To acquire computing skills	Students endorsed scheme. Authors reported tendency for students to underestimate achievements cf. marks from previous year.	Edwards and Sutton (1991)	SA by 2nd yr students of Information Systems Management
Improving programming skills	PA measures breadth of achievement. Good results achieved	Rosbottom and Topp (1993/4)	PA by HND students of information science
(d) Using SA to investigate other skills			
To investigate experiences of Black American students	SA of leadership skills and rates of participation used	Kimbrough (1995)	Membership of fraternities/ sororities = key variable
(3) Pressure			
(a) External: national bodies UK professional bodies e.g. SEDA; TDLB UK's BCS US's AAHE	General influence	Young (1999)	PG Cert in teaching and learning
	Syllabus and delivery Influence in changing focus of learning from *what* to *how* noted	Lejk (1999b) Keith (1996)	Computing science General application

US National Educational Goals Panel (1991); National Council on Educational Standards and Testing (1992)	Call for national examinations and performance assessment emphasizing complex higher order knowledge/skills	Ben-David (1999)	General application
Australasia's HERDSA	General influence		
(b) Internal: formal and mandatory			
Director of student assessment appointed	Monitored assessment procedures	Tait and Knight (1994)	Throughout a US University
(c) Internal: problems resulting from external pressure			
'National policy and institutional pressure for more cost effective learning'	This pressure drove up group sizes and increased demands on teachers' time	Lapham and Webster (1999: 184)	Information management
(d) Internal: informal and voluntary			
To fulfil university mission statement and provide students with experience necessary for careers	Technique deemed valid	Goldfinch and Raeside (1990)	Mathematics
To comply with internal credit scheme	Alignment with scheme achieved	Young (1999)	PGCert in teaching and learning
To meet employer needs for graduates with good communication skills	No correspondence found between marks awarded by students and their communication skills. See Chapter 5	Hughes and Large (1994)	Final yr pharmacology
To develop industrial and economic awareness	External industrial assessor involved. Role/outcomes not clear. See also above	Butcher et al. (1995)	1st yr biosciences
To prepare for life by developing S & PA	Skill development reported to have taken place. However, transferability assumed. Students uncomfortable	Greenan et al. (1997)	Group presentations; PG management programme

(Table 4.2 continued)

Table 4.2 Continued

Features/methods/motivation	Outcomes	Studies	Areas of implementation
(4) Measurement			
Reliability and/or validity of S &/or PA[a]	Correlations between PA and faculty high and stat. sig.	Bergee (1993)	S, P & TA of brass jury performance
	'Staff-assisted' peer marking reported as reliable as teacher marking 'if not more so'	Scott and Watson (1992: 516)	PA in engineering
	Reliability high for multiple raters, low for singletons. 'Validity concerns are rarely amenable to complete resolution'	Magin (1993b: 4)	'Community medicine and human behaviour
	Students had 'a realistic perception of their own abilities' and could 'make rational judgements on the achievements of their peers'	Stefani (1994: 69)	1st yr biochemistry lab reports
	See Chapter 5	Cheng and Warren (1999)	Oral and written tasks of Hong Kong electrical engineering students learning English
	P/T mark correlation, $r = 0.8$	MacAlpine (1999)	Engineering
(5) Addressing problems			
Non-participation in discussion	Increased involvement	Ewers and Searby (1997)	Musical composition
Encouraging and assessment of participation	S & PA ratings higher than teacher's. Some problems encountered	Gopinath (1999)	MBA
Exams 'unrealistic' and unfair	Perceptions of unfairness persisted	McDowell (1995)	Review article

(6) Investigating the process

(a) General

Open-ended investigation	Kelmar (1992)	Graduate management course
Identification of methods to permit and encourage growth in S & PA skills	Oldfield and MacAlpine (1995)	1st and 2nd yr. BEng and 2nd yr HD
	Useful information gathered	
	PA in steps effective strategy. See above	
Investigation to minimize factors outside control of students; implementation of new assessment scheme.	Tariq et al. (1998)	Assessment of honours project in Biology, Biochemistry and Biomedical sciences
	Old and new schemes compared and no statistical differences found between them	

(b) Student attitudes/satisfaction

Attitudes to S & PA	Williams (1992)	1st yr Business studies
	Exercise found useful, interesting and fun to do. Some reservations about PA. See Chapters 6 and 9	
Student perception of assessment methods	Kniveton (1996)	Students in Human, Environmental and Social science studies from 2 universities
	Overall view = continuous assessment in not more than $1/2$ grade measurement	
Attitudes to PA before vs after participation	Cheng and Warren (1997)	1st yr electrical engineering (English for academic purposes)
	See Chapter 5	
Attitudes to PA	Gatfield (1999)	International marketing management
	High levels of satisfaction	

(c) Individual differences

Preferred approaches to learning	Williams (1992)	1st yr business studies
	Participation and democratic relationships preferred	
Individual/context differences: S & PA of interpersonal problems	Hill et al. (1998)	Students recruited through psychology department volunteer pool
	Peer and self-observations of problems differed in emphasis	

(Table 4.2 continued)

Table 4.2 Continued

Features/methods/motivation	Outcomes	Studies	Areas of implementation
(d) Effects of practice			
Effects of practice on PA accuracy	Ability improved in the second half of semester	Freeman (1995)	Final year undergraduates/business/marketing degree/oral presentations
(7) Developing communication skills			
Peer evaluation of writing	Most teachers rated process as effective	Lynch and Golen (1992)	Juniors and seniors in business communication
S & PA of essay	57% students reported benefits	Mowl and Pain (1995); Pain and Mowl (1996)	Essay writing in 1st yr geography
SA of coursework essays	See Chapter 5	Longhurst and Norton (1997)	Psychology essay writing
P & SA of posters	SA over-marked cf. T, but PA & TA similar	Billington (1997)	Poster assessment; final yr biology and environmental sci.
(8) Transferring power			
Co-assessment	Co-assessed students represented higher proportions than expected by chance at the higher grade levels	Hall (1995)	2nd and 3rd yr Bachelor of Education students
Review of research into student self-evaluation processes	Student involvement seen as empowering	Klenowski (1995)	Variety, including some compulsory education
Giving students responsibility in every aspect of course (incl. assessment), and a sense of ownership and control of process	PA found useful and fair. Student involvement increased	Rafiq and Fullerton (1996)	PA of group projects in Civil engineering

'Peer evaluation also has the interesting implication of signalling a different relationship between lecturers and students' Involving students in determining method of assessment	See above	Billington (1997: 219)	Final yr biology and environmental science posters
PA & group work as vehicles for student empowerment	Author's faith in approach supported by student responses	Ritter (1997)	History teaching in Australian CAE
	'The nature of student empowerment associated with the use of these methods is difficult to monitor and, indeed, the benefits may be delayed'	Stanier (1997: 95)	2nd yr students of interdisciplinary studies
P & SA require that power and control be handed over to students	The 'instructor must have patience and faith for this method of assessment to work'	Beaman (1998: 56)	Contract SA by adult learners
S & PA. Aim to motivate and encourage students to make more effort by giving them more control	Decided to 'embrace scheme 'more wholeheartedly' and handed total control to students	Roach (1999: 193)	Oral presentations; intro HND information technology and communication assignments
SA to help break down stereotype of T and L roles	Scheme generally well received	Taras (1999)	Social and international studies
(9) Providing feedback			
S & PA and student feedback	Generally rated as successful. See Chapter 6	Falchikov (1994, 1995a,b, 1996a,b)	See Chapter 6
SA to help address lack of good quality feedback	Students found procedure useful. See Chapter 5	Anderson and Freiberg (1995)	Teacher training
PA to complement teacher feedback, particularly in very large classes	See Chapter 5	Catterall (1995)	Marketing

(Table 4.2 continued)

Table 4.2 Continued

Features/methods/motivation	Outcomes	Studies	Areas of implementation
PA feedback to moderate assessmen	Having 'a variety of different opinions decreases the likelihood of getting a rogue result and increases the confidence of those being assessed that they are being treated fairly	Ewers and Searby (1997: 7)	Musical composition
(10) Saving time/reducing workload			
PA	Schemes likely to take longer to implement and evaluate than lecturer marking on own. Student and teacher endorsements	Fry (1990)	Mechanical engineering
PA P & SA of group work: developing an effective response to increased enrolment	Some degree personal conflict noted PA rated positively by authors and students + some student reservations More time spent with Ed. Dev. unit than usually associated with implementing innovation	Kelmar (1992) Strachan and Wilcox (1996)	Graduate management course 3rd yr microclimatology
PA	See above, but authors reported that the initial scheme took longer to administer than a standard assessment	Ewers and Searby (1997)	Musical composition
Pressure on lecturing staff made weekly marking of problem sheets impossible PA seen as a solution	The PA task provided prompt feedback	Gibbs (1999)	Weekly problem sheets + exam 2nd yr engineering

(11) Dissemination/application

To recommend schemes to others	Strong relationship between peer and prof ratings. Most professors participating continue to use method	Melvin and Lord (1995)	Prof/peer method used in 7 graduate and 11 undergraduate courses
Report of dissemination of SA across university	Teachers very willing to try SA, but not yet fully established as standard procedure in institution Importance of a champion noted	Taras (1999)	Various groups across university
To explore potential of using self-reports to assess educational effectiveness	Authors concluded assessment information can be used in a set of courses	LeBold *et al.* (1998)	Beginning maths and chemistry courses
To explore utility of PA in examination of personality pathologies	Authors concluded PA has potential to explore relationships between S, P and investigator perceptions	Oltmanns *et al.* (1998)	Female college students

Note

a Other studies investigating reliability as secondary purpose: Lennon (1995); Freeman (1995); Melvin and Lord (1995); Kwan and Leung (1996); Penny and Grover (1996); Orsmond *et al.* (1996); Zoller and Ben-Chaim (1997).

Measuring reliability or validity

The desire to compare student ratings with teacher marks continues to be a feature of research in the 1990s. Examples of studies giving some measurement-related reason for their innovation are shown in Table 4.2(4).

Addressing problems

McDowell (1995) identified two reasons why lecturers have been involved in changing assessment methods in recent years, both of which are related to problems with traditional assessment. The reasons are:

(a) increased awareness of the 'unrealistic' nature of exams and loss of faith in their validity as tests of learning;
(b) growing perception of the unfairness to some students of over-reliance on exams and essays (accelerated by entry into HE of non-traditional students).

Several other authors reported similar problems. A sample of these is shown in Table 4.2(5).

Investigating the process

Several ways of investigating processes of involving students in assessment are evident in studies in the 1990s. Four main categories have been identified: general investigations, those involving student attitudes or satisfaction, individual differences and investigations of the effects of practice. These studies are summarized in Table 4.2(6).

Developing communication skills

It is possible to regard this category as a part of the wider category of skills. However, we shall look at some studies which aimed to improve communication skills separately. These are shown in Table 4.2(7).

Transferring power

A few studies, all taking place towards the end of the decade of the 1990s, began to acknowledge the power relationship which is part of traditional assessment, and to implement changes which they hoped would have the effect of transferring some power to students. Hall (1995) flagged up the beginnings of the power shift. His paper on co-assessment described student and teacher participation in assessment as a joint effort. Some studies described simple measures which have the effect of empowering students. In other studies, researchers made their awareness of the change in power relationship explicit. We shall investigate the teacher–student power relationship further in Chapter 5. However, some examples of studies are shown in Table 4.2(8).

Providing feedback

The need to provide feedback constituted the next reason for involving students in assessment. Some see this aspect of assessment as a burden. For example, Todd (2002: 21) asserted that 'feedback forms are part and parcel of the growing mountain of paperwork academics are expected to deal with'. On the other hand, Trevitt and Pettigrove (1995) reported that large numbers of their students indicated that they desired more feedback. Feedback has been identified as a key component of formative assessment (e.g. Wiliam and Black, 1996), and many teachers have identified peer assessment as a means of addressing this problem. My own work (Falchikov 1994, 1995a,b, 1996a,b), which will be described in some detail in Chapter 6, falls, in part, into this category. Studies having this rationale are shown in Table 4.2(9).

Saving time/reducing workload

The desire to reduce the workload, particularly to save time taken up by marking, featured as a reason for involving students in assessment throughout the 1990s. Of course, this reason may be under-reported, as some teachers may regard it as unbefitting to them or their profession. I should point out, however, that time saving is too often a chimera. It is, perhaps, less surprising that computer aided assessment should have saving of staff time as one of its aims. Examples are shown in Table 4.2(10).

Dissemination/application

Dissemination and application are mentioned explicitly as important features of research by a few teachers in the 1990s. This usage has a curiously traditional 'feel' to it, but places student evaluations firmly at the centre rather than teacher ratings. Examples are shown in Table 4.2(11).

The early 2000s: the rise of the machines?

So far, the new century has produced, in addition to implementations which closely resemble those of the previous years, a crop of studies which report attempts to harness information technology to support assessment. Using the categories from the 1990s, the following are represented at the beginning of the twenty-first century:

(1) Investigating and understanding the process
(2) Measurement: reliability, validity and correlation
(3) Facilitating acquisition and development of skills
(4) Benefits
(5) Addressing problems of assessment
(6) Pressure from external and internal bodies
(7) Transferring power
(8) Providing feedback
(9) Dissemination and application

Twenty-first century studies which do not involve technology seem to fit into similar categories to those in the 1990s. Many of these are concerned with investigating the process, conferring benefits, addressing problems and empowering students. However, studies involving technology differ. Since the development of the role of computers in supporting assessment, we see in such studies a similar pattern of development of reasons to that found in the review of rationales for involving students in earlier decades. In other words, assessment studies involving students working with computers are conducted, first to address concerns with reliability and validity, then to identify benefits and problems and, more recently, to investigate the process.

Investigating and understanding the process

Some studies involving information technology seem to bridge the gap between the non-technological and technological. All studies classified as falling within this category are shown in Table 4.3(1).

Measurement: reliability, validity and correlation

Studies falling within this category are shown in Table 4.3(2).

Facilitating acquisition and development of skills

Skills of reflection and team working feature in this section, as well as subject related skills. See Table 4.3(3).

Benefits

As in previous decades, teachers wish for their students to derive benefits from participation in assessment. Studies reporting benefits are shown in Table 4.3(4).

Table 4.3 Themes and features of the twenty-first century

Features / methods / motivation	Outcomes	Studies	Areas of implementation
(1) Investigating and understanding the process			
Examining process to maximize potential	Participants with previous experience / those involved in setting criteria rated PA more highly than inexperienced / those not involved. Participation → increased involvement, and autonomy and development of critical skills.	Sivan (2000)	PA of group presentations by HD, 2nd yr undergraduates & graduates in hotel human environment, research methodology & effective communication
Achieving greater understanding of criteria and identifying more effective ways of introducing S and PA	Students less challenged by own criteria cf. teacher's See Chapter 5	Orsmond *et al.* (2000)	P & SA of posters by undergraduates, level 1 modules (Common skills, Life on earth)
Student views Gender and level of study differences	Gender differences in reasons for assessment (M =grading, F = feedback). Some age differences	Adams *et al.* (2000)	Business students
Investigation of individual differences / idiosyncratic PA strategies	Two variables identified: mutual understanding of quality and deviation. Most raters correlated with 1st. Only one idiosyncratic strategy found	Sluijsmans *et al.* (2001)	PA of PBL by students of educational sciences
Investigation of student confidence in self-evaluations	Instructors had higher confidence cf. students in basic areas and lower in more complex	Safoutin *et al.* (2000)	Engineering

(Table 4.3 continued)

Table 4.3 Continued

Features/methods/motivation	Outcomes	Studies	Areas of implementation
Student perceptions of fairness of innovative assessment	<1/4 perceived PA fair	Norton and Brunas-Wagstaff (2000)	3rd yr psychology students
Investigation of PA activities which encourage students to value own/peer solutions	Students generally trustful of peers. Some discomfort/threats to self-image.	Purchase (2000)	Interface design on HCI course
Investigation of student attitudes; how system facilitated development; quality of feedback	See Chapter 10 and below.	Lin et al. (2001); Tsai et al. (2001); Davies (2003b)	Web-based PA
(2) *Measurement* Correlation Investigation of feasibility of use of Project Essay Grade (PEG)	See Chapter 10 and below.	Davies (2002); Tsai et al. (2001); Shermis et al. (2001)	Computing science Web-based essays used as placement tests
Improvement of validity and sensitivity of S & PA	S & PA instrument developed	van Duzer and McMartin (2000)	Assessment of teamwork skills in engineering education
Comparisons of S and tutor; S & P marks	See above and Chapter 5. Agreement between T, S & P marks not increased as a result of students discussing and deciding own criteria	Orsmond et al. (2000)	P & SA of posters by undergraduates, level 1 modules (Common skills, Life on earth)
Reliability of P ratings	Generalizability of ratings in 1 group showed quality of scoring to be low	Sluijsmans et al. (2001)	PA of PBL by students of educational sciences

(3) *Facilitating acquisition and development of skills*			
Development of skills of reflection	Believed to be successful. See Chapter 10	Davies (2000a)	Essays written by final year computer science students
Teamwork skills development	Little detail supplied	Housego and Freeman (2000); van Duzer and McMartin (2000)	S & PA of group work; assessment of teamwork skills in engineering education
Assessment of design knowledge and skills	Systematic approach for evaluation developed	Safoutin et al. (2000)	Freshmen level Engineering design course
(4) *Benefits*			
Encouraging reflection	See above and Chapter 5	Orsmond et al. (2000)	P & SA of posters by undergraduates, level 1 modules (Common skills, Life on earth)
Enhancing learning; promoting trust	Data confirmed trust enhanced in two ways: partner's ability to conduct PA (perceived competence)and trust developed through interaction (social component)	Butler and Hodge (2001)	Physical education
(5) *Pressure*			
UK's QAA for HE's code of practice	Student views on fairness of assessment sought	Norton and Brunas-Wagstaff (2000)	3rd yr psychology students
US Accreditation Board for Engineering and Technology	A 'design attribute framework' developed involving student self-ratings	Safoutin et al. (2000)	Engineering
Current practice in engineering education	S/PA instrument developed	van Duzer and McMartin (2000)	Engineering education

(Table 4.3 continued)

Table 4.3 Continued

Features/methods/motivation	Outcomes	Studies	Areas of implementation
(6) Addressing problems of assessment Problem = lack of participation Wished to 'ensure that each student is keeping up his or her end of the bargain'	Author's experience positive and PA recommended. Not clear whether participation rates improved	Hamilton (2000: 3)	Collaborative writing in chemistry
(7) Transferring power To be empowering, ' the very process must be open, open to debate, negotiation and change, as learners have different and ever-changing views about empowerment in assessment'	Varied. See Chapter 5	Leach *et al.* (2001: 301)	Students choose categories and method of assessment
(8) Providing feedback Aimed to provide additional formative feedback. Model answers provided, peer review	Seemed to have succeeded	MacDonald (2001)	2nd level IT and society course, UK's OU
(9) Dissemination and application Aimed to survey practical applications of PA	Review provided	Butler and Hodge (2001)	Physical education

Pressure

As in the 1990s, institutions are under pressure from external bodies to change assessment practices to involve students to a greater extent. The UK's QAA features as a pressure, along with professional bodies for engineering in both the UK and US. These pressures on assessment and the ways students have been involved are summarized in Table 4.3(5).

Single examples of the remaining categories have been found, so far. However, the decade is, if no longer young, not too far advanced, and other examples are likely to be added. Remaining categories (addressing problems; transferring power; providing feedback; dissemination and application) are shown in Table 4.3(6)–(9).

Addressing problems of assessment

It should be noted that, in Hamilton's (2000) study, peer assessment may be seen as taking on a policing function as well as having some benefits to students.

Transferring power

In the study by Leach *et al.* (2001) designed to empower learners described, student views varied from demanding a share of control to strong resistance to the possibility of taking it. Some were sceptical about the process. We shall discuss this study further in the Chapter 5.

Providing feedback

In addition to the example shown in the table, feedback also features in some Computer Assisted Assessment schemes which are discussed in Chapter 10.

Dissemination and application

Butler and Hodge (2001) reviewed some practical applications of peer assessment, mostly from the area of physical education (e.g. facilitating fitnessgram testing).

Overview

Now that the survey of reasons researchers and teachers have given for involving their students in assessment has been completed, it is interesting to look at the changes that have come about decade by decade.

Table 4.4 Key to abbreviations used in Tables 4.2–4.3

AAHE	American Association for Higher Education
BCS	British Computer Society
CAE	College of Advanced Education (Australia)
ESL	English as a Second Language
HCI	Human–computer interaction
HE	Higher education
HERDSA	Higher Education Research and Development Society of Australasia
HND	Higher National Diploma
HOCS	Higher order cognitive skills
LOCS	Lower order cognitive skills
MBA	Master of Business Administration
OU	Open University (UK)
PA	Peer assessment
PBL	Problem-Based Learning
PG	Postgraduate
PGCE	Postgraduate Certificate of Education
SA	Self-assessment
SEDA	Staff and Educational Development Association
T	Teacher/tutor
TDLB	Training and Development Lead Body

Figures 4.1–4.6 illustrate trends. Charts show percentages of the total number of reasons given for involving students in each category.

In the 1950s, the desire to carry out measurement, to calculate reliability or validity statistics constituted the main reason for involving students. These activities are all examples of what Serafini (2000) calls 'assessment as measurement'. The proportion of measurement reasons decreases over the

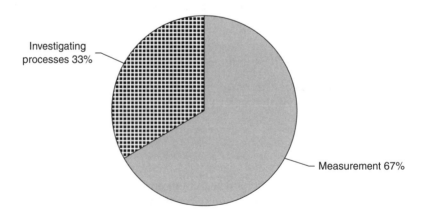

Figure 4.1 Reasons for involving students in assessment: 1950s

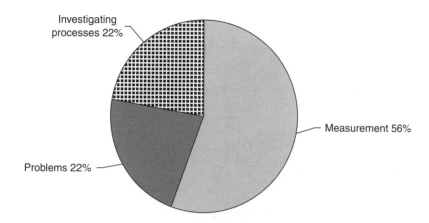

Figure 4.2 Reasons for involving students in assessment: 1960s

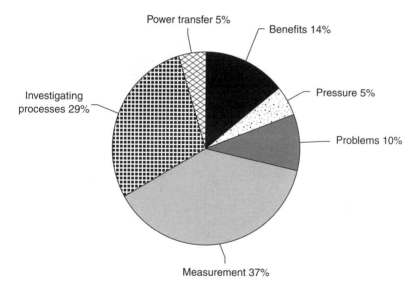

Figure 4.3 Reasons for involving students in assessment: 1970s

decades, as we progress from assessment as measurement to assessment as enquiry. The dramatic increase in variety of reasons for involving students is well illustrated. The two reasons given in the 1950s, concerning measurement and investigating processes expand to eleven categories by

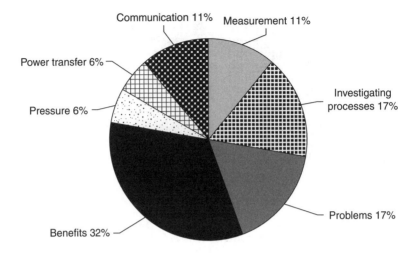

Figure 4.4 Reasons for involving students in assessment: 1980s

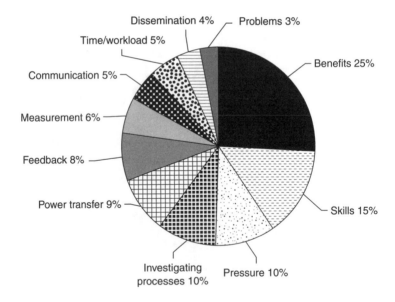

Figure 4.5 Reasons for involving students in assessment: 1990s

the 1990s. The 1990s in particular saw, not only a proliferation of studies, but a proliferation of reasons for conducting them. A few teachers adopted self- or peer assessment with the aim of reducing their marking load and saving time. Few achieved this aim. A trickle of researchers

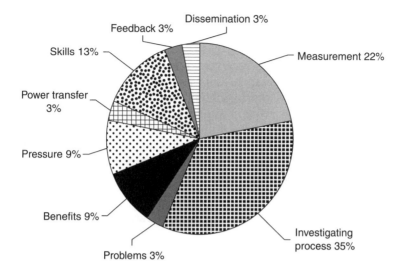

Figure 4.6 Reasons for involving students in assessment: 2000s

aimed to disseminate results and urged application of peer and self-assessment schemes in areas other than their own.

Another key trend is the growing emphasis, from the 1960s to 1990s, on benefits that student involvement confers. The particular benefits of involving students in assessment for formative purposes were being acknowledged, and the usefulness of student feedback took prominence. Also interesting is the decrease in emphasis on problems and their investigation which might indicate that teachers are growing in knowledge and confidence, that both teachers and students are less troubled by problems or that assessment practices are becoming more sophisticated.

With the arrival of the new millennium came the use of technology to support student involvement, and a return to earlier patterns of reasons for involving students. Once more we see an increase in the proportion of studies conducted in order to calculate reliability, validity or correlation statistics. There is also an increase in the proportion of studies which investigate processes. It is, perhaps, not surprising that the new methods of delivering self- and peer assessment require the same degree of scrutiny given to non-technological versions in previous decades, to ensure that the processes are as reliable or valid as possible. It will be interesting to monitor the progress of CAA. I predict that, once researchers have worked to achieve reliability and validity for their schemes, to convince themselves and others, we shall see a fresh flowering of reasons for implementing such studies.

Summary: benefits of involving students in assessment

As we have seen, many reasons given for involving students in assessment, particularly in recent years, are associated with direct and indirect benefits to participants. Unfortunately, many claims are unsupported. However, some studies provide compelling statistical evidence to support their claims. These are largely studies investigating improved performance in terms of grades or scores on tests and examinations. Numerous other studies provide information derived from questionnaires and other forms of student self-reported data.

Benefits supported by statistical evidence

Bangert's (1995) study provided ample statistical evidence of benefits. Analyses indicated that peer assessors scored significantly higher on Performance Based Assessment (PBS) tasks than students who did not participate in the exercise. Peer assessors also exhibited significant increases in mathematics self-efficacy and significant decreases in mathematics and test anxiety.

In Greer's (2001) study of the impact of feedback and the importance of criteria on course assessment outcomes, examination marks for the experimental cohort were compared with those of previous cohorts and found to be better. In addition, Greer also supplied data from questionnaires and focus groups which indicated that students found the feedback helpful.

Benefits supported by questionnaire and other self-reported methods

Many studies include data derived from student self reports and analyses of questionnaire data. For example, Edwards and Sutton (1991) concluded that student responsibility for learning can be fostered in the right environment, based on an analysis of questionnaire responses. Price and Cutler (1995), also using data derived from questionnaires, found that, although students identified a number of problems with peer assessment (to which we shall return in Chapter 6), large numbers of students felt they had gained confidence and improved their presentation skills. Lennon's (1995) questionnaire data led her to assert that the learning objectives of her scheme had been achieved and the educational benefits of self- and peer assessment had been confirmed. Trevitt and Pettigrove (1995) reported action research into autonomous criterion-referenced and self-assessment conducted with third year undergraduates of fire science and forestry at a State University in Tasmania. Their analysis of open-ended questions suggested that students rated 'criterion referenced understanding/abilities' as the most important reason for assessment, and 'continuous, incremental assessment' as the best approach. In addition, analysis of the end of semester course evaluation questionnaire found that in excess of 90 per cent of students agreed (or agreed strongly) that the form of assessment they had experienced was appropriate, a valuable learning experience and relevant to future careers; 86 per cent of students rated themselves as being more aware of the significance of criteria and standards after the experience of self-assessment than at the outset.

Sivan (2000) reported descriptive data and results of an analysis of variance of questionnaire responses relating to a study of peer assessment. Results indicated that a large number of students felt more confident using the method for the second time and an overwhelming majority stated that students should participate in establishing the criteria. Participants with previous experience consistently rated peer assessment more highly than new participants in terms of fairness and clarity of explanations of the methodology. Similarly, students who participated in criteria setting rated the experience more highly than peers who were not involved. Interviews found differences between experienced and inexperienced peer assessors. While all students recognized the importance of peer assessment, inexperienced students expressed reservations about the fairness of the procedure mostly in terms of personal inadequacies. Experienced students were more concerned with ways in which the procedure might be improved. Students reported an increased involvement in learning and development of critical and independent thinking skills as a result of participation in both forms of peer assessment.

Davies (2000b) reported results of analysis of an online questionnaire responses completed by students using the Computerized Assessment with Plagiarism (CAP) system which involved peer assessment. Davies compared scores on a pre-test with those on the post-test and noted that participating students had improved by a small percentage. He also noted that students benefited differently according to their report mark. Those students who had achieved a poor mark for their report benefited most from using the CAP system. Sitthiworachart and Joy (2003) also discussed the results of an analysis of data derived from an online questionnaire. In their case, results indicated that most students agreed that seeing a variety of programs written by others helped them learn programming. Two-thirds of their group were reported to have agreed that the act of marking helped them see mistakes in their own work and develop their understanding of computer programming. We shall return to the topic of computer assisted peer assessment, and to the work of Davies, and Sitthiworachart and Joy, in Chapters 6, 9 and 10.

Summary

We have seen that, particularly in the 1990s, the benefits of involving students in assessment constituted a major reason for conducting studies. However, benefits have also been reported in other decades. Thus, benefits claimed for involving students in assessment derived from the whole corpus, categorized according to type of benefit, are summarized in Table 4.5.

Table 4.5 Summary: benefits of involving students in assessment

Type of benefit	Examples
Cognitive and meta-cognitive competencies	
Aids problem solving	Dochy *et al.* (1999) (review); Oliver and Omari (1999)
Brings about unspecified educational/ learning benefits	Armstrong and Boud (1983); Boud and Holmes (1981); Boud and Knights (1994); Brehm (1974); Davies (2000b, 2003a); Denehy and Fuller (1974);Freeman (1995); Gray (1987); Lennon (1995); McDowell (1995); Oldfield and MacAlpine (1995); Orsmond *et al.* (1996); Powell *et al.* (1987); Sitthiworachart and Joy (2003); Stefani (1992, 1998); Williams (1995)
Encourages development of higher order cognitive skills	Zoller and Ben-Chaim (1997)
Encourages reflection	Alverno College (2001); Anderson and Freiberg (1995); Askham (1997); Boud and Knights (1994); Brew (1999) (review); Challis (1999); Chang (2001); Davies (2003a); Falchikov (1996a,b); Holt *et al.* (1998); Horgan (1997); Jordan (1999); Kwan and Leung (1996); Lapham and Webster (1999); MacDonald (2000); McDowell (1995); Mansell (1986); Safoutin *et al.* (2000); Sluijsmans *et al.* (1999) (review); Stefani (1998); Woodward (1998)
Encourages transfer of learning	Catterall (1995)
Improves critical thinking	Ewers and Searby (1997); Falchikov (1986); Oliver and Omari (1999); Sivan (2000)
Improves understanding/ mastery	Catterall (1995); Falchikov (1986); Lapham and Webster (1999); Ney (1991)
Skills development	
Brings about unspecified benefits to professional skills	Topping (1998) (review)

(Table 4.5 continued)

Table 4.5 Continued

Type of benefit	Examples
Enhances listening skills	Falchikov (1995a,b)
Enhances vocational skills	McDowell (1995); Trevitt and Pettigrove (1995)
Improves presentation skills	Price and Cutler (1995)
Improves writing skills	Topping (1998) (review)
Promotes learning skills/ abilities	Dochy *et al.* (1999) (review)
Promotes lifelong learning skills	Challis (1999)
Performance	
Enhances experience of trainee teaching	Anderson and Frieberg (1995)
Improves academic performance	Dochy *et al.* (1999) (review); Davies (2000b); Hassmén *et al.* (1996); Tsai *et al.* (2002)
Improves grades/ test scores	Bangert (1995); Dochy *et al.* (1999); Gibbs (1999); Greer (2001); Hunt (1982); Shortt (2002)
Personal/ intellectual development	
Brings about unspecified benefits	Fry (1990); McDowell (1995)
Increases autonomy/ independence	Beaman (1998); Falchikov (1986); Lapham and Webster (1999); McNamara and Deane (1995); Sivan (2000); Stefani (1998)
Increases responsibility	Dochy *et al.* (1999) (review); Edwards and Sutton (1991); Heathfield, M. (1999); Lapham and Webster (1999)
Increases self-efficacy (in context of mathematics)	Bangert (1995)
Social competencies	
Enhances diplomatic skills	Falchikov (1994, 1995a,b)
Improves co-operation	Lapham and Webster (1999); MacDonald (2000)
'Affective dispositions' (Birenbaum, 1996: 4)	
Decreases test anxiety (particularly mathematics anxiety)	Bangert (1995)
Increases confidence	Lapham and Webster (1999); Falchikov (1986); Foubister *et al.* (1997); Price and Cutler (1995); Sivan (2000)
Improves internal (intrinsic) motivation	McDowell (1995); Oliver and Omari (1999)

(Table 4.5 continued)

Table 4.5 Continued

Type of benefit	Examples
Reduces stress	Zakrzewski and Bull (1998)
Benefits to assessment Brings unspecified benefits	Davies (2002)
Enhanced appreciation of importance of criteria	Trevitt and Pettigrove (1995)
Saves time	Ngu *et al.* (1995)
Benefits to teachers Unspecified (associated with need to prepare model answers)	Gray (1987)

As Table 4.5 indicates, the benefits claimed to be derived from involving students in assessment are many and varied. Cognitive and meta-cognitive competencies have been found to improve, as has the development of a variety of skills. Some studies point to improvements in performance, while others suggest enhancements to personal or intellectual development or social competencies. Involving students appears to be equally effective in the area of what Birenbaum (1996: 4) calls 'affective dispositions'. Finally, involving students in assessment may have the power to improve assessment itself and to benefit teachers.

Chapter 5

How may students be involved in assessment?

Students may be involved in assessment in a wide variety of ways. The Assessment Strategies in Scottish Higher Education (ASSHE) project (Hounsell *et al.*, 1996) identified the following:

- peer assessment
- self-assessment
- feedback provision
- self- or peer testing
- negotiation or collaboration with lecturers concerning some aspect of the process.

The most frequently occurring form was peer assessment, mentioned by over half the examples encountered in the survey, often in the context of group work and/or the provision of feedback. We shall, therefore, start with peer assessment.

Peer assessment

The literature abounds with examples of peer assessment in higher education. Many take place in the context of group work. We shall delay full discussion of these until Chapter 9. The examples chosen for discussion here do not generally involve groups. They may seem very varied, but they share a number of features. They also differ in some respects. Let us look more closely four examples taken from differing contexts, presented chronologically, and attempt to identify some of their key features.

Peer assessment of pharmacology students' oral communication skills (Hughes and Large, 1993)

Hughes and Large (1993) reported results of peer assessment of oral communication skills by final year students of pharmacology at the University of Leeds. Students attended a one-hour teaching session during which common mistakes in presentation were illustrated as preparation for the exercise. Before presentations were made, students discussed and agreed the criteria for judgement and the proportion of marks to be allocated to each. Peer and staff marks were found to be highly significantly correlated. Mean values for the two groups were close, with students being slightly tougher than staff. No correspondence was found between marks awarded by students and their own communication skills.

Peer assessment in a marketing class (Catterall, 1995)

Catterall's (1995) study of peer assessment of class tests by part-time students studying marketing at the University of Ulster involved marking multiple choice questions and answers to five short essay questions. A marking scheme was provided by teachers. Students completed a questionnaire on peer assessment after the marking had been completed. Results demonstrated little difference between marks awarded by students and those awarded by the lecturer. Analysis of questionnaire responses indicated that students tended to endorse peer assessment. However, Catterall (1995: 57–8) concluded that 'the real pay-off for students may come from being able to transfer that learning to their own work and being able to assess their own work more objectively and critically as a result'. Students reported some reluctance to fail peers, but some did so, as fairness was deemed important. More than half the respondents noted lack of confidence in their ability to mark fairly due to insufficient knowledge and lack of experience.

Peer assessment in musical performance studies (Hunter and Russ, 1996)

Second year students were given training in a study of peer assessment of musical performance reported by Hunter and Russ (1996). A preliminary session introducing the exercise was followed by a session during which criteria were discussed and agreed. Teachers and panels of students then assessed the performance of other students independently, before meeting together to discuss marks. Teacher marks tended to be a little lower than student marks and covered a wider spread. In cases where differences were 3 per cent or less, students were awarded the higher mark. Greater disparities were resolved by negotiation. Students were reported to be enthusiastic and knowledgeable, and it was thought that the experience of acting as assessor helped them in terms of their own future performance. However, students were found to be not entirely happy about assessing peers. Hunter and Russ (1996) responded to this concern by requiring students from third year to assess second year students in future implementations. This was thought to result in more objective reporting.

Peer assessment in electrical engineering (Cheng and Warren, 1997)

Cheng and Warren (1997) conducted a research project at Hong Kong Polytechnic University in order to find out students' attitudes to peer assessment. Electrical engineering students took part in a training session in which advantages and disadvantages of peer assessment were discussed and at which assessment criteria were examined. Students were also given some practice in peer assessment. Attitudes were measured before the peer assessment exercise, and again once it was completed. Students who displayed a 'marked change' were subsequently interviewed. The authors reported that students were generally positive towards peer assessment both before and after the exercise, but that the experience was not consistently positive. Some students changed their ratings in both directions. The authors concluded that the results might suggest that practice at peer assessment acts to reduce students' feelings of discomfort, in that an overall shift towards feeling more comfortable was noted. However, some students remained unsure whether they would make or had made 'a fair and responsible assessment' of their peers.

Common features of peer assessment

Features that crop up regularly in these peer assessment studies are

- the *relationship between peer and teacher marks*;
- the *benefits to students*;
- *criteria*;
- *preparation and training*.

Some further examples also highlight issues such as *methods of measurement, student evaluation, benefits to teachers* (e.g. Ewers and Searby, 1997), *student attitudes* (e.g. Denehy and Fuller, 1974; Williams, 1992; Keaten and Richardson, 1993; Cheng and Warren, 1997) or *problems* (e.g. Fineman, 1981; Falchikov, 1995a; Greenan *et al.*, 1997). More recent studies emphasize *feedback* (to which we shall return later in the chapter), *negotiation* (e.g. Leach *et al.*, 2001; Hunter and Russ, 1996; Sluijsmans *et al.*, 2001) or *ongoing modifications to schemes* (e.g. Ewers and Searby, 1997).

As we shall see in the next section, self-assessment shares most of the key features of peer assessment. Thus, a generic pattern of 'how to do peer and self-assessment' is shown in Figure 5.1, after the discussion of self-assessment.

Self-assessment

The Saphe project (1999) defined 'self-assessment' as

- a way for students to become involved in assessing their own development and learning;
- a way of introducing students to the concept of individual judgement;
- involving the students in dialogue with teachers and peers;
- involving individual reflection about what constitutes good work;
- requiring learners to think about what they have learned so far, identify gaps and ways in which these can be filled and take steps towards remediation.

Boud (2000) sees self-assessment as requiring re-working throughout life in order to meet new challenges. Being an effective lifelong learner involves being an effective lifelong assessor. Boud (2000) also argues, along with others, that we should focus more on the role of formative rather than summative assessment.

Self-assessment is typically combined with peer assessment. In this section, in cases where both self- and peer assessment are featured, we shall concentrate on the self-assessment aspect in the examples cited. We shall start with what, for me particularly, is a classic study.

'Struggling with student self-assessment' in engineering (Cowan, 1988)

Cowan (1988) provided an account of an innovation carried out at Heriot-Watt University, Edinburgh, in which first year students of engineering volunteered to participate in a venture of self-assessment recognized by the Education for Capability Scheme. Cowan noted the influence of the work of Carl Rogers' 'Freedom to learn' (1969). Participants entered into an agreement which stipulated that each student would

- have complete control over choice of objectives, criteria and assessment;
- give and receive comments on objectives and activities of others if requested to do so;

- carry out two formal self-appraisals which would be open to question and comment and which would require a response;
- make her or his learning available to other members of the group on request.

After the first term, the scheme appeared to be a disaster. Cowan reported that the students didn't know where or how to start. He felt that he had 'tried too hard to be non-prescriptive' (Cowan, 1988: 195) and concluded that his lack of knowledge about how to facilitate fully autonomous learning or self-assessment had been a problem, as was the absence of de-briefing or co-counselling mechanisms to support himself as facilitator. However, the evaluation of the scheme indicated that all students had moved up the class ranking, by an average of almost 15 places (out of 60). Cowan also asserted that self-assessment had led learners to a higher level of commitment and to a questioning approach, which he argued is a major step towards adoption of a deep learning strategy. The following year the experiment was repeated on a compulsory third year course with more participants. Some changes were made. Even more problems were encountered in the second year of operation, due, suggested Cowan, to the compulsory nature of the course, the greatly increased numbers, which made personal contact with all impossible, and to some changes which gave rise to unpredicted reactions. Further changes were made. Cowan (1988: 209) listed some practical advice to colleagues, concluding that, '. . . the lesson to be learnt from this . . . is that innovators need to be devious strategists, and to exploit the circumstances of a particular situation'.

Using self-assessment as a reflective tool to enhance the student teaching experience (Anderson and Freiberg, 1995)

Anderson and Freiberg (1995) described a study of self-assessment, involving a small group of students seeking certification in a variety of subjects, which was designed to help solve the problem of lack of good quality feedback during training. The focus of such self-assessments was on formative development rather than summative evaluation. The authors described the instrument they used during this study, the Low Inference Self-Assessment Measure (LISAM). The instrument identifies useful teaching behaviours such as questioning skills, the ratio of teacher to student talk, numbers of positive statements made by teacher and teacher use of student ideas.

The study consisted of six stages:

(1) participants recorded themselves teaching a lesson;
(2) the LISAM analysis procedures were used to analyse the audio tapes;

(3) participants attended a meeting to discuss effective use of LISAM teaching behaviours;
(4) participants developed written goals based on their own analyses;
(5) participants taught and recorded a second lesson incorporating their new strategies;
(6) in-depth, semi-structured interviews were conducted with each student teacher.

Student evaluation of the procedure illustrated that all participants found their use of the LISAM to be worthwhile and beneficial. The authors concluded that, in some cases, the use of LISAM may have served as a catalyst to accelerate student development. They also suggested reasons why the procedure was effective: it empowers students; it may be used immediately after the teaching; the teaching behaviours identified in the LISAM are observable and alterable.

Self-assessment of coursework essays (Longhurst and Norton, 1997)

Longhurst and Norton (1997) reported the results of a study involving self-assessment of essays by second year psychology students which was designed to find out whether tutors who claim to reward students who take a deep approach to studying actually do so. Students were asked to grade their own work using the system used by tutors. 'Deep processing criteria' were supplied by teachers. These were

- addressing the question throughout;
- clearly organized with appropriate structure;
- quality and relevance of argument;
- depth of understanding in relation to psychological issues;
- evaluation of theoretical concepts and research evidence.

Results suggested that tutors did reward students for taking a deep approach. Correlations between tutor and student grades were positive and significant. The authors found equal amounts of over- and underestimation by learners and concluded that students were reasonably accurate at grading their own essays. Further analysis indicated that, while the overall deep processing mark students awarded themselves correlated positively with overall mark, when split into constituent criteria, the only one to be correlated positively was that relating to depth of understanding of psychological issues. Thus, students may not be as accurate in judging their performance on individual criteria as on overall performance. Some evidence that weaker students tend to over-estimate their essays was found.

Self-assessment in sociology (Hahlo, 1997)

Hahlo (1997) reported results of a study of self-assessment carried out by first year students of sociology who were told about the exercise well in advance. The itemized marking schedule used by staff was included in the course document. Essays were submitted in the usual way and returned to students along with marking schedules completed by teachers. Teacher marks were withheld at this point. Students were then asked to award themselves a grade, and informed that they might earn a bonus of 5 per cent if their marks were the same as the teacher's marks. Marks were compared in one-to-one sessions. Hahlo found that 78 per cent of students gave themselves a lower mark, and 21.9 per cent a higher mark, than those awarded by the teacher. Only one student and teacher mark corresponded exactly, but seven students came within 5 per cent of the teacher mark. The requirement for this degree of similarity seems draconian, particularly given the lack of reliability of teacher marking. However, both the teacher and the students found the exercise valuable.

Self-assessment by students of foreign languages (Jordan, 1999)

Jordan (1999) described a case study of self- and peer assessment carried out with second year students of foreign languages at Thames Valley University, in which the self and peer assessment component contributed 40 per cent of the marks for the module. Criteria were negotiated rather than imposed. The self-assessment form was reported as functioning rather like a learning contract. It contained a short rationale for including a self-assessed element and prompts to reflection, as well as practical information. Students were required to award themselves a numerical grade, based on the criteria agreed. They were also given the opportunity to make open-ended comments. Both students and tutors were required to be able to justify marks awarded.

Assessments were conducted twice: in week 6 (halfway through the process) and at the end of the module. Thus, some data relating to the repeated experience of self and peer assessment were provided. Jordan (1999: 175) reported that, in the first round of assessments, the move from private to public assessment not infrequently led to conflict, due to students' 'unrealistic (usually inflated) perception of the value of their own contribution'. The second assessments were deemed to run more smoothly than the first: students were more confident and comfortable, and tutors were required to intervene less than on the first occasion. Students were reported to have demonstrated maturity in analysing differences in performances and made 'illuminating statements' (Jordan, 1999: 177) about the value of self-assessment. Students appreciated the experience, seeing it as 'a part of learning to learn, and beneficial even when it is problematic' (Jordan, 1999: 178).

Common features of self-assessment

The studies featured earlier, taken in the context of many other self-assessment studies, have a number of characteristics in common:

- *Feedback*
  (e.g. Cowan, 1988; Anderson and Frieberg, 1995; Hahlo, 1997; Jordan, 1999; Taras, 1999);
- *Benefits to students*
  (e.g. Cowan, 1988; Anderson and Freiberg, 1995; Lennon, 1995; Oldfield and MacAlpine, 1995; Price and Cutler, 1995; Jordan, 1999);
- *Evaluation, problems and improvements*
  (e.g. Cowan, 1988; Dickinson, 1988; Lennon, 1995; Price and Cutler, 1995; Hahlo, 1997; Taras, 1999);
- *Criteria* (both student and teacher derived)
  (e.g. Cowan, 1988; Edwards and Sutton, 1991; Lennon, 1995; Penny and Grover, 1996; Longhurst and Norton, 1997; Jordan, 1999; Taras, 1999; Roach, 1999);
- *Comparisons between teacher and student ratings*
  (e.g. Morton and Macbeth, 1977; Rezler, 1989; Lennon, 1995; Price and Cutler, 1995; Longhurst and Norton, 1997; Hahlo, 1997; Lejk, 1999b; Sullivan *et al.*, 1999).

Some studies involve *summative assessment* (e.g. Cowan, 1988; Jordan, 1999), while others emphasize *formative* aspects (e.g. Anderson and Freiberg, 1995; Taras, 1999). Others debate the advantages and disadvantages of each (e.g. Lejk, 1999b). Several different *methods of measurement* are mentioned – a topic to which we shall return later in the chapter. The *effects of practice* are being researched (e.g. Edwards and Sutton, 1991).

Other factors found include: *application of psychological principles* to the study of self-assessment (e.g. Hunt, 1982; Hassmén *et al.*, 1996); *attitudes to self-assessment* (e.g. Stefani *et al.*, 1997); *effects of psychological, demographic and biological factors* (e.g. Chatterji and Mukerjee, 1983); *moderation and reliability* (e.g. Price and Cutler, 1995); *negotiation* (e.g. Serafini, 2000).

Self-assessment studies involve differing amounts of *student control*, from total control (e.g. Cowan, 1988; Edwards and Sutton, 1991) to predominantly teacher control (e.g. Taras, 1999). We shall return to consider issues of control and power later in the chapter.

Self- or peer testing may be seen as a special case of self- or peer assessment which involves students using model answers or marking schemes to grade their own work or that of their peers. They need to make few, if any, judgements about whether criteria have been achieved. They need, simply, to apply what the teacher supplies to what they find in front of

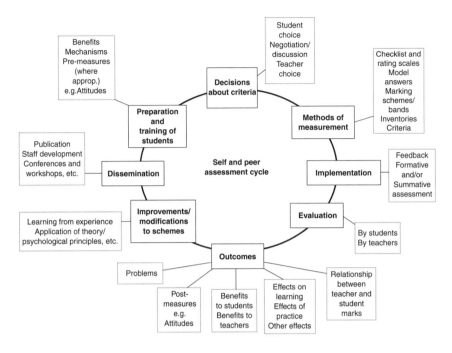

Figure 5.1 How to carry out peer and self-assessment

them. This simple exercise, however, may have some benefits, if only in requiring students to engage with material for an additional time.

Thus, the body of self-assessment studies is rich in themes.

A generic pattern of 'how to do peer and self-assessment' is shown in Figure 5.1.

Collaborative assessment

The term *'collaborative assessment'* is often used to indicate that students and teachers share the responsibility for selecting criteria (e.g. Falchikov, 1986). Similarly, Hall (1995) defines *co-assessment* as student and teacher participating in assessment as a joint effort. He also points out that many examples of self-assessment studies from the literature are really co-assessment, in that students and teachers share in the selection of criteria. Another term used to describe assessment partnerships is *'participative assessment'* (Reynolds and Trehan, 2000).

Dickinson (1988) described an experiment in collaborative assessment involving experienced language teachers studying for a Postgraduate Diploma in Linguistics and English Language Teaching. Criteria were supplied by tutors, though some discussion was expected and encouraged. Unfortunately, Dickinson (1988: 127) reported a 'rather disappointing' number of participants. She noted that almost all students 'were initially out of sympathy with the concept of collaborative assessment'. She also suggested the power relationship between tutors and students 'in which the tutor's views, particularly with regard to assessment of work, are regarded as beyond discussion' (Dickinson, 1988: 127) constituted a reason for student reluctance. Dickinson noted that some tutors were less enthusiastic than others about the scheme, and that a few did not offer it at all. Thus, as with any innovation, collaboration requires careful preparation and conviction on the part of all participants.

However, collaborative assessment sometimes signifies more than agreement over criteria or marks, particularly when used in specialized contexts. For example, Keith (1996) included collaboratively developed *goals* as part of *portfolio development*. Marshall and Mill (1993) argued that assessment should be collaborative when involving learners in the development of *learning contracts* and that assessment systems should include mechanisms to support collaboration between learners and teachers and, in the case of *work-based learning*, the employers.

Pain *et al.* (1996), at a conference on *Artificial Intelligence in Education*, described collaborative assessment of language learning. However, the role of the teacher is automated, providing students with a virtual person with whom to negotiate. Thus, in this case, student and system collaborate over a final, agreed assessment. The authors argued that collaborative assessment involving modelling, as in non-computerized contexts, requires that explicit criteria be known to both students and teacher (system or human). 'The end product is a joint and agreed assessment of the learner's knowledge in relation to the criteria (possibly with some points flagged with "unresolved disagreement")' (Pain *et al.*, 1996: 1). They discovered that, once the process was completed, students were able to defend their assessments to the teacher.

Finally, Lapham and Webster (1999) identified some negative effects associated with the introduction of peer assessment of seminar presentations. Among these were 'Prejudice, favouritism, friendships and ethnic division' which led to 'collaboration over marks and mark fixing' (Lapham and Webster, 1999: 188). This *not* what is meant by collaborative assessment!

Feedback provision

Students are increasingly being asked to give verbal and written feedback to their peers as part of peer assessment. We shall delay discussion of this topic until Chapter 6.

What is the level of student involvement?

Reynolds and Trehan (2000) argued that assessment, more than any other aspect of education, embodies power relations between tutors and students, due to its function in providing the basis for granting or withholding qualifications. Tutors act as custodians of the institution's rules and practices and the effect of tutor judgements, 'ensures that assessment is experienced by students as being of considerable significance' (Reynolds and Trehan, 2000: 268). Leach *et al.* (2001) pointed out that, although, traditionally, teachers have been all-powerful in assessment, things are beginning to change as more people come to be critical of the status quo. In particular, they argued that there is a 'growing recognition that adult learners have a legitimate role in an assessment partnership' (Leach *et al.*, 2001: 293). However, Reynolds and Trehan (2000) argued that, although it is often assumed that questions of power and authority are less problematic in participative assessment than in traditional assessment, this may not be the case. 'If self-awareness, consciousness-raising or reflexivity are introduced into the assessment process without power, authority and judgement-making being examined or changed, students have even less control than in more traditional methods' (Reynolds and Trehan, 2000: 271).

Leach *et al.* (2001) explored three aspects of empowerment:

(1) an individual learner can be empowered to make decisions about a course of action;
(2) empowerment takes place within a wider social, economic and cultural context of inequality;
(3) empowerment is not the same for all and difference and identity are acknowledged.

The authors claimed to reflect all three traditions in their assessment practice. Although self- or peer assessment are usually seen as a move towards greater empowerment of students, Leach *et al.* (2001: 296) pointed out that self-assessment is usually imposed, which 'reinforces the hegemony of the dominant teacher'. This situation is avoided when self-assessment is made optional. In addition, assessment practices designed to empower learners use a version of criterion referencing in which students select the evidence they wish to provide in their portfolios, choose or negotiate criteria and assess their own work. Leach *et al.* (2001: 298) claimed that learners are provided with information which enables them 'to decide what role they want in the assessment process'. Learners choose teacher, self or peer assessment, all of which require the use of categories. A six item 'standard set' is offered to participants, along with a longer list.

Students may choose either the standard set or construct their own set from the list. The method of assessment is negotiable. However, it appears that, in Leach's approach, students are not given the option of opting out of assessment altogether. Thus, some power continues to reside with the teacher, or with the institutional regulations under which we all have to operate. Many of us acknowledge the benefits and necessity of assessment. For us, there seems no escape from this dilemma.

There seems to be a strongly held view that assessment is more reliable, students are more involved and learning enhanced when students take part in deriving their own criteria. This view is supported to some extent by the work I did with Judy Goldfinch (Falchikov and Goldfinch, 2000) which found that, if you wish for a close correspondence between peer and teacher marks, then you would do well to involve your students in generation of criteria. Feedback from McDowell's (1995: 310) students suggested that this is the view of some students, too. 'Someone else's criteria is always difficult to assess. A bit like answering an exam question.' Similarly, other students reported that knowledge of the criteria in a self- and peer assessment task was helpful for stimulating thought (McDowell and Sambell, 1999).

Brew's typology

We shall make use of Brew's (1999) typology to enable us to classify self and peer assessment studies according to the level of student involvement. This typology was derived from Habermas (1987) and involves three levels of 'knowledge interests': technical, communicative and emancipatory. Brew argued that the ability to assess oneself and one's peers in each of these three areas is essential for the development of autonomous independent professional judgement.

Level 1

Self or peer assessment which requires students to check knowledge, performance or skill level against a model answer or to use criteria provided by the teacher may be said to represent the first, lowest level. Other examples of assessment involving students at this level is the use of marking schemes or teacher identified criteria or competency statements.

Level 2

At the second level, involvement is greater, and students are allowed or encouraged to discuss and negotiate criteria or consider what constitutes a good answer before applying these standards to their own or each other's work.

Level 3

The third level has an emancipatory component, in that, at this level of involvement, students are required to give critical attention to the criteria. Meta-level skills such as critical reflection may be developed through teaching strategies which encourage this practice. In the context of assessment of competencies, Brew argued that it is expected that the competencies themselves should be questioned and critiqued. 'Learning comes about through an iterative process where the criteria inform the assessment and then the assessment informs the student's understanding of the criteria and so on' (Brew, 1999: 167).

We shall now examine studies of self, peer or collaborative assessment and attempt to categorize them according to the degree of student involvement in the derivation of criteria and other 'emancipatory' features, starting with some studies where criteria do not seem to have been made explicit at all.

Studies with no explicit criteria

Few studies fall into this category. One example of such a study was conducted by Chatterji and Mukerjee (1983: 30) who argued that, as students 'would not be able to evaluate the performance of others on a variety of distinct dimensions, as they had no prior training or experience in this field', they would not be asked to use the several dimensions of assessment criteria made available to teachers. Nonetheless, peer and teacher assessments were found to be highly correlated. Earl (1986), on the other hand, described a self and peer assessment study in which there were no explicit criteria by design. They were not explicitly stated because the teaching team involved wished 'to reflect the shift from staff-sponsored instruction to self/peer sponsored perception of relationships' (Earl, 1986: 60). General guidelines were supplied to students, however and the scheme rated as effective for group assessment.

Studies at level 1: checking knowledge, performance or skill

We shall look at some subcategories within this level: teacher prepared model answers, marking schemes, rating scales or evaluation forms. In addition, we shall identify some studies in which criteria are provided by teachers.

Model answers

There are several examples of self- or peer assessment studies in which model answers are provided. For example, Gray's (1987) first year engineering students marked their own examination script and that of a peer. Students were provided with a set of model answers and suggestions about marking and priorities. Gray argued that the exercise had been a qualified success, in that, although students tended to be more generous to themselves than to their peers, teachers had also benefited from the requirement to produce model answers. Similarly, Fry (1990) reported results of a study in which mechanical engineering students took part in a scheme of peer marking using a model solution to closed questions. Peer marks were found to be in close agreement with the tutor's, which Fry took as a demonstration of the validity of peer assessment. Student evaluations also endorsed the scheme, as was the case in Trevitt and Pettigrove's (1995) self-assessment study which also supplied students with a model answer.

Marking schemes

A marking scheme was provided by teachers in Catterall's (1995) study of peer assessment of class tests which involved marking multiple-choice questions and answers to five short essay questions. As we saw in Chapter 4, students endorsed the scheme.

Rating scales/evaluation forms

In an early peer evaluation study in a pre-clinical dental course (Brehm, 1974), students evaluated their own work, using the same evaluation form as that used by faculty members. The form identified a number of things for assessors to look out for and evaluate (e.g. 'occlusion', 'margins', 'contours and contacts'). Results indicated that, as a group, students were more critical than faculty members, and student remarks were more candid. A large percentage of students rated the exercise as a meaningful learning experience. In the study of peer, supervisor and self-ratings of counselling performance early in graduate training by Fuqua *et al.* (1984), ratings were made using a standardized instrument prepared by a panel of experts. As we learned in Chapter 4, results were variable and Fuqua *et al.* (1984) concluded that self-constructed rating scales are problematic, in that their validity has not been tested. More recently, in Bergee's (1993) study of teacher, peer and self-assessment of musical performance, brass jury performances were evaluated using the author's Brass Performance Rating Scale. Self-assessments were found to resemble teacher assessment to a lesser degree than peer assessments.

Studies in which criteria were supplied by teachers

Studies which use teacher supplied criteria are also common in the literature. Examples of these are summarized alphabetically in Table 5.1.

Table 5.1 Examples of self- and peer assessment studies involving teacher supplied criteria

Study identifier	Type of study	Details of teacher input
Billington (1997)	PA of poster presentations	Criteria provided and explained clearly to students, as in the absence of 'agreed criteria' students may be overly influenced by impressive graphics at the expense of other aspects.
Butcher *et al.* (1995)	P & SA of a group project in bioscience (poster)	Students and tutors supplied with (different) marking proformas.
Cheng and Warren (1999)	PA of group project tasks	Criteria supplied before commencement of exercise.
Deeks (1999)	PA of an information systems group project	Form supplied to students. Criteria 'elaborated', though students do not appear to have any input into this part of the process.
Denehy and Fuller (1974)	Peer evaluation of pre-clinical dental laboratory skills	Students given evaluation criteria.
Goldfinch and Raeside (1990)	PA for obtaining individual marks in a group project	Students supplied with assessment form with a list of skills just before assessment took place. 'This had the advantage of inhibiting prior discussion among students about how they would mark each other' (Goldfinch and Raeside, 1990: 213).
Hammond and Kern (1959)	PA of competence as a physician	Five dimensions supplied by staff.
Horgan (1997)	Examination of interrelationships among self, peer, and instructor assessments	Assessment instruments with five criteria supplied by teacher.
Kegel-Flom (1975)	Peer and self-ratings of intern performance	Four dimensions supplied by teachers.
Kelmar (1992)	PA on a graduate management course	Criteria provided, but discussed so that a 'common understanding of dimensions could be achieved' (Kelmar, 1992: 84). No evidence of modification as a result.

(Table 5.1 continued)

Table 5.1 Continued

Study identifier	Type of study	Details of teacher input
Korman and Stubblefield (1971)	Peer ratings of medical internship performance	Twelve variables supplied by staff.
Lawrence and Branch (1974, referred to in Lawrence & Branch, 1978)	'Peer panel procedure'	While the authors claim that the procedure assumes students to be 'co-producers rather than consumers', a measuring instrument with a set of 'relatively objective categories' was supplied.
Lawrence and Branch (1978)	Peer managed assessment of competencies in a micro-teaching situation	The peer panel verifies the completeness of evidence supplied by peers in support of their objectives according to given criteria.
Lin *et al.* (2001)	Web-based PA	Six criteria provided by teachers.
Longhurst and Norton (1997)	SA of coursework essays	'Deep processing criteria' supplied by teachers.
Lopez-Real and Chan (1999)	PA of group project in primary mathematics education course	Criteria supplied by teacher. Some discussion to achieve common understanding.
Mathews (1994)	Peer evaluation in group projects	Criteria were included in a completion guide supplied to students.
Orsmond *et al.* (1996)	PA of a poster	Students provided with guidelines and criteria which were expanded and explained.
Penny and Grover (1996)	Study of student grade expectations and marker consistency	Criteria provided by teachers.
Purchase (2000)	PA	Assessment sheet with criteria supplied.
Sitthiworachart and Joy (2003)	PA	Marking scheme and 'well explained criteria' supplied.
Sivan (2000)	PA conducted in three phases	Criteria supplied in phases 1 and 2, but established by students in 3.
Taras (1999)	Student SA	Criteria provided by teacher.
University of Dundee's Centre for Learning and Teaching (2003)	Creation of personalized online S & PA exercise	Teachers required to supply a question to be assessed and set of marking criteria.

Notes
PA = peer assessment.
SA = self-assessment.

Some hint of power transfer is indicated in two of these studies. Purchase (2000) described the peer assessment procedure employed by third year students within the School of Computer Science and Electrical Engineering at the University of Queensland in which criteria were supplied to students. A mark allocation was also supplied for each. The researcher emphasized that

- Peer assessment grades were recommendations only and the lecturer would make the final decision.
- It was essential for students to participate fully. Those students who did not submit an assessment sheet, duly completed and signed, would not receive their own mark.
- Students were being trusted to be responsible.
- Any student unhappy with their final peer assessment mark was welcome to seek an independent assessment by the lecturer.

Here we see that the researcher wishes to give over some power to her students, but we also note some reluctance to do so. For example, there are two references to the teacher having the final say. Similarly, stating that students are being trusted to be responsible suggests to me some uncertainty about the issue. However, the exercise contributed 10 per cent towards the final mark. Qualitative feedback from students suggested that many perceived the criteria to be objective, while others saw them as subjective and ambiguous. Some students perceived that the criteria got in the way of making aesthetic judgements. Thus, the hint of power may have resulted in some students beginning to question the process – the first step to 'emancipation'.

This tendency is also demonstrated in Sivan's (2000) study, where the method of selecting criteria 'jumps' from the teacher's choice to student determination. The study involved five groups of students who participated over a three phase process. Three of the five groups had no previous experience of peer assessment. Two types of peer assessment of group work were used: intra- and inter-group. Criteria were supplied by teachers in the intra-group peer assessment and in cycles one and two of the inter-group peer assessment. However, criteria were established by students in the third cycle. As we saw in Chapter 4, students who had participated in criteria setting rated the experience more highly than peers who had not been involved.

Studies at level 2: discussion and negotiation of criteria

There are many examples of studies in which students take part in discussions with teachers and negotiate the criteria by which they then judge their work. Examples of these are shown in Table 5.2.

Table 5.2 Examples of self- and peer assessment studies involving negotiation/discussion

Study identifier	Type of study	Details of discussion/negotiation
Chang (2001)	Web-based learning portfolio (WBLP) system, characterized as 'authentic assessment'	Criteria of assessment agreed by teachers and students together.
Cowan (2001)	'Plus/minus marking scheme', where derivations from a previously defined 'sound standard' (benchmark) are identified, explained and marked positively or negatively.	The 'sound standard' description is discussed until a shared understanding has been achieved. Cowan noted that this method readily lends itself to SA.
Davies (2002)	SA involving final year students of computer science	Criterion transparency was established by distributing guidelines to students which made clear what was expected of different grades of performance. Marking categories were discussed with students prior to the exercise.
Dickinson (1988)	Collaborative assessment in PG language course	Criteria supplied by tutors, though some discussion was encouraged. It was expected that students volunteering to take part in the scheme and their tutors would agree over the criteria before the assignment was started.
Falchikov (1988) and Falchikov (1993)	PA and group process analysis on a developmental psychology module	Modifications to Johnson and Johnson (1985) checklist were made in response to students' suggestions, following discussion of the categories and their meaning.
Falchikov (1996a)	PA on a general social science course	Criteria discussed and agreed between students and teacher.
Hughes and Large (1993)	PA of oral communication skills by final year students of pharmacology	'There was extensive discussion as to how the broad criteria. . . . should be defined and quantified' (Hughes and Large, 1993: 80).

(Table 5.2 continued)

Table 5.2 Continued

Study identifier	Type of study	Details of discussion/negotiation
Hunter and Russ (1996)	PA in musical performance studies	List of agreed criteria drawn up by teachers and students jointly.
Jordan (1999)	S & PA	Criteria negotiated rather than imposed. Those chosen by students ranged from the quantitative, such as frequency of attendance to the qualitative (e.g. effective group work).
Lennon (1995)	P & SA of practical simulations in physiotherapy	Nine assessment criteria jointly devised by students and tutor.
Ngu *et al.* (1995)	Computer assisted PA system, 'Peers', used to help the marking of postgraduate assignments within an Information Science course at the University of New South Wales.	In the first part of the system, the assessment criteria are developed. Criteria and weightings entered into the system by the lecturer are inspected by students who have the power to suggest new criteria or new weights for existing criteria.
Roach (1999)	P & SA in a basic Information Technology and communication skills module	Students involved in generation of criteria and discussion of standards and in choice of topics for the presentation.
Sluijsmans *et al.* (2001)	PA in problem-based learning	Four criteria defined by students in negotiation with the tutor.
Strachan and Wilcox (1996)	P & SA of group work in a third year course in microclimatology	'Students appeared responsive to the idea of being included in the process and debated enthusiastically the merits of various criteria' (Strachan and Wilcox, 1996: 347). A PA form was developed from Miller's (1992) model using students' ideas.
Tariq *et al.* (1998)	Assessment of project work	Approach stressed that criteria should match learning outcomes and be shared with students. Measuring instruments were 'new objective proformas with . . . explicit criteria, descriptors and grades' (Tariq *et al.*, 1998: 233). However, students and supervisors completed different versions of these.

Notes
PA = peer assessment.
SA = self-assessment.

As we saw in Chapter 4, Ewers and Searby (1997) used peer assessment in musical composition at Kingston University. Their scheme was planned as one involving discussion between students and teachers, but, in practice was one in which students identified their own criteria. The researchers reported that students worked in small groups to identify criteria to encourage ownership of these, but that the lecturer had the power to intervene if 'any serious oversights were being made' (Ewers and Searby, 1997: 6). However, no such intervention was found to be necessary in practice.

Studies at level 3: student choices

Brew suggests that level 3 of student involvement requires the presence of an emancipatory component. Students are given the power to make important decisions of their own: selection of criteria; weightings of marks awarded; the mark itself. We have already encountered the work of John Cowan, whose students were required to take responsibility for their own assessment, from the selection of criteria to the grade they awarded themselves (Cowan, 1988). As we learned earlier, Cowan's students had complete control over choice of objectives, criteria and assessment. Moreover, they were required to take responsibility for giving and receiving comments to and from their peers and for publicly defending their self-appraisals. Although Cowan reported difficulties, the benefits to participants seemed great.

Other examples of level 3 studies are to be found in Table 5.3.

A cautionary note

There is some evidence that there may be fundamental limitations to the amount of power we can effectively cede to students regarding selection of criteria. For example, Orsmond *et al.* (2000) reported results of a study involving self- and peer assessment of posters which aimed to explore and compare the use of student and teacher supplied criteria. Two weeks after being introduced to the idea of self- and peer assessment, students were required to construct suitable criteria for marking their posters. Criteria chosen varied slightly from group to group, but four criteria per group were agreed upon. All students were supplied with a marking form containing their own criteria. Tutors then marked all posters. Results indicated that students were *less able to discriminate* using their own criteria than previous cohorts had been using criteria supplied by the tutor. Orsmond *et al.* (2000: 23) concluded that allowing students to construct their own criteria 'may lead to different learning outcomes compared to providing students with marking criteria'. However, the authors noted that, during the exercise, students were actively engaged in discussions

Table 5.3 Examples of assessment studies involving students with a significant emancipatory component

Study identifier	Type of study	Details of emancipatory component
Boud and Tyree (1979)	S & PA of class participation in a small first year undergraduate class in Law at the University of New South Wales.	Before carrying out assessments, students were asked to identify criteria for making judgements; 148 criteria were identified by students, subsequently categorized by teachers into three groups.
Edwards and Sutton (1991)	SA on an Information Systems for Management course.	At beginning of the course, students identified own objectives which were discussed with other students. Achievements matched against objectives three months later. Feedback encouraged, but final mark remained the responsibility of each individual.
Falchikov (1995a)	PA in Psychology	Students discussed and drew up their own list of criteria for assessing peer presentations.
Fineman (1981)	Peer teaching and PA of student-run sessions involving third year students of Business Administration.	Students identified five criteria relevant to judging the quality of a presentation, as Fineman (1981: 84) argued that it seemed 'inconsistent with the spirit and purpose of self-determination' for criteria to be supplied by teachers.
Gatfield (1999)	Group PA project, involving students of International Marketing Management. PA carried 40% semester marks.	Students were given a peer mark allocation sheet with five equally weighted categories, developed by themselves earlier in their course.
Magin (1993)	Peer ratings and summative assessment.	Two main criteria (with several subdivisions) for assessing individual contributions developed and agreed by students.
Stefani (1994)	S, P and tutor A	Students drew up the marking schedule. Stefani (1994: 70) argued that, 'as it can be extremely difficult to obtain agreement between lecturers and tutors on appropriate marking criteria, it seemed unfair to thwart the student efforts by introducing modifications'.
		NB Criteria were limited to structural categories relating to a laboratory report (e.g. 'Aims and hypothesis', 'Method', 'Discussion of results', etc.). No indication of quality within categories was suggested.

Notes
PA = peer assessment.
SA = self-assessment.

about their own criteria and built on material that was their own. Nonetheless, it was felt that students were *less challenged by their own criteria* than by those supplied by teachers, and that they did not engage sufficiently in deep thought about the exact meaning of their own criteria. In spite of this, feedback from students suggested that they felt themselves to have benefited from the exercise.

More recently, Miller (2003: 383) compared the effects of the specificity of criteria used in self- and peer assessment and found that, by increasing the number of criteria from 5 to 24, the mean scores decreased and the standard deviations of the peer and self-assessments increased, 'providing a wider range of scores and increasing the sensitivity of the instruments'. This supports one of the conclusions drawn from a meta-analysis of quantitative self-assessment studies (Falchikov and Boud, 1989). In this, we found that the number of discriminations required in self-assessment studies varied enormously, but that the greatest degree of association between self- and teacher assessment seemed to be associated with more detailed measuring instruments which used a full 100 marks range. However, results also suggested that extremely long instruments requiring much discrimination produced less good correspondence and are, therefore, less reliable or valid than shorter ones requiring fewer discriminations.

Newkirk (1984) raised another important issue in his report of results of a study comparing instructor and peer evaluations of student writing. He concluded that the two groups were using *different criteria* when judging work and that, even when teachers are careful to go over criteria with students, these *criteria may be applied in different ways* by the two groups. 'The teacher's "detail" may differ from the student's "detail" ' (Newkirk, 1984: 310). This view was supported by Topping *et al.* (2000) who found little evidence for conflict between the overall views of teachers and students, but did note a tendency for the two groups to focus on *different details*. Similarly, Magin (2001a) argued that, when reliabilities of averaged peer scores is high but peer–tutor correlations low, teacher and student values may differ and criteria may be being applied differently. He recommended that either peer ratings be dropped from calculations or that procedures for training students to understand and apply criteria be instituted. Alternatively, he pointed out that it is possible to argue that student interpretations 'have an equal claim to legitimacy' (Magin, 2001a: 148). However, as a friend pointed out, given the choice, one would choose a registered professional with recognized qualifications over a raw recruit to conduct surgery on one's nearest and dearest.

Penny and Grover (1996: 173) found that *students tended to be pragmatic and technical* and to emphasize 'lower order criteria' such as style and presentation and ignore criteria concerned with theoretical and conceptual understanding, reflection and quality of discussion in their research report. I also noted a similar tendency for students to focus on practical, observable factors rather than more conceptual ones in a study which compared student and teacher feedback (Falchikov, 1995b).

Norton *et al.* (1996) explained the mismatch between teacher and student perceptions of criteria used in marking essays in terms of *the hidden curriculum*, which was discussed in Chapter 2. Sambell and McDowell (1998) also discussed the construction of the hidden curriculum in the context of alternative assessments. They concluded that individuals are active 'in the reconstruction of the messages and meanings of assessment' (Sambell and McDowell, 1998: 391). Not only did teachers and students see things differently, there appeared to be *a range of views within the student body*, too. While students hear and understand explicit instructions and communications about assessment, 'they are also aware of the embodied sub-texts and have their own individual perspectives all of which come together to produce many variants on the hidden curriculum' (Sambell and McDowell, 1998: 400). Sambell and McDowell argued that familiar assessment methods such as exams can influence ideas and approaches to alternative forms of assessment.

What do students assess?

As I noted elsewhere (Falchikov, 2004), it is possible to involve students in the assessment of work or performance in three distinct areas: traditional (and non-traditional) academic activity, performance in academic settings and professional practice. The first category is differentiated from the second two in that the outcomes are products rather than processes. The Assessment Strategies in Scottish Higher Education (ASSHE) survey (Hounsell *et al.*, 1996) found that assessment of educational products occurred about twice as frequently as assessment of processes. The survey also found that assessment of professional and personal transferable skills occurred less frequently.

Traditional academic products

Contained within this category are

- *coursework essays* (e.g. Williams, 1992; Catterall, 1995; Mowl and Pain, 1995; Ngu *et al.*, 1995; Price and Cutler, 1995; Longhurst and Norton, 1997; Hahlo, 1997; MacDonald *et al.*, 1999; Davies, 2000a; Shermis *et al.*, 2001; Davies, 2002; Davies, 2003a);
- *examinations* (e.g. Jacobs *et al.*, 1975; Burnett and Cavaye, 1980; Gray, 1987; Zoller and Ben-Chaim, 1997);
- *group projects* (e.g. Goldfinch and Raeside, 1990; Conway *et al.*, 1993; Keaten and Richardson, 1993; Mathews, 1994; Butcher *et al.*, 1995;

Cheng and Warren, 1999; Price and Cutler, 1995; Rafiq and Fullerton, 1996; Deeks, 1999; Gatfield, 1999; Lejk, 1999a; Lopez-Real and Chan, 1999);
- *laboratory reports* (e.g. Stefani, 1994);
- *multiple-choice tests* (e.g. Catterall, 1995).

Relatively recent additions to this category are

- *portfolios* and *journals* (though these combine elements of process, too, and generally involve students engaging in self-assessment at a formative level) (e.g. Wolf *et al.*, 1991; Arter and Spandel, 1992; Ashcroft and Foreman-Peck, 1994; Halsall, 1995; McNamara and Deane, 1995; Keith, 1996; Woodward, 1998; Challis, 1999; Young, 1999; Ben-David, 2000; Gosling, 2000; Chang, 2001; Leach *et al.*, 2001).
- *posters* may also be included in this category, though it is their presentation that is usually the focus of assessment. Thus, we shall consider them in the next section.

Performance in academic settings

Assessment of performance in academic settings includes

- *analysis of group processes* (which can result in a product) (e.g. Falchikov, 1993; Webb, 1995);
- rating *class participation* (e.g. Boud and Tyree, 1979; Armstrong and Boud, 1983; Lyons, 1989; Melvin and Lord, 1995; Kimbrough, 1995; Gopinath, 1999; Sullivan *et al.*, 1999);
- evaluation of *discussion, oral presentations* and *communication* (e.g. Siders, 1983; Greenan *et al.*, 1997; Lopez-Real and Chan, 1999; MacAlpine, 1999; Cheng and Warren, 1999);
- *interpersonal skills* (e.g. D'Augelli, 1973);
- *poster presentations* (e.g. Orsmond *et al.*, 1996; Billington, 1997; Akister *et al.*, 2000; Orsmond *et al.*, 2000).

Competence at conducting *interviews* may also be assessed, though this seems to take place in a professional skills context. This is discussed in the next section.

Professional practice

Assessment of professional practice typically occurs in places of work such as medical, paramedical, clinical dental or teaching contexts. Professional practice may be assessed by means of *exhibitions*, defined as *live performances* of artistic or technical skill or demonstrations of the products of learning. In the context of medicine and related disciplines, the focus of assessment may be

- *competence as a physician* (e.g. Hammond and Kern, 1959);
- *dental anatomy* (e.g. Denehy and Fuller, 1974);
- *diagnostic radiography* (e.g. Hounsell *et al.*, 1996);
- *internship or residency performance* (e.g. Korman and Stubblefield, 1971; Kegel-Flom, 1975);
- *occupational therapy skills;*
- *performance during medical training* (e.g. Gough *et al.*, 1964; Linn *et al.*, 1975);
- *physiotherapy* (e.g. Lennon, 1995);
- *practical surgical clinical or anaesthetic skills* (e.g. Morton and Macbeth, 1977; Burnett and Cavaye, 1980).

Professional practice also takes place in the contexts of

- *counselling performance* (e.g. Fuqua *et al.*, 1984);
- *interviewing skills* (e.g. Friesen and Dunning, 1973);
- *music* (e.g. Bergee, 1993; Hunter and Russ, 1996; Ewers and Searby, 1997);
- *teaching* (where students typically assess their own performance) (e.g. Pease, 1975; Manning and Payne, 1984).

How are assessments carried out?

We have already encountered some of the ways in which assessments are carried out: model answers, marking schemes, rating scales, evaluation forms, lists of criteria. Self, peer and collaborative assessment may also involve the use of checklists. These instruments may have been designed by potential users, using criteria identified by students and agreed with the teacher. However, pre-existing instruments may also be used or modified to suit particular purposes. We shall look at the latter category in the section headed 'Inventories'.

We shall now outline each of the main types and then look at some examples from the literature.

Checklists and rating scales

Checklists are, as their name suggests, lists of statements or words which users are invited to endorse. The checklist is presented to respondents who are asked to rate each item following a set of written instructions. These instructions may request respondents to simply tick (or check) items that are present, or with which they agree. Sometimes rating on a five-point scale is required to gain a picture of the extent to which items are present (or agreed with). This is the *Likert technique* which is a form of attitude testing. Sometimes, different numbers of points are presented, though five seems to be the most common. There is also a view that an even number of possibilities prevents respondents from the easy mid-point choice. However, my opinion is that sometimes the mid-point represents respondents' views and to force them to come down on either a positive or negative side misrepresents those views. There are other ways of dealing with the tendency to choose the mid-point, such as to request that respondents avoid this unless absolutely necessary or to discard any completed checklist where all or a large majority of ratings take the mid-point position. Asking respondents to justify their ratings may also be useful here, too, though this takes us away from the simple checklist.

In a Likert scale, as each degree of agreement is given a numerical value (usually 1–5), the responses may be converted into a number. However, as Mogey (2003) argued, it makes no sense to simply add a response of 'agree' (coded as, say, 2) to a response of 'undecided' (coded as 3) to get a 'mean' response of 2.5, as such a number is meaningless. Moreover, Mogey also pointed out that as such data are ordinal, having order or sequence, it is not wise to make any assumptions about them. For example, the difference between agreeing strongly and simply agreeing may be different from the amount of change in attitude represented by the difference between 'undecided' and 'disagree'. In other words, analysis of such data requires application of common sense, and often takes the form of descriptive statistics such as reporting the modal response or the range of responses. Sometimes the distribution of responses is reported. Mogey (2003) also suggested that simple inferential techniques might also be used, such as investigating differences or associations between comparable groups using non-parametric statistics.

In other cases, the checklist may take the form of a *semantic differential* which presents respondents with two poles with single words (e.g. 'Clear' vs 'Unclear') or statements (e.g. 'Supported by evidence' vs 'No evidence provided') and boxes in between in which they record their views. Such a format brings another possible problem: the arrangement of positive and negative pole statements. While having all positive on one side and negative on the other facilitates scoring and interpretation, it can lead to response bias. Respondents may get into a pattern of responding which they follow throughout the form (including taking the middle way throughout). Mixing positive and negative statements helps minimize response bias and may stimulate reflection in respondents, but it adds to your problems when it comes to scoring and analysis.

Checklists have been described as a quick way of getting a lot of information (e.g. Milligan, 2003), and this is certainly true. Moreover, the collection and simple analysis of data can be automated. However, for the information to be useful, the items on the list need to be chosen carefully. For example, you need to be sure that they reflect your concerns and enable you to gain answers to the questions you pose. Even the simplest checklist will benefit from piloting in order to reassure yourself that everything you need is included and that everything included is necessary. Piloting also allows you to detect any ambiguities of wording.

Examples of assessment studies using checklists

Checklists have been used in studies of student involvement in assessment over a long time period. Obah (1993) described how pair work and peer feedback at Seneca College of Applied Arts and Technology in Toronto makes use of a four-point checklist provided by the teacher. Students work in pairs and small groups throughout the writing process, from topic selection to exchange of outlines and drafts to provision of feedback using the checklist. The list appears to consist of four simple prompts: Content – is it clear?; Organization – is it visible?; Expression – is it acceptable?; Mechanical accuracy – is it correct? This checklist appears to be the simplest 'Yes'/'No' type. Powell *et al.* (1987) reported results of a self- and peer assessment exercise designed to help dental students develop skills in the use of videotapes to present cases to their teachers and peers. This also used a simple 'Yes'/'No' type checklist which contained 23 'Yes/No' questions relating to different aspects of a student presentation (e.g. rapport development, patient involvement, explanation of disease process, etc.). Evaluation of the initiative found that 86 per cent of students found the checklist useful.

Freeman (1995) reported the results of a peer assessment exercise in which final year undergraduates business studies students rated the quality of a group presentation, using a presentation checklist with 22 criteria grouped under six main headings provided by the teacher. This checklist was of the semantic differential type, with bi-polar descriptions (e.g. 'Rigorous critique of key concepts' vs 'Lack of demonstration of key concepts') and five categories between representing percentage mark ranges. However, Freeman concluded that peer marks are not reliable enough to be used on their own. The full checklist is included in Freeman's paper.

Eisenberg (1965) completed an early study of peer rating in the context of doctoral comprehensive examinations at the University of Maryland, using a Likert-type checklist rating scale which listed four areas of knowledge to be tested in the examination. Raters were instructed to use a three-point scale to indicate the degree to which students were qualified in these areas. As we saw in the previous chapter, a high correlation between predication and criterion data was found. Kwan and Leung (1996) described a simulation training exercise, assessed separately by tutor and peer group, which also used a checklist of the Likert type. The checklist, a copy of which is included in their paper, includes questions (e.g. 'Was the question technique effective?') which require an answer on a five-point scale ranging from 'good' = 5 to 'poor' = 0. It should be noted that, although the meaning is clear, a simple re-wording to 'To what extent is . . . ?' and 'very' = 5 to 'not at all' = 0 would have been an improvement. As we learned in Chapter 4, they concluded that the educational benefits outweigh the risks of unreliability, in spite of finding only a moderate degree of agreement between teacher and peer marks. The system of web- based peer assessment, by Lin *et al.* (2001), to which we referred earlier, made use of a ten-point Likert scale (1 = poor, 10 = satisfactory) to rate performance on each criterion.

A summary of the different types of checklist items taken from the self- and peer assessment literature is included in Table 5.4.

Model answers, marking schemes and marking bands

We have already encountered several uses of model answers, marking schemes and marking bands in the section on level 1 of student involvement. These are typically used to check the level of knowledge, performance or skill and are prepared and supplied by teachers.

Inventories

Inventories are generally pre-existing measurement forms, often of a checklist format, which have been designed and tested for use in a particular context. Well-designed examples will have had their reliability and validity checked before use, and will report these and other statistics along with the instrument itself. Self- and peer assessment studies sometimes make use of such instruments. For example, Friesen and Dunning (1973) conducted a study in which small numbers of counselling practicum students, professional counsellors and lay people rated videotaped counselling interviews. All raters used the Rating Scale of Counselor Effectiveness which comprised 25 semantic differential items with Likert-type scaling. The validity of the scale had been established by its originator, Ivey. As we saw in the previous chapter, graduate practicum students could reliably evaluate their peers using it. More recently, Tamir (1996) reported use of a Self-Report Knowledge Inventory (SRKI) for self-assessment. Students were required to rate themselves on a five-point scale on a list of concepts and/or skills they expected to master. The SRKI was used to measure levels of prior knowledge before students embarked on new courses. It could, thus, help teachers plan effective teaching and provide a base line against which to measure the success of teaching/knowledge and skills increase. No mention was made of validity or reliability of

Table 5.4 Examples of checklist items used in self- and peer assessment

Item type	Examples	Study
Presence vs absence (simple 'Yes'/'No' or '✓')	Content – is it clear? **Y/ N** Organization – is it visible? **Y/ N** Expression – is it acceptable? **Y/ N** Mechanical accuracy – is it correct? **Y/ N**	Obah (1993)
	Rapport development – ✓(present) or **X** (absent)? Patient involvement – ✓ or **X**? Explanation of disease process – ✓ or **X**?	Powell *et al.* (1987)
Likert scale	Students rated four areas of knowledge: 1 General and theoretical material 2 Measurement and methodological areas 3 Specialist topic I 4 Specialist topic II as '**Pass**' or '**Fail**', and then used a three-point scale (**1 = most qualified, 2 = moderately qualified, 3 = least qualified**) to rate their confidence in their judgement.	Eisenberg (1965)
	Students rated 20 group activities, organized into 'Task' and 'Maintenance' functions (plus an 'Other' category): e.g. 2 'Information and opinion seeker: asks for facts, information, opinions, ideas and feelings from other members to help group discussion' (Task) 9 'Encourager of participation: encourages everyone to participate' (Maintenance)	Falchikov (1993)
	Level of activity of group members rated as '**High**', '**Medium**' or '**Low**'.	
	Raters used ten-point scale (**1 = poor, 10 = satisfactory**) to rate performance on each of six criteria (framed as questions): e.g. 1 Is there a high correlation between survey content and operating systems? 2 Is the survey complete? Other questions related to adequacy of the introduction of theory and background knowledge, clarity of discussions, the robustness of conclusions, and adequacy of referencing.	Lin *et al.* (2001)

(Table 5.4 continued)

Table 5.4 Continued

Item type	Examples	Study
Semantic differential	22 criteria grouped under six main headings:	Freeman (1995)
	Structure (e.g. 'objectives achieved' vs 'objectives ignored')	
	Argument (e.g. 'convincingly argued' vs 'argument lacks credibility')	
	Originality (e.g. 'original and creative thought' vs 'little evidence of originality')	
	Personal style (e.g. 'succinct delivery' vs 'unnecessarily repetitive and unclear')	
	Presentation (e.g. 'clear and effective use of media' vs 'media aids irrelevant or used as a crutch')	
	Mechanics (e.g. 'effective changeovers' vs 'changeovers handled poorly')	
	Five-point scale with percentage ranges specified.	
	The scheme of SA *makes you*:	Falchikov (1986)
	Independent ⬚⬚⬚⬚⬚ Dependent	
	Not think ⬚⬚⬚⬚⬚ Think more	
	Lack confidence ⬚⬚⬚⬚⬚ Confident	
	Critical ⬚⬚⬚⬚⬚ Uncritical	
	Unstructured ⬚⬚⬚⬚⬚ Structured	
	The scheme *is*:	
	Time saving ⬚⬚⬚⬚⬚ Time consuming	
	Not enjoyable ⬚⬚⬚⬚⬚ Enjoyable	
	Easy ⬚⬚⬚⬚⬚ Hard	
	Challenging ⬚⬚⬚⬚⬚ Not challenging	
	Unhelpful ⬚⬚⬚⬚⬚ Helpful	
	Beneficial ⬚⬚⬚⬚⬚ Not beneficial	

the instrument, however. Hill *et al.* (1998) described the use of a self-report measure, the Inventory of Interpersonal Problems-Circumplex (IIP-C), to obtain peer report data.

Assessment criteria

Finally, as we saw previously, it is very common for assessment criteria to be used as an aid to assessment. These may be supplied by the teacher, agreed or generated by the students themselves.

Recommendations to help combat bias in alternative assessments

Van Daalen (1999) suggested a number of strategies to maximize reliability in alternative assessments. These included the requirement to design multiple tasks that lead to the same outcome, the need for trained judges, the use of clear criteria, the need to monitor periodically to ensure that criteria and standards are being applied consistently and the desirability of using triangulation. These suggestions are echoed by others in the field. We shall look at each briefly.

Design multiple tasks

Birenbaum (1996: 14) quoted Moss (1994) as arguing that an 'hermeneutic approach' which involves integration of many evidence-based interpretations is more appropriate for alternative assessment than a psychometric one which is typically based on a single performance. However, this suggestion is not as straightforward as might appear at first glance. As we learned earlier, Birenbaum (1996) pointed to the trade off between breadth of domain and reliability. Research shows that correlations among tasks drop as tasks become more heterogeneous (Birenbaum, 1996). She argued that increased specificity, which we might interpret as being represented by multiple tasks, undermines validity, whereas a narrow domain, which we might interpret as being few tasks or a single task with high specificity, gives rise to higher reliability than a wide one.

Use trained judges

Broadfoot (1999) argued that experienced teachers and assessors, as well as new teachers in training can benefit from support in the assessment process. While van Daalen (1999) may have been referring to the skill of teachers and instructors when she suggested this strategy, it is equally applicable to student assessors. Numerous self- and peer assessment studies have pointed to the need for preparation and training of students prior to their undertaking assessments (e.g. Friesen and Dunning, 1973; Lawrence and Branch, 1974; Fuqua *et al.*, 1984; Obah, 1993; Webb, 1995; Hunter and Russ, 1996; Cheng and Warren, 1997; Magin, 2001a).

Use multiple judges

Van der Vleuten *et al.* (2000) argued that, in the context of competency assessment, reliability may be compromised in two main ways. First of all, competence measurement is situation-specific and second, assessors may be prone to subjective judgements. The authors recommend multiple assessors as a means of minimizing subjectivity of judgement. This strategy may have wider application.

Van Duzer and McMartin (2000) noted that the literature on self- and peer assessment indicates that biases to reliability may be reduced by correlating self-assessments with scores of multiple raters.

Average peer marks

Chatterji and Mukerjee (1983) noted that averaged peer ranks possessed much higher reliability than single peer ranks. This view is echoed by other teachers and researchers (e.g. Magin, 1993). Magin (2001a) described a novel application of ANOVA techniques to compare the reliability of multiple peer ratings with single tutor ratings. Results of an analysis of data indicated that reliability of multiple assessments was 'moderate to high' compared with that of individual student raters which was described as 'very low' (Magin, 2001a: 146). Magin also found that the reliability of tutor ratings was consistently superior to figures obtained from individual students and, generally, closely aligned with averaged peer assessments. He argued that the addition of a single tutor rating was equivalent to adding two peer ratings.

Use clear criteria

There is some evidence to suggest that assessment is more reliable, that students are more involved, and that learning is enhanced, when students take part in deriving their own criteria (e.g. Fineman, 1981; Falchikov, 1986; Hughes and Large, 1993; Ewers and Searby, 1997). The work I did with Judy Goldfinch (Falchikov and Goldfinch, 2000) also found some support for this view. It is not uncommon for students to report finding the process of deriving and using explicit criteria as useful (e.g. McDowell and Sambell, 1999; Sivan, 2000; Magin, 2001a).

Monitor use of standards and criteria

Given that teachers and students may vary in the ways they interpret and apply criteria and standards (e.g. Magin, 2001b), it is good practice to check that all involved are 'singing from the same hymn sheet' to borrow a current phrase. As we all know, it is too easy to fall back into familiar patterns, so van Daalen's advice to monitor usage is prudent.

Employ triangulation

Triangulation technically requires three sources of data, results of which may be compared. However, Cohen *et al.* (2000: 112) define it as 'the use of two or more methods of data collection'. Triangulation of data may be achieved by using input from learners, from teachers and other individuals such as employers. It is, according to Cohen *et al.* (2000) a technique subscribed to frequently in theory, but implemented seldom. Van Daalen (1999) suggested that portfolios may be seen as a kind of triangulation instrument, containing as they do, a variety of work samples.

Other researchers have suggested further strategies to help minimize threats to reliability and validity of alternative assessments.

Value learners and increase their power and control

As we saw earlier, assessment has been identified as embodying power relations between teachers and students. We also saw that change is afoot, and that a growing number of people wish to devolve some power and control to students. Many now argue that the quality of learning and assessment is enhanced when learners are taken seriously and helped to understand how they learn. Quality is also enhanced when students take ownership of their learning and assessment and 'when they are seen as partners in evaluating the quality of learning outcomes' (Shaw and Roper, 1993: 124).

These recommendations are summarized in Table 5.5.

Conclusion

Tracing the use of self, peer and collaborative assessment in higher education in recent years, we perceive a move toward more transparency and openness. As we have seen, this is sometimes the direct result of a desire on the part of the teachers to give over some power and control to students. However, sometimes teachers find themselves in conflict over assessment and the needs and rights of students, and the demands of the system.

Setting up a self- or peer assessment study requires careful preparation, monitoring and follow-up. The key stages are illustrated in Figure 5.1.

As I have reasoned elsewhere (Falchikov, 2004), preparation requires application of many of the principles of good experimental design. Evaluation requires that variables be identified: dependent variables such as the degree of agreement between teacher and student marks, the inter-rater reliability of peer marking or some more qualitative measure of the effects of the experience, and independent variables such as participant experience or gender. It is always wise to learn as much as possible about outcomes of other research studies. In the case of student involvement in assessment, information provided by the two meta-analyses referred to earlier (Falchikov and Boud, 1989; Falchikov and Goldfinch, 2000) is particularly relevant. Use of a control group is possible, though it has been argued (e.g. by Kember, 2003) that genuine control is impossible in naturalistic studies. Practical preparation requires that students be provided with full explanations of what is being proposed, examples of successful implementations, practice, if this is possible, and clear written instructions to take away. Every effort should be made to ensure that students are thoroughly informed and reassured that they are capable of carrying

Table 5.5 Recommendations to practitioners for minimizing bias in alternative assessments

Recommendation	Examples of sources of further information
Design multiple tasks	Birenbaum (1996); Moss (1994); van Daalen (1999)
Train assessors	Broadfoot (1999); Cheng and Warren (1997); Friesen and Dunning (1973); Fuqua *et al.* (1984); Lawrence and Branch (1974 in 1978); Magin (2001a); Hunter and Russ (1996); Obah (1993); Webb (1995); van Daalen (1999)
Use multiple judges	Van Daalen (1999); van der Vleuten *et al.* (2000); van Duzer and McMartin (2000)
Average peer marks	Chatterji and Mukerjee (1983); Magin (1993); Magin (2001a); van Daalen (1999)
Use clear criteria/ involve students in generating them	Ewers and Searby (1997); Falchikov (1986); Falchikov and Goldfinch (2000); Fineman (1981); Hughes and Large (1993); Magin (2001a); McDowell and Sambell (1999); Sivan (2000); van Daalen (1999)
Monitor use of criteria/ understanding of standards	Magin (2001b); van Daalen (1999)
Employ triangulation techniques	Cohen *et al.* (2000); van Daalen (1999)
Value learners and increase their power and control	Boud and Tyree (1979); Brew (1999); Chang (2001); Cowan (1988), 2001); Davies (2002); Dickinson (1988); Edwards and Sutton (1991); Falchikov (1988, 1993); Falchikov (1995a); Falchikov (1996b); Falchikov and Goldfinch (2000); Fineman (1981); Gatfield (1999); Habermas (1987); Hughes and Large (1993); Hunter and Russ (1996); Jordan (1999); Leach *et al.* (2001); Lennon (1995); Magin (1993); Ngu *et al.* (1995); Reynolds and Trehan (2000); Roach (1999); Shaw and Roper (1993); Sluijsmans *et al.* (2001); Stefani (1994); Strachan and Wilcox (1996); Tariq *et al.* (1998)
Be self-critical/ evaluate innovations	Crooks *et al.* (1996); Leach *et al.* (2001)

out what is required of them. It is also important to anticipate and discuss possible areas of disagreement and to make explicit procedures for resolving any such problems. As I have advised before, teachers would be wise to 'have a ready response to suggestions that "marking is the teacher's job, not mine" ' (Falchikov, 2004). We shall consider some possible responses to this and other frequently asked questions in the next chapter.

Chapter 6

Practical peer assessment and feedback: problems and solutions

As illustrated in the previous chapter, peer assessment seems to be the most popular way of involving students in assessment. Many teachers are aware of its benefits and student evaluations of peer assessment schemes suggest they perceive it to be beneficial to them, too. However, as with most approaches, there appear to be some problems associated with peer assessment. This chapter poses a number of frequently asked questions (FAQs) relating to such problems. Each question will be discussed, using research-based information wherever possible, and answers suggested.

Frequently asked questions

1 Isn't it my job as a teacher to undertake assessment?

Some colleagues may argue that teachers are neglecting their duties if they involve students in assessment. Assessment is certainly part of our job. However, as teachers in the twenty-first century, many of us also have the aim of helping our undergraduates develop into critical, thoughtful autonomous learners. Assessment is a commanding tool, one which may be used as an instrument of power or a powerful aid to learning. The more students are involved, the greater the potential of assessment to improve learning and encourage personal, academic and professional development. Current thinking also demands that, when they graduate, our students have lifelong skills, including self and peer assessment. Sometimes, assessment may be 'used' to help achieve these ends. Involving students in assessment is not the same as washing our hands of it. Although we are giving students more control, we continue to be involved in the processes of education and assessment.

Colleagues who ask this type of question may have difficulty in changing their role in response to current ideas about students-centred learning and teaching.

What can be done?

Our colleagues need to be persuaded that our role is changing and, and that the new one is every bit as important as the old one. As Dochy (2001: 11) argued, the responsibility of the teacher today is to act as a key to open the door 'to domains of knowledge and experience' rather than to be the source of all knowledge. The traditional role, in which the teacher has power to make all decisions relating to the education of students, is evolving into a partnership. In this partnership, students are encouraged to take control of many aspects of their education, including some involvement in assessment. MacDonald (2000: 10) argued that this shift in the balance of power can have unnerving consequences for teachers, as, 'students will find a communal voice, and express their views, questioning the authority of what they have read'. Serafini (2000), among others, noted that teachers require support during this process. Staff developers, as well as colleagues already committed to self-, peer or collaborative assessment, have a role to play here. New responsibilities need to be explored. Sceptical teachers need to be reassured that, by allowing student to be more actively involved in assessment, we are supporting their learning and not compromising standards. There are new tasks to perform. For example, before students can take part in assessment, teachers must provide them with training and guidance. We remain deeply involved in the process once the scheme is underway, monitoring it and, where appropriate, carrying out quality checks. Teachers still have a very important role to play.

If 'letting go of students completely is overwhelming', Beaman (1998: 56) suggested using another self-assessment technique, the Sequential Criterion-Referenced Evaluation System (SCREE). This is a self-administered repeated measure which requires students to rate themselves each week on class objectives and learning outcomes (supplied by the teacher). This has no place in grade determination. They record their competence (1 = acquired, 0 = not yet developed) and can watch their development over time.

2 Students may argue that it's not their job to carry out assessment, as this is what teachers are paid to do. Some students also argue that, nowadays, they, themselves, are doing the paying. How do I respond to that?

Weaver and Cotrell (1986) argued that, while on the surface, this may seem a legitimate concern, it is sometimes a smokescreen for anxiety provoked by a new and different procedure. I have encountered examples of this argument, both from my own students and from talking to many colleagues. I have also encountered this type of objection in the context of resistance to peer tutoring. As with the previous question, this may also be a response to current challenges to the traditional roles of teachers and students.

What can be done?

We have seen that teachers require reassurance that their role is changing, but that the new one is no less important and challenging than the traditional. Students also need to know why they are being asked to expand their role. They need to be given explanations, and evidence that carrying out some activities traditionally the province of the teacher carries benefits for them. Teachers also need to make explicit to students what they see as their role and responsibility in relation to students' education. It is *not* our responsibility to award degrees to passive consumers, however much they may pay us, but, rather, to provide as rich a learning environment as possible for students and to support them in their own efforts. As has been noted (e.g. Falchikov, 1996b), once students get involved, this particular objection is seldom raised again.

3 Students say that peer assessment is just a way of saving the teacher's time. Is this true?

Anyone who has attempted to introduce an innovative assessment technique into her or his teaching programme will know that this assertion could not be further from the truth. However, some students seem to labour under this misconception. McDowell (1995), for example, reported case study research which indicated that some students, both beginners and final years, held the view that self-marking and self- and peer assessment are a time-saving mechanism for lecturers.

What can be done?

Should this query arise, it is best to deal with it head on. You might want to reiterate some of the benefits that involvement in assessment can bring to participants, and point out that you are attempting to help students acquire a desirable skill that is sought by many future employers. The fact that the preparatory session is taking place will speak for itself. You value the scheme enough to give over precious time to support it. You might also point out that, when assessment has a summative component, you, as well as the students, are going to be doing the marking as usual. Treat the suggestion with the levity it deserves, but avoid laughing it off summarily or sounding either defensive or petulant. You might also wish to give a simple (and brief) account of the time you have taken preparing for the exercise. The background research information you presented to support your scheme has not selected or organized itself. The guidelines you supplied to your students, similarly, were prepared by you for them with the express purpose of increasing the chances of the success of the venture.

4 Won't students simply agree to award each other high marks?

Before proceeding further, it is necessary to differentiate between examples of peer over-marking as a deliberate collusive strategy, as indicated in the question, and over-marking for other reasons. Students may err on the side of generosity when asked to grade their friends, in the absence of any agreement to do so. This kind of over-marking has been noted by a number of researchers, myself included. We shall discuss this issue further later on.

McDowell (1995), to whose work we referred above, identified some examples of the negative impact of self- and peer assessment which included the opportunity for cheating in the form of agreement between self- and peer second markers. Nonetheless, this was mentioned as a possibility by only a small proportion of students and no evidence of it having actually happened was provided. Lapham and Webster (1999: 188), on the other hand, reported that, '[p]rejudice, favouritism, friendships and ethnic division led to collaboration over marks and mark fixing' in their study of peer assessment of seminar presentations.

My review of the literature suggests that collusion which results in student over-marking may not be very common (or be under-reported or undetected by researchers). In fact, there is a hint of evidence that some students may award *lower* marks than teachers, though sometimes for reasons unconnected with the work being assessed. For example, Tsai *et al.* (2002: 249) reported that some students gave very low scores to a peer so as 'to keep his or her achievement at a relatively high level'. However, this kind of occurrence seems rare in the literature, at least. Many students seem to take the task seriously, to the extent that they question their own ability to be objective. For example, student evaluation of model of learning, by Greenan *et al.* (1997: 74), which involved self- and peer assessment, indicated that students were uncomfortable, seeing the main problem as the impossibility of achieving the objectivity for which they were striving, given that they knew each other well. This, of course is another problem, to which we shall return later. Suffice it to say that Greenan *et al.* continued to implement their model, believing that students develop assessment skills with practice, and learn to apply them to other modules.

What can be done?

My exploration of the literature suggests that potential collusion may be over emphasized, as the brief discussion given earlier indicates. Nevertheless, fears surrounding the possibility of collusion need to be addressed. First of all, it may be useful to present as much evidence as possible on the extent of the problem in order to allay such fears. Next, in order to prevent the problem developing, peer assessment schemes should be designed so as to maximize student responsibility and ownership (e.g. of criteria). If students are required to justify their decisions, they may desist from collusion. Mathews (1994: 23–4) suggested that, if evidence of collusion is found which indicates systematic victimization of one individual, 'then perhaps there is good argument to penalise the group as a whole for their lack of action to cope with the deviant behaviour'. It may be that, if the marks generated by students have a significant influence on their final marks, the pressures to maximize grades by any means may be increased. In fact, Boud (1989) questioned whether marks derived from self-assessment should be used for grading purposes. He proposed some strategies for improving reliability of student marking as well as ways of using student generated marks indirectly. For example, as well as requiring students to justify their marking, he suggested that staff should moderate self-assessment marks where necessary. Other proposals made by Boud included the re-marking of work by teachers where student peer marking gave rise to discrepancies. Boud also put forward the idea of marking students on the quality of their self-assessments, and not using student-generated marks formally until students had demonstrated that they could be reliable appraisers of their own work.

We shall return to consider other types of bias in later questions.

5 Won't some students use the opportunity to assess peers as a way of settling old scores?

This is seen as a problem by some students and teachers (e.g. Beaman, 1998), though I have found no hard evidence one way or the other. This question is closely linked with the following one. Consideration of what might be done to ameliorate this potential situation will be delayed until the end of the next section.

6 Won't students fear reprisals from peers to whom they've awarded low marks?

This situation, which may be described as fear of retaliation, has been noted by some researchers. For example, Lin *et al.* (2001) noted that some students dislike peer assessment as it involves rating people who are their competitors. The authors reported examples of retaliatory behaviour on the part of students who, on receiving an unexpectedly low grade from peers, 'immediately jump to reduce the previous scores they gave to others' (Lin *et al.*, 2001: 4). Purchase (2000) recorded fear of retaliation as a potential problem noted by her students. Similarly, Beaman (1998) reported encountering retaliation in relation to peer assessment.

What can be done?

Beaman (1998) stressed the importance of evidence, criteria and of collective decision-making as a way of dealing with retaliation, or fear of retaliation. This seems a step in the right direction. It would also be wise to require students to justify and defend their ratings. Additionally, in cases where grades are central to the assessment, taking an average of several peer assessments can serve to increase the reliability of such ratings. For example, Magin (1993) analysed results from two case studies of peer assessment. He calculated reliabilities of peer marks derived by averaging marks of several students using analysis of variance techniques for measuring inter-observer agreement. He concluded that, 'peer assessments based on multiple ratings can be highly reliable, even where individual rater reliability is low' (Magin, 1993: 5). Similarly, Sluijsmans *et al.* (2001), having calculated generalizability of ratings in a peer assessment study, found that quality of scoring to be low. However, when scores from at least three students were used to calculate a final score, a 'somewhat acceptable level' (Sluijsmans *et al.*, 2001: 159) was reached.

7 Isn't it the case that students lack the knowledge or experience to carry out the task?

There can be little doubt that this is, indeed, the case. In this respect, students may be no different from a beginner teacher who also lacks experience. Both may be helped to become knowledgeable and skilful. Students are aware of this limitation, and not infrequently note it as a reason not to engage in peer assessment or as a factor that had made the experience less than satisfactory. For example, some of Fineman's (1981) students questioned their own competence. Lapham and Webster (1999: 188) also noted that students feared marking inappropriately due to lack of specialist knowledge, and reported experiencing difficulty in marking objectively.

Similarly, Sluijsmans *et al.* (2001) reported that evaluations completed by students indicated that they had some doubts about their capability of assessing each other in a fair and responsible way. In fact, only 7 per cent of their sample felt comfortable when assessing peers. Nonetheless, over 70 per cent said they were in favour of implementing peer assessment and 66 per cent felt they knew what peer assessment was about. Tsai *et al.* (2002), on the other hand, noted that students believed that their peers may lack adequate knowledge to evaluate the work of others. Similarly, feedback from a small study of computer aided peer assessment by Ngu *et al.* (1995) suggested that 80 per cent of the sample wanted peer assessment to remain part of the course, though most stated a preference for lecturer marking due to lack of confidence in peer marking. Most said the experience had helped them learn some more about the subject.

The tutor's role can be problematic in this context. Lin *et al.* (2001) reported that students often believe that only the teacher has the ability and knowledge for the job. Similarly, Reynolds and Trehan (2000: 272) cited an example of assessment shared between a tutor and a group of students, in which a student reported that the tutor submitted her mark first and that, 'everybody then kind of fell in with because . . . we just weren't experienced, not up to arguing'. The authors cited other examples of unquestioned deference to tutors' authority on the part of students. Thus, tutors helping their students to become competent self and peer assessors need to be aware of this problem and structure sessions so as to prevent everyone falling into old traditional role patterns.

In a study conducted by Safoutin *et al.* (2000: 196), in which students were required to rate their own problem-solving abilities, student ratings of confidence were found to be 'relatively flat' across categories, in contrast to the more varied instructor ratings. Instructors tended to have higher confidence in students' abilities in the more basic areas than the students, and lower confidence in more complex and advanced areas.

Sluijsmans *et al.* (2001) argued that, as students are novices when it comes to assessment, rating errors can occur. They identified five sources of error:

(1) personal differences in standards and rating styles;
(2) differences in raters in the extent to which they distribute;
(3) the halo effect of basing overall rating on effects caused by one single dominating aspect;
(4) diverging opinions of groups of individuals regarding rating tasks;
(5) evaluation policy where judges differ in the ways they employ criteria.

What can be done?

Students need support in order to become partners in assessment. They need to learn how to become thoughtful and reliable assessors, in the same way that beginner teachers do. What might we do to help our students gain these skills and confidence in their ability to use them? First of all, they need *training* in self- and peer assessment, so they can begin to develop the necessary skills. Giving students training in peer assessment, and the opportunity to *practice* it, has been found to be beneficial (e.g. Cheng and Warren, 1997). Similarly, Lapham and Webster (1999) found that practice in presenting and assessing increased confidence. Thus, repeating the experience of self or peer assessment may already go some way towards increasing student confidence. Dochy *et al.* (1999), in their review of 63 studies of 'new' assessment forms, reported that increased student confidence was one of the positive effects of participating in self-, peer and co-assessment.

Some researchers and teachers *design studies* with the aim of encouraging students to develop confidence and the ability to assess their own work or that of their peers (e.g. Catterall, 1995). However, this may not always have the desired effect. Catterall found that, at the end of the study, more than half the respondents still reported lack of confidence in their ability to mark fairly due to insufficient knowledge and lack of experience. We were not told whether this was an improvement. Nonetheless, improvement is hinted at, in that Catterall (1995: 57–8) concluded that 'the real pay-off for students may come from being able to transfer that learning to their own work and being able to assess their own work more objectively and critically as a result'.

Re-designing the *mechanics of assessment* may help increase student confidence. For example, Ewers and Searby (1997: 7) modified their peer assessment, replacing single student assessments with those by small groups and concluded that, 'having a variety of different opinions decreases the likelihood of getting a rogue result and increases the confidence of those being assessed that they are being treated fairly'.

Finally, we need to be aware of *potential sources of rating errors* (cf. Sluijsmans *et al.*, 2001). The more transparent our procedures, the less likely are personal differences in standards and interpretation to influence marking.

8 Won't some students be better at this than others?

As with teachers, students may vary in their ability to apply marking standards consistently. Magin (2001b) explored the potential for biases of several kinds in the context of peer assessment, including *variation in marking standards* between raters. 'This criticism holds particular force where a peer mark is based on an individual peer rating' (Magin, 2001b: 54). Biases due to rater leniency and rater severity have been reported (e.g. Swanson *et al.*, 1991). Mathews (1994: 24) noted that perceptions vary between people and that some peer marks were what he described as 'out of kilter'. This seems to indicate that some *individuals think they have done more than others* in the group, Mathews (1994) supported Magin's (1993) conclusions and argued that averaged group assessment may give a more consistent evaluation than individual assessment.

Sluijsmans *et al.* (2001) reported results of studies carried out in order to test reliability of peer ratings and to investigate *idiosyncratic strategies* in peer assessment. Analysis of data indicated that the systematic variance in peer ratings could be accounted for by two latent variables. The first variable, which contributed about two-thirds of variance, was interpreted as mutual understanding of the quality, and the smaller, second variable, which contributed around 10 per cent, was seen as deviation. Most raters were found to have a 'substantial and positive correlation with the first principle component' (Sluijsmans *et al.*, 2001: 160). It may be, therefore, that similarities far outweigh differences.

Some *cultural differences* have been found, and others may exist. Lin *et al.* (2001), for example, reported research that had found a preference in Chinese speaking students for group harmony that worked to prevent critiquing of peers' work. In addition, Lin *et al.* found that some students experienced greater pressure when assessment is by peers than when it is conducted by a teacher. The authors reported that, in peer assessment, 'to perform better is to avoid shame and to maintain self-esteem in front of their peers' (Lin *et al.*, 2001: 4). However, I have also encountered this phenomenon in male Scottish students.

What can be done?

As already noted, both Mathews (1994) and Magin (1993, 2001b) suggest that marks derived from multiple assessors are more reliable than single marks. In addition, self- or peer assessment skills may improve with practice. Cultural differences that make peer criticism difficult need to be handled sensitively, but explicit instructions and reassurances can go a long way. A little more preparation and practice may be necessary for non-Western students than in cases of their Western counterparts.

9 Won't existing friendship patterns interfere with peer assessment?

This also seems to be a legitimate concern. Magin (2001b: 53) argued that the most persistent criticisms of peer assessment, voiced by teachers and students alike, is that peer ratings, particularly in group settings, are prone to bias which 'is seen to arise as a result of friendships and social interactions accompanying group task activities'. This bias can give rise to inaccurate and unfair marking. Tsai *et al.* (2002: 241) also suggested that 'interrelations of others', along with other factors such as complex interactions among background knowledge and individual preferences, might reduce the validity of using peer assessment. Sluijsmans *et al.* (1999), analysing 62 studies involving self-, peer or co-assessment, also identified problems which included friendship marking which can give rise to inflated grades. However, Magin (2001b) noted a dearth of empirical studies into the actual extent of this kind of bias.

A number of students have indicated that rating peers had been a strange experience, particularly if the peers were also friends. As illustrated in Chapter 3, Fineman (1981) reported over-compensation on the part of students resulting from friendships and tensions within the group. Similarly, Williams (1992) found the most common problem with peer assessment was students' dislike of criticizing friends.

There may be other relational effects that impact on peer assessment. Montgomery (1986) argued that peer rating behaviours are influenced by the characteristics of rater and ratee, and that 'reciprocity effects' can occur which impact on reliability and validity of peer assessments. Magin (2001b: 55) reasoned that the notion of reciprocity 'implies that assessments and judgements are influenced by relational effects which extend beyond those which can be attributed simply to friendships'. He described his method of detecting presumed reciprocity effects, an analysis of multiple peer assessment ratings, based on a cell-by-cell correlation analysis of reciprocal (rater/ratee) pairs. However, Magin calculated the proportion of variance accounted for by the presumed reciprocity effects and found these effects to be negligible.

What can be done?

When preparing students for self- or peer assessment, it is important to stress the necessity for realistic assessments. Provide students with an explanation of what marks mean. It might also be useful to point out that relatively few people perform at a first class (or third class) level. Magin's (2001b) methodology provides a means of investigating any reciprocity effects that you suspect might exist. If any are found, then a direct approach to the students concerned may be necessary. It may also be possible to inform students of the possibility of investigating such effects in your introduction to your implementation, in the hope that this will reduce the likelihood of their arising.

Lejk (1999b) argued that peer assessment is open to abuse and sometimes abused. He noted that friendship groups seemed to contribute to lack of objectivity. Many students expressed a preference for secret peer assessments and Lejk found that peer assessment seems to be 'more honest' when conducted in secret than in open agreement within the group. Lejk (1999b: 91) concluded that, 'peer assessment is frequently a "white lie" '.

10 Won't students find assessing themselves or their peers stressful?

McDowell (1995) noted that stress and anxiety were sometimes associated with innovative assessment. Some students have been found to experience greater pressure when assessment is by peers than when it is conducted by a teacher. For example, Purchase's (2000) students pointed to potential or actual problems with peer assessment. Some mentioned discomfort when encountering work better than their own, while others talked of threats to self-image or of embarrassment. As we saw earlier, Lin *et al.* (2001) reported a different type of pressure: avoidance of shame and maintenance of self-esteem acted as a spur to good performance.

Reynolds and Trehan (2000) also noted that, even though tutors intend that students will share the work of grading, the process can cause students anxiety and frustration.

Poor time management and organization may also cause stress (McDowell, 1995).

What can be done?

Any change is stressful, even change for the better. Thus, some degree of anxiety at the onset seems inevitable. Knowing that their feelings of apprehension are 'normal' may help students become more able to live with stress at this time. As poor time management and organization have been implicated in student stress, particular care should be taken to make sure that schemes are well planned and executed. We are asking our students to be more open and public about assessment than has been the case traditionally, which can threaten both self-esteem and self-image. It is important, therefore, to ensure that participants gain some satisfaction from the increased responsibility and power peer assessment affords them. Once again, this points to very thorough preparation and monitoring of the scheme. Students should be complimented for their honesty and helped to reinterpret what they may see as failure as perceptive self-appraisal. The kind of pressure to avoid shame reported by Lin *et al.* (2001), referred to earlier, may well work to improve both performance and assessment.

11 It takes me long enough to get through my marking. Won't students doing it just take too long?

Tsai *et al.* (2002) reported that students engaged in a networked peer assessment system found it time and effort consuming. Anyone who has implemented a face-to-face classroom-based self- or peer assessment scheme will probably have had the same experience. As with many activities, involving students in assessment in such a way that they will benefit cannot be done quickly, and such a venture will take time. It may be quicker to continue with the old ways, but this option is becoming less and less tenable if our students are to be prepared for lifelong learning. Initial involvement of students in assessment will take time to set up, yours and theirs, but the potential benefits are great and make the venture worthwhile. As with so many things, practice will improve things and speed up the process.

What can be done?

I'm afraid there are no quick fixes here. The answer is to exercise patience and plan schemes carefully. The second time round, implementation will take less time. If you value the exercise, so will your students.

12 My students don't want to be involved in assessment. How can I persuade them to give it a try?

This is another issue with which I am very familiar. I have found some students very willing to try something new, usually smaller groups of students whom I know well and who know me. However, I have also encountered other students who are not so open to novelty. I am not alone in this. For example, Gibbs (1999) noted that learners are sometimes not accepting of alternative marking procedures such as peer assessment. Weaver and Cotrell's (1986) explanation is that students are lazy, preferring to do as little as possible and perceiving peer assessment as demanding of time and effort. This seems a little uncharitable and, even if true, not applicable to all students.

What can be done?

Clearly, the answer here is (forgive the parallels with recent UK Labour Party education policy) preparation, preparation, preparation. Much may be achieved by spending time and energy at the preparatory stage. We have already discussed ways of combating the, 'It's your job, not mine', issue in question 2. If students are made aware of the benefits to them of their participating in assessment, they may become more willing to give it a go. If you have any evidence from studies within your own institution, department or discipline, this will be more persuasive than evidence from another country, culture or subject area. Students also need to be supplied with a detailed set of procedures, preferably written down for them to take away. It also seems that the problem of student reluctance to participate solves itself once they have engaged in the activities and given and received feedback. Weaver and Cotrell (1986) also noted that, having experienced it, students perceive the process as meaningful and useful and begin to find participation in assessment challenging and stimulating.

13 I tried peer assessment with my students who didn't like it. I am convinced that peer assessment is very beneficial and don't want to drop it. What should I do?

This statement will not be surprising to some who have implemented an element of peer assessment into their teaching. Sluijsmans *et al.* (2001) noted that only 7 per cent of their sample of students felt comfortable when first assessing peers. Similarly, Tsai *et al.* (2002) found that their students hesitated to criticize their peers, even though the assessments were done anonymously. Furthermore, Reynolds and Trehan (2000) discovered that participative approaches to assessment might be experienced by students as a more subtle technique for disciplining them. Much student reluctance seems to stem from their dislike of grading friends and acquaintances, as we have seen. However, researchers (e.g. McDowell, 1995) reported that some students hold beliefs that self-marking is tokenistic.

Nonetheless, there is a lot of evidence to suggest that many students find self and peer assessment a positive experience. Let's digress, briefly, to look at some research into the topic.

Research into attitudes to self- and peer assessment

Given that much self- and peer assessment seems to take place in the context of group work, it may be important to differentiate attitudes to group work from attitudes to self- or peer assessment of it. It is possible for students to have favourable attitudes to one aspect while holding more negative views on the other. Keaten and Richardson (1993) investigated this relationship and provided information relevant to this discussion. They reported that student attitudes to peer assessment were independent of attitudes towards group working, being more positive for peer assessment than for group working. Attitudes toward peer assessment were also found to be independent of group process and outcome variables.

Studies reporting generally favourable student attitudes to peer assessment

A number of researchers report student evaluations of self- and peer assessment which indicate positive attitudes. For example, Denehy and Fuller's (1974) analysis of an attitude questionnaire, completed by all freshmen dental students involved in a study of peer evaluation of preclinical laboratory skills, indicated that those who had been active participants as evaluators had more positive attitudes to peer evaluation than non-evaluators. Similarly, the results of an analysis of data derived from an online questionnaire conducted by Sitthiworachart and Joy (2003) indicated that most students agreed that seeing a variety of programs written by others helped them learn computer programming. Two-thirds of the group agreed that the act of marking helped them see mistakes in their own work and develop their understanding of programming. The aim of the study by Lin *et al.* (2001) of web-based peer assessment, 'NetPeas', used by students of computer science at a research university in Taiwan, was to discover whether or not most students have a positive attitude to peer assessment. The study also set out to investigate the relationships between achievement and attitude and between attitude and quality of feedback, as we saw in Chapter 4. Here, we shall limit ourselves to their findings relating to attitudes. Results indicated that 65 per cent of students held a positive attitude towards peer assessment and that those with positive attitudes had significantly higher achievement than those with negative attitudes. Quality of feedback given by those with positive attitudes was better than that provided by students with less positive attitudes. Lin *et al.* (2001) discussed possible reasons for the relationship between attitude and achievement, noting that attitudes may have been influenced by scores achieved. It is unfortunate that attitude measures were not taken before completion of the exercise and receipt of grades. Further details of this study are to be found in Chapter 10.

Gatfield (1999: 366) carried out 'an empirical test . . . to evaluate the perceptions of the students' acceptance of the process' of peer assessment. Analysis of data from an evaluation form indicated high levels of satisfaction with both the group work and the assessment method.

Studies reporting generally unfavourable student attitudes to peer assessment

Oliver and Omari (1999) reported that while students were satisfied with their online problem-based learning scheme overall, their response to the peer assessment element was less than positive. Concerns were expressed about the effects of rivalries and competition. However, even here, Oliver and Omari (1999: 11) reported that the use of peer assessment, 'appeared to provide a means to motivate and encourage students' critical thinking and involvement in synthesising the various solutions'. Personal experience, as well as many discussions with colleagues, suggests that students' initial attitudes to peer assessment may often be less than positive, if not actually negative. Common sense might also suggest that attitudes will change as students become more practised in the art of peer assessment. My own experience has been that this happens and that students become more favourably disposed to participation once they have experienced it, but changes in the opposite direction are also possible. We shall now look at some studies to try to get a feel for what seems to be happening in practice.

Does practice bring about attitude change?

As indicated previously, research by Cheng and Warren (1997) investigated the effects of practice on attitudes to peer assessment. Although they concluded that, overall, effects were beneficial, the pattern of attitude change was complex. The authors reported that students were generally positive towards peer assessment both before and after the exercise, but that the experience was not consistently positive. Some students changed their ratings in both directions. Responses to different questions suggested that different aspects of the process influenced ratings in different ways. For example, one question revealed that almost 60 per cent of those who had agreed that students should be able to assign grades responsibly in the pre-test changed their response to 'No' in the post-measurement. However, 6 of the 16 who had responded negatively first time said, 'Yes' in post-test. Cheng and Warren conducted interviews with students who had changed their mind, and identified a number of reasons for a change in a negative direction:

(1) students felt themselves not to be qualified to carry out the work;
(2) some students doubted their own objectivity;
(3) the objectivity of peers was questioned;
(4) the even split between teacher and peer grades was felt to place too much responsibility on shoulders of students;
(5) students claimed to have had no training for the task.

Some of these reasons refer back to earlier questions. For example, the first two points have a direct bearing on students' lack of knowledge or experience to carry out the task (question 7). The last point suggested to the authors that students *felt* unprepared for the task whatever the reality of the situation.

Sivan (2000) also reported results of the evaluation of a peer assessment study which indicated that a large number of students felt more confident using the method for the second time. As we shall see later, in Chapter 9, Jordan (1999) also found that practice led to more positive attitudes and an increased appreciation of the potential of peer assessment.

What can be done?

Beaman predicted that peer and self-assessment may give rise to complaints about the role of the teacher and requests to revert to the old way of doing things. She acknowledged that the 'instructor must have patience and faith for this method of assessment to work' and noted that things begin to change as the students become familiar with the system and 'get a grip on their purposes' (Beaman, 1998: 56).

The brief review of research also suggests that Beaman's conclusion is justified. It has also been my experience, and that of a number of Scottish teachers who contributed to the ASSHE survey (Falchikov, 1996b; Hounsell *et al.*, 1996), that students settle down and begin to see the benefits of self and peer assessment as they practice them.

14 How do I prepare my students for the task?

Sluijsmans *et al.* (2001) reported evaluations of a peer assessment task by students that highlighted problem areas they had encountered. Several of these related to the *preparation* they had received for the task. For example, some found the criteria difficult to interpret. More fundamentally, it was felt that peer assessment had not been introduced sufficiently well in general. Many rated the task as difficult because of lack of prior experience. Purchase (2000), too, reported that some students saw the criteria as subjective and ambiguous.

What can be done?

Beaman (1998) also acknowledged that peer assessment requires a great deal of preparation, particularly in the planning stages. She devised the 'Egg Game' to help students experience peer assessment in an unthreatening context, while, at the same time, discover (and solve) some of the problems. The Egg Game enables students to rehearse peer assessment. She argued that the relaxed environment of a game setting allows students to make mistakes and discover potential problems. In the game, grading is not an issue.

The Egg Game

The Egg Game 'enables students to think about what is involved in peer assessment and, at the same time, to raise any problems or issues such as collusion, fairness and validity' (Beaman, 1998: 54). Students are provided with materials and asked to make an egg container that can be dropped from a certain height without breaking. However, before they start, students have to make decisions about the criteria that they are to use for assessment and on the weightings of each criterion. Beaman argued that, in order to do this, students need to differentiate between process and product. They must also decide who is to do the assessing on completion of the task. Beaman recommended that an 'issues' board be maintained by the teacher throughout the game, on which comments are recorded for future discussion.

Beaman also recommended using peer assessment to provide feedback without grading. She also described another game designed to help groups differentiate between members, the 'You get a raise!' game. We shall learn more about this in Chapter 9.

FAQ summary

Pond *et al.* (1995) reviewed some of the problems associated with peer assessment considered earlier, and suggested possible remedies for them. They found that student ownership of assessment criteria was very important. If present, it had the power to reduce bias. Another remedy was to require assessors to justify their marking. This was found to be effective in all cases except collusive marking, though it is difficult to see why it should not have an effect here, too. Making the responsibility for determining the final mark be shared by teachers and students was also suggested as a means of reducing friendship and collusive marking.

Questions, issues and suggestions for solution are summarized in Table 6.1.

There are other problems associated with peer assessment, in addition to those discussed. These frequently relate to the problem of differentiating between students working in a group. Sluijsmans *et al.* (1999) identified two such problems:

(1) 'decibel marking' (individuals dominate groups and get highest marks)
(2) 'parasite marking' (students benefit who don't contribute).

We shall return to consider these, and others, in Chapter 9.

Peer feedback marking

One final question needs to be asked: 'Why do researchers emphasize marks, when we know that this is not the most important aspect of assessment?' There are many studies of self and peer assessment that emphasize and investigate the relationship between teacher and student marks. While such a venture has its place, as it is useful to have empirical evidence to help persuade colleagues to give alternative assessments a try, grading is not the most important aspect of involving students in assessment. Sluijsmans *et al.* (2001) found that many students were not happy with awarding a score, feeling that *feedback* would have been more useful. I also came to this conclusion during the 1990s when I was developing peer assessment into an approach that attempted to capitalize on the

Table 6.1 Summary: FAQs and suggestions for action

Question	Action
1 Isn't it my job as a teacher to undertake assessment?	• Stress importance of new role to teachers. • Spell out new role responsibilities. • Support teachers during necessary role change. • Use SCREE.
2 Students may argue that it's not their job to carry out assessment, as this is what teachers are paid to do. Some students also argue that, nowadays, they, themselves, are doing the paying. How do I respond to that?	• Give explanations and provide evidence of benefits to students of participating in assessment. • Make roles and responsibilities of both teachers and students explicit.
3 Students say that peer assessment is just a way of saving the teacher's time. Is this true?	• Reiterate benefits to students. • Value the exercise by giving it adequate time. • Be prepared to account for new usage of time.
4 Won't students simply agree to award each other high marks?	• Try to put problems in context. Seek/present evidence about extent of problem. • Design schemes to maximize student responsibility and ownership. • Require students to justify their decisions. • Reward groups for dealing with problem members/penalize them for lack of action. • Reduce extent to which marks 'count' towards final grades.
5 Won't some students use the opportunity to assess peers as a way of settling old scores? and 6 Won't students fear reprisals from peers to whom they've awarded low marks?	• Stress importance of evidence and criteria. • Require students to justify ratings. • Use averages of several peer ratings rather than single ratings to increase reliability.
7 Isn't it the case that students lack the knowledge or experience to carry out the task?	• Provide training in self, peer, collaborative assessment. • Design studies and assessment mechanisms to encourage development of student confidence and skills. • Design studies that allow students to learn by repeating the experience. • Use multiple assessors rather than singletons to increase student confidence as well as reliability.

8 Won't some students be better at this than others?

- Provide sufficient training and practice.
- Provide explicit instructions.
- Provide reassurances to students with different cultural values regarding peer criticism.
- Use marks derived from multiple assessors.

9 Won't existing friendship patterns interfere with peer assessment?

- Discuss this potential problem with students before they engage in assessment.
- Stress the need for realistic assessments. Provide students with an explanation of what marks mean. Point out that relatively few people perform at a first class (or third class) level.
- Use Magin's (2001b) methodology to discourage/detect presumed reciprocity bias.
- Use secret peer assessments.

10 Won't students find assessing themselves or their peers stressful?

- Ensure that schemes are well planned and executed.
- Ensure that participants gain satisfaction from the increased responsibility and power peer assessment affords them.
- Compliment students for their honesty and help them to reinterpret failure as perceptive self-appraisal.

11 It takes *me* long enough to get through my marking. Won't students doing it just take too long?

- Plan and implement schemes carefully.
- Value the experience yourself and be patient.

12 My students don't want to be involved in assessment. How can I persuade them to give it a try?

- Give time and energy to setting up the exercise and preparing students for it.
- Stress benefits to students (and employers?).
- Use evidence of benefits 'close to home' where possible.
- Supply detailed written procedures and guidance.

13 I tried peer assessment with my students who didn't like it. I am convinced that peer assessment is very beneficial and don't want to drop it. What should I do?

- Exercise more patience and have faith in your implementation. Student attitudes will change, as students become more familiar with the system.

14 How do I prepare my students for the task?

- Explain why you are introducing your scheme e.g. stress benefits to students, potential employers, etc.
- Provide training.
- Use the Egg Game.

benefits while helping minimize the problems. By focusing on the formative aspects of assessment, it is possible to reduce the discomfort students often experience. I called the variant procedure that I developed Peer Feedback Marking (PFM) (Falchikov, 1994, 1995a,b). This, as the name suggests, involved, and emphasized the importance of, feedback. I carried out three studies which are discussed in more detail later on.

In Chapter 1, we learned that, according to Black and Wiliam (1998), feedback about performance must contain three elements: identification of the goal, evidence about the current position and understanding of the way to close the gap between the two. We also learned that feedback must be timely, related to assessment criteria and used (QAA, 2000). To what extent do we, as teachers, meet these criteria? Magin and Helmore (2001) reported analyses of written feedback provided by teachers to fourth year engineering students on their oral presentations made as part of their project assignment. Assessments had formative and summative components in the form of a single global percentage mark, together with written comments and ratings on eight skill components. These components were predominantly concerned with the mechanics of presentation such as audibility, use of English, use of visual aids, eye contact. Two focused on the content and organization of the presentation, requiring evaluation of the logical organization of the content and the extent to which the audience was informed about the project topic. Another component related to the handling of questions. Magin and Helmore (2001: 410) reported that the use of audio visual aids attracted the greatest number of comments (29 per cent), followed by 'inform topic' and 'logic of presentation' (19 per cent each). Virtually all comments about use of aids contained practical advice on more effective use. Critical comment on the adequacy of information on the topic was often connected to time management, and that relating to the logic of presentation to lack of preparation. Thus, teacher feedback tended to be very practical indeed, and limited to relatively low-level cognitive outcomes. Of course, this may have been an artefact of the study, in that presentation skills were being assessed. Nonetheless, the practical emphasis of these teachers resembles that of the students found in my second Peer Feedback Marking study (described later).

I think that, if we ask students to give each other feedback, it is important to look closely at the kind of feedback they give, as indicated in the analysis of Study 3 data. It is in no-one's interest for students to mislead each other. Tsai *et al.* (2002), for example, reported that their students found peer feedback was often ambiguous or not relevant. This has not been my experience, having repeated Study 3 several times with comparable groups. Each time, reflective statements did not suggest that students found that their peers mislead them or they lacked the ability to supply useful feedback. Similarly, Catterall (1995) whose study aimed to encourage students to develop confidence and ability to assess their own or their peers' work and to complement teacher feedback, concluded that students found the exercise useful. Gibbs (1999) argued that students pay more attention to feedback that has a social dimension than to a tutor mark supplied confidentially. In other words, they care about what other people, including their peers, think about them.

Study 1

I conducted a small pilot investigation of PFM involving third year students studying psychology as part of a degree in biological sciences (Falchikov, 1995a,b). I hoped to be able to capitalize on the benefits of peer assessment in terms of improving the learning process, sharpening critical abilities and increasing student autonomy while also addressing problems encountered in earlier studies. Dislike of marking friends was greatest of these. I also planned to help the development of listening skills and make learning in audience members more active. Students began by identifying criteria of excellence relating to oral presentations. They then used these criteria, incorporated into evaluation forms, in rating presentations made by individual members of the class. In this example of PFM, students awarded marks (out of 20) as well as providing feedback, but this step is not essential, or even desirable, some might argue. Students noted the 'Best feature' of each presentation along with one 'Weakness', in writing, on their evaluation forms. Suggestions for improvement were encouraged.

Oral feedback based on what had been written down was given immediately after each presentation was concluded, starting with the 'Best feature'. This had the benefit of increasing the confidence of those who were threatened by being asked to make an oral contribution. They had the reassurance of their own written feedback in front of them, and so had something to say. It also boosted the confidence of presenters who derived considerable pleasure hearing compliments about their work. This seemed to make them more receptive to the constructive criticism that followed.

I later learned that Jacobs (1974: 408), who reported some early research into the effects of positive and negative feedback, had also noted that the delivery and receipt of feedback involves more than 'an objective transfer of information'. Positive feedback, or feedback describing what Jacobs called 'assets', leads to feelings of well-being and energy in recipients, while feedback which identifies deficiencies arouses anxiety and depression. Jacobs (1974) also found that feedback 'ordinarily rated as highly undesirable becomes less undesirable when preceded by positive feedback' (Jacobs, 1974: 433–4). This effect had been noted even earlier, in the early 1950s, by Rogers (1951, cited by Jacobs, 1974) who had established that individuals are more receptive to positive self-enhancement than to feedback which threatened the self-image. In addition, Jacobs (1974: 445) identified what he termed a 'credibility gap', in that students rated positive feedback as more accurate than negative. He also noted that perceptions of believability and accuracy seem to be enhanced if positive feedback is delivered before negative. Jacobs argued that such results may be predicted from dissonance or balance theories in social psychology (e.g. Festinger, 1957; Heider, 1958). Additionally, he found that positive feedback, being perceived as desirable, may lead to greater intentions to change than negative feedback. Research by Jacobs and colleagues (Jacobs *et al.*, 1973 in Jacobs, 1974) also found that group members tended to dilute negative feedback by means of qualifications and denials. I observed this effect, too. However, I digress.

In PFM Study 1, I completed a rating for each presentation, using the same assessment form students had used, and took part in the feedback session once peers had delivered their feedback. Forms were collected when the process was completed. I analysed the type of written feedback supplied by peers. Unsurprisingly, it reflected the four criteria identified. Most students' presentations were rated as having a variety of strengths, and raters suggestions varied considerably. Fewer weaknesses were identified than strengths, but there was greater inter-rater agreement over these. Evaluation sheets and summaries were returned to students the following week.

Student evaluation of the exercise indicated that they valued the fairness of the PFM system and felt it to have acted as an aid to learning. As with much peer assessment, some problems over discomfort at rating peers, particularly friends, persisted. Some students found the task hard and doubted their own analytical skills. Of course, this may have been due to the requirement to produce a numerical grade.

Study 2

The second PFM study was a 'replication' of the first, but this time involved a larger group of students (Falchikov, 1994). There were other slight differences between the two studies. The pilot study had involved third year students, while the replication involved first years. While, in the first study, individual presentations were assessed, the second study involved assessment of group presentations. In the replication, I looked more closely at the sort of feedback students were giving each other, comparing it with the feedback supplied by the three tutors involved. However, the methodology was identical with that of the first study. As before, students were required to identify the 'Best feature' and one 'Weakness'. Once again, marks were also required, though this time I asked for percentages. I now see that I may have some difficulty relinquishing my need for statistical verification! Or maybe old habits die hard. Nonetheless, students value marks, and both new tutors and students alike seem to be reassured when comparisons of marks point to frequent similarities and very few differences. This time was no exception. Mean peer and lecturer marks and standard deviations were found to be almost identical.

All feedback statements were subjected to a content analysis, using 11 categories: amount of information; content; delivery and presentation; quality of information; methodology; amount and quality of preparation; structure; support material used; teamwork; demonstration of understanding; zero response or 'nothing'. Two raters were involved and inter-rater agreement was found to be nearly 90 per cent. Students and two of the tutors provided slightly more 'positive' than critical feedback. However, the most striking finding was the prominence students gave to the delivery aspect of presentations. We know that students, particularly first years, find giving an oral presentation very stressful, so it is not surprising that they should be concerned with this feature. While students emphasized presentation and delivery, tutors gave more emphasis to methodological issues and understanding. I suggested that there might be an hierarchy of feedback, 'with "Delivery" being an initial hurdle, through which one must pass before being able to attend to more detailed and complex issues' (Falchikov, 1994: 415).

Study 3

The most recent study in this series (Falchikov, 1996a) was a modification of Bruffee's (1978) Brooklyn Plan which involved the use of peer criticism of student writing. In Study 3, peers gave feedback to student writers in a series of stages. This study involved fourth (final) year students of biological science studying a module on the topic of 'Sexuality, behaviour and society'. This PFM scheme differed from that used in the previous two studies in that feedback relating to individual essays was given before the product was handed in and assessed. The scheme was more modest in scale than Bruffee's original, but involved more organization and a greater investment of time than the previous PFM studies.

I have since discovered that similar schemes are in use in other institutions. For example, Obah (1993) described pair work and peer feedback used at Seneca College of Applied Arts and Technology in Toronto, concluding that the exercise was successful and that students learned from each other. She perceived that students made fewer mechanical errors than previous groups and produced essays which were more 'fluent and packed with meaningful content' (Obah, 1993: 13) than had been the case in previous cohorts.

My PFM Study 3 took place over an eight week period and consisted of five stages:

1 Essay titles, reading lists and brief notes on essay writing were supplied to students who were required to choose one topic from the list.
2 Students completed first drafts of their written assignments.

3 Unevaluative criticism took place. A peer made a short description of the main points of each paragraph and of the whole paper.
4 Evaluative criticism took place. Using agreed criteria, further criticism was made by a peer, which emphasized ways of improving the paper. Strengths were identified, and hints for improvement supplied.
5 Reflections on the scheme were made. Each student was required to submit a reflective statement on their experiences as reviewers and receivers of feedback. This statement contributed 20 per cent of the final coursework assessment mark (the remaining 80 per cent being awarded for the essay).

Stages 1 and 3 took place during normal lecture/tutorial time and were separated by five weeks. During this time students wrote their first drafts (stage 2). Stage 4 followed one week after stage 3. Students then had a further two weeks in which to complete both their essays and reflective statements.

My main concern over this study was to ensure that students were not being given useless or misleading information by their peers, so I asked for the evaluative feedback they had received to be submitted along with essays and reflections. The reflections themselves also contained views on the quality of the advice given, information about the extent to which students acted on advice and details of any changes made as a result. Thus, the tutor was able to take into account this information when grading the essay and ensure that students were not penalized in case any peer reviewer had provided misleading information.

The reflective statements provided interesting reading. Although there were relatively few males in the class, I got a strong impression that there were gender differences in the response to the exercise. For example, a female student wrote in support of the scheme:

1 There are many errors which you make when writing an essay, but it takes someone else to actually notice them.
2 The input from someone else can only serve to help. Two heads really are better than one.
3 The exercise spurs you on to write a good essay and not leave it until the last minute.

(Falchikov, 1996a: 215)

A male student's reaction was rather different.

The fact that a peer is going to read your essay and be invited to rip it to shreds makes demands upon you to take extra care. There is nothing worse than somebody quietly smirking to themselves at your expense, and an attempt to avoid this becomes a priority when writing the essay.

(Falchikov, 1996a: 215)

This difference in emphasis, in which the female student welcomes co-operation and the male perceives competition, requires further investigation. Results of a study conducted by Adams *et al.* (2000) may be relevant here. Gender differences were evident in the top ranked reasons given by students for assessment. Males were found to consider the primary reason for assessment to be 'to provide a unit mark representing their capabilities' (Adams *et al.*, 2000: 238), while females regarded the provision of feedback as their first choice.

Returning to PFM Study 3, inspection of the ratio of positive to negative statements provided by peers and, subsequently by tutors, indicated that, as in Study 2, students provided more positive than 'negative' (critical) feedback. This time, the reverse was found to be true for tutor markers, though, in Study 3, the students being assessed were in their final rather than first year. However, on this occasion, students provided more prompts and suggestions for improvements than tutors.

Further details of the analysis are to be found in Falchikov (1996a).

To what extent does student feedback resemble teacher feedback?

As discussed earlier, students vary in their ability to conduct peer assessment. There are also likely to be similar individual differences in the context of feedback provision. Indeed, there is some evidence to support this assertion. Lin *et al.* (2001) conducted a study to find out whether feedback supplied by students with a positive attitude was better than that given by those with negative attitudes. Analysis of their results found that the quality of feedback given by those with positive attitudes was, indeed, better than that provided by students with less positive attitudes. It would be strange if other differences did not exist.

Let us now look again at the three PFM studies.

Features common to peer and teacher feedback and features that differentiate between the two groups are shown in Table 6.2.

As can be seen from Table 6.2, teacher and peer feedback have been found to have a greater number of features in common than features that differentiate between them. Similarities may have resulted from the organization of the studies that produced them. Without the opportunity to discuss and agree criteria, fewer criteria may have been held in common than seems to have been the case in the three PFM studies and in many studies of self and peer assessment. Similarly, involving students in assessment makes explicit the relationship between objectives, criteria and assessment. Both students and teachers espouse the ideal of timely feedback, and PFM enables this ideal to be realized. For example, PFM Study 3 required students to attend to all elements listed by both Black and Wiliam (1998) (discussed in Chapter 1) and by the QAA (2000). It

Table 6.2 Features held in common and those that differentiate between student and teacher feedback

Shared features

- Some aims of feedback e.g. preference for minimizing time between demonstration of learning and feedback. Feedback functions as a motivator (cf. Rowntree, 1987), particularly for male students.
- Identification and understanding of criteria shared.
- Feedback related to assessment criteria.
- Feedback contains positive (Strengths) and negative elements (Weaknesses) and suggestions for improvement.
- Feedback generally believed to be, and found to be useful (cf. Tsai *et al.*, 2002 who reported peer feedback sometimes ambiguous or not helpful).

Features that differentiate

- Application of criteria may differ (e.g. In PFM 1 students emphasized 'practical' criteria and teachers 'understanding' and 'methodology'. However, Magin and Helmore (2001) found teachers also emphasized practical issues.)
- Different balances between positive and negative feedback found. Some suggestion that students provide both more positive encouragement and more suggestions for improvement than teachers. However, time on task differed for the two groups.

ensured that feedback be available before work was ready for hand-in, and separated feedback from summative assessment. Some differences in emphasis persist. After all, most teachers have more experience of assessment than most students. However, while we may help students learn skills of assessment, we, too, can learn from the experience. As I argued elsewhere (Falchikov, 1994), the transparency associated with involving students in assessment helps alert us to our own 'hobbyhorses'. In addition, McDowell (1995) found an unintended outcome of innovative assessment, including self- and peer assessment, was an increased awareness of the subjectivity of assessment, even when undertaken by lecturers. We are not infallible.

Final comment

In spite of the many and various problems we have considered in this chapter, we should not lose sight of the fact that involving students in assessment carries many benefits (see Chapter 4). The experience has been found to be beneficial for students. I believe it to be beneficial for teachers, too. Even the processes of identifying problems and searching for solutions have the power to improve assessment procedures and encourage development in students and teachers alike.

Chapter 7

How well are students able to judge their own work?

The question of the chapter title immediately begs other questions, namely, 'How is student performance to be judged? Against what standard are we to judge student marking? With what do we compare student grades?' There seem to be two main contenders for a standard against which to judge student grading, though other less frequently employed possibilities also exist. Student marks are most often compared with teacher marks for the same piece of work. However, student marks may also be compared with other marks awarded by teachers for different pieces of work. It is the former, teacher–student comparison, that is most commonly used when teachers or researchers wish to be sure that student participation in assessment is either reliable or valid.

Of course, other questions altogether may be asked in this context. Why does student involvement in assessment have to focus on marks? I have much sympathy with this enquiry, as the learning benefits to be derived from participating in assessment are great. We have already looked at these in Chapters 4 and 6.

Another question concerns whether, by comparing student and teacher marks, we are investigating reliability or validity. It should be noted that many teachers who compare their marking with that of self- or peer assessments of their students, report that they are investigating reliability. Simply comparing teacher and student generated marks is, in fact, far from simple, and there are those who prefer to conceptualize the comparison as a measure of validity. However, at the end of the day, I believe it is more important to get on with the venture than to debate the niceties of such a question. Thus, I will leave it to individuals to decide what it is that is being investigated.

We shall now look at two studies which explored the relationship between student self-assessment and teacher marks. In 1989, I worked with David Boud on two papers: a qualitative review of student self-assessment studies in higher education and a meta-analysis (Boud and Falchikov, 1989; Falchikov and Boud, 1989). Both reviews identified the conditions under which student and teacher ratings were most likely to agree.

A qualitative review of self-assessment studies

Our first study focused on the aspect of self-assessment that looked at statistical comparisons between teacher and student ratings. It did not investigate the multiple benefits to be gained from this procedure. Instead, we wished to identify the methodological and conceptual limitations of the studies reviewed.

Methodology

We obtained our studies by a number of methods: from searches of electronic databases such as ERIC, Psychological Abstracts, Sociological abstracts and MEDLINE; from conventional literature searching; from following up citations; and from direct contact with authors. Having collected together our corpus, we were faced with a choice of ways to proceed. It was necessary to conduct some form of integrative review, and we chose the traditional qualitative method. The first step was to develop an understanding of the relationships between student and teacher marks and of the variables thought to affect this relationship.

Findings

Weaknesses and problems

We identified a large number of methodological weaknesses in our corpus. The key problems were as follows:

- student and teacher ratings were often derived using different methods;
- results were reported in a variety of ways (in the majority of studies, we learned either 'how much' agreement there is, or in 'how many' cases agreement occurs, but rarely both);
- explicit criteria were frequently missing;
- there appeared to be little or no replication;
- some studies included rating of effort;
- very many different scales had been used;
- some studies required students to predict performance levels;
- self-grading was often not defined.

In addition, we often found the description of the context was inadequate, such that replication by interested readers was impossible.

We also found conceptual limitations. The unreliability of teacher ratings causes a major difficulty. It is reasonable to suppose that teachers have limited access to the knowledge of their students. In addition, students and teachers may have different perspectives and ideas about what is important. Nonetheless, we appreciated that teachers needed to have some evidence about what was happening in self-assessment.

Over- and under-rating

We experienced some difficulty in trying to establish the degree of over- or under-rating by students, due to the variety of definitions of 'agreement' we encountered. However, we found that in most studies, greater numbers of student marks agreed than disagreed with teacher marks. We briefly described 17 studies which had reported over-rating, and 12 which reported under-rating. However, we concluded that, on balance, as there were more studies with methodological flaws in the former group, no clear tendency was evident.

Ability effects

We found a general trend in the studies for high-achieving students to be more realistic, in terms of agreement of their marks with those of teachers, than their lower-achieving peers. We also noted that high-achievers tended to underestimate and low-achievers to overestimate their own performances.

Level of course effects

Here, we found a trend for undergraduate students in later years of their courses and graduates to be more accurate in their judgements than students in earlier years. Students in later years also showed a slight tendency to underestimate their performance.

Using marks for formal assessment purposes

It was difficult to find out whether using marks for formal purposes affected rating performance, as studies did not report the use to which self-derived marks were put in any consistent fashion.

Gender effects

The few studies of gender effects we encountered were also inconclusive.

A meta-analysis of student self-assessment studies

Before looking at the findings of our second study, it would be useful to explain what a meta-analysis is. Those who are familiar with this technique might skip this section.

What is a meta-analysis and why is it useful?

The traditional critical literature review allows synthesis of the results of many studies, and can, thus, provide insights into trends and patterns in the data. It can also indicate gaps in our knowledge and in the research. However, such qualitative research syntheses are subject to bias. Original researchers may interpret findings in ways not shared by others. Authors sometimes over-generalize their results. Reviewers, too, may introduce further bias. Meta-analysis circumvents many problems of bias, in that it uses statistical results rather than interpretations of these. It then synthesizes quantitative information for the purpose of comparing study results.

How is meta-analysis carried out? What methodology is used?

Four procedures are necessary in order to carry out a meta-analysis. They are

(1) selection of studies;
(2) coding of study characteristics;
(3) quantifying the experimental effect;
(4) correlation of common metrics with context variables.

We shall look briefly at each in the context of our meta-analysis.

(1) Selection of studies.   Self-assessment studies for the meta-analysis were found by searching a wide range of databases, as with the qualitative review. To be included in our corpus, each study had to have taken place within higher education and to have reported some quantitative measure of teacher–student agreement. These data had then been subjected to statistical analysis by the researcher reporting them. Studies varied in terms of their quality, but no quality filter was applied at this point.

(2) Coding quantitative peer assessment study characteristics.   We attempted to identify those variables that might influence the outcomes of the studies located (independent variables), as well as the findings (dependent variables). We then classified each study, using the following headings:

- Study identifiers (i.e. name of researchers and date)
- Population characteristics (i.e. number of participants, gender, level of students)

- What is assessed
- The level of the module or course (e.g. introductory or advanced)
- How the assessment was carried out and the nature of the criteria used (if known)
- The design quality
- Number of peers, and number of faculty involved in assessments.

We measured design quality by evaluating the adequacy of reported information, the degree of inference required of the reader, the appropriateness of tasks involved and the quality of instrumentation. This procedure is described in greater detail in Falchikov and Goldfinch (2000).

(3) Quantifying the experimental effect. In order to compare results of studies, it is necessary to express the statistics in a common form. Some outcomes were already reported as correlation coefficients which required no conversion. Other statistics needed to be converted to effect sizes, using a calculation formula. At the time, the formula by Glass *et al.* (1981) was deemed suitable. A newer formulation is described in Chapter 8. Those studies which reported only the proportion of students whose marks corresponded with teacher marks were treated as a separate subgroup. This was a problematic grouping, given that different researchers had used different definitions of 'agreement'. Sometimes, identical ratings were required, while in other studies, agreement was taken to be present when marks fell within a pre-agreed range. Less than 10 per cent difference was a common definition used.

(4) Correlating common metrics with variables. Once we had sets of common metrics, we were able to examine the relative importance of the variables we had identified. We made a number of predictions, based on the critical literature review reported earlier which are shown in Table 7.1.

In addition to these predictions, we also anticipated that studies carried out in different subject areas would differ in the accuracy of student ratings, and that both the nature of the assessment task and the measuring instrument used would also influence self-assessment accuracy.

Results

Predictions and results of the tests carried out are shown in Table 7.1.

Thus, we learned that self-assessment is more likely to produce accurate ratings when studies are well designed. This entails students being well prepared for the task. Good agreement also occurs between teachers and students when criteria are discussed and agreed, and exclude effort. When students engaged in self-assessment have some experience within a subject area and have, presumably, internalized some of the standards of the discipline, again, agreement between teacher and student is likely to be high. Finally, accurate ratings seem to be found when self-assessment is conducted within a science context,

Table 7.1 Predictions and degree of support provided by analyses

Prediction	Whether supported by meta-analysis
(a) Studies with good design quality will give rise to better agreement than those with poor design.	Supported in 2 of the 3 subsets. In effect sizes and proportions subsets, high quality studies produced better teacher–student agreement than low quality ones.
(b) More recent studies will be better designed than older ones.	Supported
(c) As effort is an inappropriate criterion against which to judge performance, its use as a criterion will give rise to poor agreement.	Supported
(d) Studies with explicit criteria, particularly criteria 'owned' by students, will produce better agreement than imposed or absent criteria.	Supported in part
(e) Senior students will be more accurate raters than juniors.	Supported, but no clear pattern found across common metrics.
(f) Those studying advanced level courses will be better raters than those on introductory courses.	Supported
Subject area differences	Evidence that more accurate self-assessments occur in Science than in Social Science when effect size or proportions used for comparison (too few examples in Art to include).
Effects of instrumentation	Use of range that includes 100 (i.e. percentages) recommended. Better to avoid use of extremely long instruments.
Effects of what is being assessed	When correlational techniques used, better teacher–student agreement achieved when traditional academic products were being assessed than in the case of assessment of performance or professional practice.

though this does not imply that it should not be implemented in other disciplines.

However, we also noted some variation in outcomes associated with the statistical method used for comparing student and teacher marks and concluded that the choice of statistic for the analysis of self-assessment studies can influence the pattern of results. For example, subject area differences tended not to show up when correlational techniques were used. Correlations, but not other statistical techniques, also pointed to better teacher–student agreement when traditional academic products were being assessed and poorer in the case of assessment of performance and professional practice. Of course, while correlation involves judgements of the relative worth of a product or performance, an effect size derived from a comparison of means and standards deviations is concerned with absolute difference or similarity.

We shall now examine some recent self-assessment studies in the light of the results of the qualitative critical review and the meta-analysis.

Recent self-assessment studies

As we saw in Chapter 4, some recent studies which involve students in assessment emphasize the formative advantages, and do not dwell too closely on statistical comparisons. However, we shall look next at examples of recent self-assessment studies which do report the level of agreement between teachers and students, bearing in mind the recommendations derived from the meta-analysis. In other words, we shall look out for presence or absence of features found to be associated with good teacher–student agreement. We would expect to find the following features to be associated with good student–teacher agreement:

- studies well designed;
- use of explicit criteria, particularly those 'owned' by students and which avoid inclusion of effort;
- students studying at an advanced level;
- use of measuring instruments and procedures that avoid too much detail and which use the percentage range;
- studies conducted in the broad academic discipline of science.

However, we would also expect some variation due to choice of statistical technique chosen for comparisons.

Answers to two questions are required:

(1) Do the characteristics of studies with good teacher–student agreement in recent years resemble the ideal conditions identified by the meta-analysis? If not, what might explain the findings?
(2) Are the characteristics of studies with poor teacher–student agreement different from the ideal conditions identified by the meta-analysis? If so, in what ways? If studies with poor agreement follow the advice offered by the results of the meta-analysis, what might explain the poor agreement?

Recent studies reporting good student–teacher agreement

We shall examine two case studies under this heading.

Williams (1992)

Williams (1992) reported the results of a Welsh self- and peer assessment study involving 99 first year students of Business Studies. Students submitted written anonymous assignments which were distributed to the group to mark in line with an agreed marking scheme. A few critical comments on each essay were also requested. Marks were agreed between authors and first markers. Analysis of the self- and peer assessments found that while peer assessments tended to be inflated, self-assessments were usually in close agreement with teacher assessments.

While, at first sight, a study involving first year students in a non-science area might not seem a likely candidate for producing good teacher–student agreement, Williams found close correspondence between the teacher and students for self-assessments. However, the marking scheme was agreed in advance of assessments being carried out, assessments were conducted anonymously and discussion between markers took place. These factors could have worked together to produce the good agreement reported.

Oldfield and MacAlpine (1995)

Oldfield and MacAlpine (1995) reported results of a Hong Kong study of peer and self-assessment conducted within a group context. On the first implementation, when self-assessment appeared to be a voluntary activity, one student only submitted and assessed individual work. This self-assessment was reported as being quite accurate.

We cannot assume that all students would perform as did the self-assessor in this study. However, in the abstract of their paper the authors reported finding 'high correlations between students' and lecturers' assessments of individual essays and presentations' (Oldfield and MacAlpine, 1995: 125). Unfortunately, no details appear in the main body of the paper. We can compare features of this study with those identified as likely to encourage good teacher–student agreement. This self-assessment exercise was well introduced, involving students gradually, as their confidence grew. However, other features of the study are not as auspicious. No criteria are reported, and the measuring instrument used a five-point scale initially. Participants were first year engineering students. If, indeed, good agreement between teacher and student marking occurred, then much must be attributed to the introduction of, and preparation for, the exercise.

Other authors (e.g. Longhurst and Norton, 1997) have seen their studies as confirming the findings of our critical review discussed previously (Boud and Falchikov, 1989). Longhurst and Norton's study has been discussed in Chapter 5.

Recent studies with mixed or ambiguous results regarding student–teacher agreement

Let us now look at three self-assessment case studies in which ambiguous or mixed results were reported.

Gopinath (1999)

Gopinath's (1999) study involved student assessment as an alternative to instructor assessment of class participation in an MBA course at an east coast American university. It aimed to compare self- and peer assessment with instructor assessment in three different situations: single self-assessment score counting towards final grade (no practice); second self-assessment score counting towards final grade; second peer assessment score counting towards final grade. Results indicated that both self- and peer assessments were higher than instructor assessments. The difference was significant in two of the three cases, the exception being the self-assessment with practice condition.

This study has some attributes that have been associated with good teacher–student agreement and others that have not. Students seemed to have been well prepared and to have been given some control over the decision-making process. Grading, however, used a ten-letter range. The most telling feature is that, while teacher–student differences were significantly different in two experimental conditions, in the self-assessment with practice condition, instructor and student ratings did not differ significantly.

Sullivan *et al.* (1999)

Sullivan *et al.* (1999) reported the results of a study of self; peer and faculty evaluations of problem-based learning in the context of a third year surgical clerkship in a west coast American university. Highest correlations were between peer and faculty ratings which, although low, were all found to be significant. Lowest correlations were between self- and faculty. The authors noted that, although correlation between most variables reached statistical significance, the overall proportion of variance explained was quite low. The authors concluded that students are not routinely taught self-evaluation skills and that practice is required.

Once again, there are a number of other factors which might account for the findings. The need for better preparation of students for the task is evident. In addition, the assessment form was provided rather than discussed and agreed. A global score was required, which we discovered in Falchikov and Boud (1989) did not appear to be associated with good agreement between teacher and student ratings. Students were told that their endeavours would not affect their grade. On the positive side, in the study by Sullivan *et al.*, students were in their third year of study and might, thus, be expected to perform better at self-assessment than less experienced peers.

Jordan (1999)

Jordan (1999) described two self- and peer assessment exercises carried out with second year students of foreign languages at an English University. Assessments were conducted twice: the first halfway through and the other at the end of the module. Jordan (1999: 175) reported that, in the first round of assessments, students had an 'unrealistic (usually inflated) perception of the value of their own contribution'. The author concluded that students were not able to judge themselves or their peers objectively. She acknowledged the problems inherent in tutor modification, and expressed a strong desire for students not to feel that tutor evaluations were being imposed, thus invalidating the exercise. The second assessments were reported to run more smoothly: students were more confident and comfortable and tutors were required to intervene less than on the first occasion. No marks were modified this time.

This study seems to have a number of features that have been associated with good teacher–student agreement. It seems to have been well designed and conducted. Criteria were negotiated, and student generated criteria included. Students were supplied with ample documentation which included a rationale for the study and background information, as well as prompts to reflection. Although it does not concern us here, students were also provided with a framework to help them manage group interactions. Both students and tutors were required to justify their decisions. The study also encouraged students to improve their self-assessment skills, in that two self-assessment sessions were built in. Jordan reported that teacher–student agreement had improved by the end of the exercise.

Recent studies reporting poor student–teacher agreement

Finally, let us look at three studies which reported poor teacher–student agreement.

Penny and Grover (1996)

Penny and Grover (1996) reported results of a study of self-assessment by final year students of education. Criteria were supplied to students. A poor match between student and tutor grades was found. Students tended to be pragmatic and technical, and to emphasize 'lower order criteria' (Penny and Grover, 1996: 173) such as style and presentation. They also tended to ignore criteria concerned with theoretical and conceptual understanding, reflection and quality of discussion in their research report. The authors suggested that the poor match between students and teachers may have related to the following:

(1) little formal preparation being provided for students;
(2) insufficient emphasis on theory by teachers;
(3) the 'cultural norm and the cultural form of the course' (Penny and Grover, 1996: 182).

Comparing the overall features of Penny and Grover's study with the ideal conditions identified by the meta-analysis, we see that more features seem to be absent than present. The one feature likely to give rise to good agreement present in the study was the degree of expertise of the students involved, being in their final year of study. However, Penny and Grover themselves identify the lack of preparation as a significant factor in the poor agreement they found. Moreover, it should also be noted that students did not appear to have been involved in identification or discussion of criteria. The study was conducted in an educational context rather than in a science-based discipline and professional practice was being assessed.

Hahlo (1997)

Hahlo (1997) reported results of a study of self-assessment carried out by a group of first year students of sociology at an English Institute of Higher Education. At the beginning of the semester, students were informed that they were to mark their own work, in class at a later date. The marking schedule used by staff was included in the course document. Essays and marking schedules completed by teachers were returned to students, but marks were withheld. Students were then asked to award themselves a grade, and informed that they might earn a bonus of 5 per cent if their marks were the same as teacher marks. Marks were compared in one-to-one sessions. Over three-quarters of students gave themselves a lower mark than that awarded by the teacher. Only one student and teacher mark was the same, but seven students came within

5 per cent of the teacher mark. Students and the teacher both found the exercise valuable.

Given the somewhat draconian measure of 'agreement' used in this study, I feel that there may be an argument to place it in the 'mixed' section rather than the 'poor agreement' one. As with many other studies, it contains elements likely to lead to good teacher–student agreement, and others that are less likely to have this effect. On the negative side, we see that participants in the exercise were first year students, presumably inexperienced in their discipline. They were given the teacher's marking schedule for information, but seemed not to have a say in the generation of criteria. No discussion was reported to take place, and it seemed as though the teacher's decision was final. On the positive side, students seemed to be well prepared for the experience, receiving written information in the course document. The incentive of the bonus is interesting, and may have helped students make realistic (or low) self-assessments.

Roach (1999)

Peer and self-assessment of oral presentations were introduced by Roach (1999) into an introductory taught module on information technology and communication involving two classes of Higher National Diploma (HND) students at an English university. The students were involved in the generation of criteria and discussion of standards, and in the choice of topics for the presentation. Self-assessment was implemented first. Roach found that students awarded themselves higher grades than he expected or would have awarded. Roach was unable to interpret this finding, and concluded that changes were needed. He expressed concerns over standards, particularly the lack of previous marks against which self- and peer assessments might be compared. He recommended three modifications:

(1) Make sure that marks awarded reflect performance.
(2) Take more care in 'constructing the rules for assessment' (Roach, 1999: 197), including more clarity over criteria and standards.
(3) Introduce more follow-up exercises to continue the reflection stage.

This study, too, contains a mixture of features associated with good teacher–student agreement and those which are not. For example, while students were involved in choice of topics and criteria generation, they were studying an introductory course and assessing oral presentations. Roach himself identified a number of ways in which the exercise might be improved. He clearly wished to give over more control to his students, but may have handed over too much too soon.

Conclusion

We have looked at a selection of recent self-assessment studies and attempted to relate their perceived success or failure to findings of the meta-analysis described earlier in the chapter. While many findings support our meta-analysis findings, the venture has also proved problematic in some respects. Those studies categorized as illustrating good teacher–student agreement do not uniformly display all the features identified in the meta-analysis. Similarly, those which reported poor teacher–student agreement were not devoid of features identified as likely to be beneficial. There are at least two factors at work here. As we saw in Chapter 4, the reasons teachers are involving their students in assessment change over time, and we are now less concerned with the formal relationship between teacher and student marks than was the case in the early decades of self- and peer assessment development. That is not to say that we are less concerned with standards and quality. Perhaps we now better appreciate the wider benefits of involving students in assessment. Most of the authors whose studies are discussed here were both aware of these benefits and concerned to maximize them for their students. The other factor which characterizes these studies is that they are prone to interpretation bias, which is one of the reasons that led us to carry out the meta-analysis in the first place.

Many studies conducted since the completion of the two integrative reviews concern themselves with problems and possible solutions. Preparation and training are beginning to be acknowledged as important if students are to value self-assessment skills. I was pleased to note that the authors featured here, particularly when reporting studies with modest to poor teacher–student agreement, displayed considerable critical reflection on the reasons for their results and identified ways in which their next implementation might be improved. This way lies progress.

However, it is not easy to answer the question which forms the title of the chapter. Some students seem to be able to judge their own work in similar ways to their teachers. Others do not. Students appear to be able to acquire and develop these skills, but not all have the opportunity to practice them. More importantly, authors are likely to continue to interpret their findings in light of their preconceptions, their previous experience and their overall educational world view. Maybe the time has come for someone to conduct another meta-analysis. Finally, I continue to believe that the main benefits of involving students in assessment reside in the potential for improving learning and stimulating personal and academic development. It still seems wise, however, when designing and implementing studies, to follow advice derived from the integrative reviews discussed here, in the absence of any competing evidence.

Chapter 8

How reliable or valid are student peer assessments?

In the last chapter, we looked at two integrative reviews relating to self-assessment, carried out to provide research-based information for teachers wishing to involve their students in self-assessment about where and when the practice is likely to succeed. As is the case with self-assessment, many colleagues are similarly concerned about how student peer ratings might resemble their own. Unless teachers are reassured about reliability or validity of peer ratings, they are unlikely to allow their students to try it, thus depriving them of its many learning benefits.

In this chapter, we will look at the findings of a meta-analysis of peer assessment studies which compared teacher and peer marks which was conducted by myself and Judy Goldfinch (Falchikov and Goldfinch, 2000). As we learned in the last chapter, a meta-analysis is a synthesis of quantitative information for the purpose of comparing study results. This procedure is particularly useful when, as is often the case, studies use a variety of different statistical techniques which make direct comparisons of results problematic. The meta-analysis discussed here systematically compared peer marks with those awarded by teachers. We have already learned that meta-analysis involves four procedures: selection of studies; coding of study characteristics; quantifying the experimental effect; correlating common metrics with context variables. Let us look briefly at each in the context of the peer assessment meta-analysis.

A meta-analysis of peer assessment studies

1 Selecting studies for inclusion

Selection procedures were followed as in the earlier meta-analysis, and in excess of 100 studies were located in total. However, not all were suitable for inclusion in our study. For example, a large number were review papers or qualitative accounts of peer assessment in higher education. However, 48 were quantitative studies which included a comparison of grades awarded by peers and teachers, and, thus, met the criteria for inclusion. These spanned the period from 1959 to 1999. In each study, the peer score was typically a mean value derived from several individual peer assessments.

2 Coding quantitative peer assessment study characteristics

Studies were classified in the same way as described in Chapter 7. However, this time, the rating of design quality was further refined, using the advice by Bangert-Drowns *et al.* (1997), which was that

- criteria for judgements of study quality must be explicit;
- the procedure for determining quality must be systematic;
- the criteria used should have face validity and reflect consensual opinions in the research community.

As before, we agreed that, for any study to be rated as of high quality, it should report enough information to enable replication. In order to ascertain this, we used the same categories as in the meta-analysis of self-assessment studies reported in the previous chapter. Total numbers of study faults were calculated and each study rated as of high or low quality on the basis of these totals.

3 Quantifying the experimental effect: calculation of common metrics

As before, numerical information took the form of means, standard deviations, correlations or percentages of agreement between peer and teacher marks. Thus, the common metrics used were the effect size (d), correlation coefficient (r) or percentage agreement (%). We used the formula provided by Cooper (1998) to convert means and standard deviations into effect sizes:

$$d = \frac{(E \text{ group mean}) - (C \text{ group mean})}{(E \text{ group sd} + C \text{ group sd})/2}$$

where C = Control (teacher), E = Experimental (peer).

Ten studies reported the proportion of comparisons that indicated 'agreement' between teachers and students rather than other statistics. However, given the tremendous variation in the definition of what constituted 'agreement', these studies were omitted from analysis.

4 Correlating common metrics with context variables

The final step in a meta-analysis is to investigate relationships between key variables and study outcomes. The following variables have been identified by researchers as mediating the correspondence between faculty and peer ratings:

- ability of student raters (Jacobs *et al.*, 1975);
- practice effects (Orpen, 1982; Fuqua *et al.*, 1984; Hunter and Russ, 1996);
- number of student raters related to the reliability of marking (Magin, 1993);
- methodologies employed (Falchikov, 1986);
- the type of assessment involved (Mowl and Pain, 1995).

In addition, the earlier meta-analysis of student self-assessment studies (Falchikov and Boud, 1989) had identified a number of significant variables. It seemed reasonable to suppose that similar relationships might exist in relation to peer assessment. This proved not to be the case, but this is skipping ahead in the story. The variables found to influence self-assessment were

- the level of course;
- the complexity of measurements used;
- the explicitness of criteria and student ownership of these;
- the subject area in which the assessment takes place.

Hypotheses

Previous research in the area led us to hypothesize that

1 There would be *subject area differences* in the reliability of peer assessment (defined as the similarity between peer and faculty marks), with higher reliabilities being associated with science and engineering areas than with social science and arts (Falchikov and Boud, 1989).
2 Peer assessment carried out in *advanced level courses* would be more reliable than that in introductory courses (Falchikov and Boud, 1989).
3 The greater the *number of students involved* in each peer assessment, the better the reliability (Magin, 1993).
4 *Explicit and student-owned criteria* would be associated with better peer assessment reliabilities than other criteria or absence of criteria (Fineman, 1981; Falchikov, 1986; Stefani, 1994).
5 More reliable assessments would be associated with *higher quality studies* than those deriving from studies with poor experimental designs (Falchikov and Boud, 1989).

6   Different *bases for ratings* might result in different levels of teacher–peer correspondence (e.g. whether or not large or small numbers of dimensions are involved or familiar ranges such as 100 per cent are used). Some researchers argue that ratings based on large numbers of dimensions will lead to closer correspondence between peer and teacher ratings (Harris and Schaubroeck, 1988), while I have argued the reverse (Falchikov and Boud, 1989).

In addition, we believed that the *nature of the assessment task* would influence reliability of peer assessment, with assessments carried out in traditional academic areas within the classroom (e.g. essays, tests, presentations) having better reliabilities than those in areas of professional practice (e.g. intern performance, counselling skills, teaching practice).

Now we shall look at what happened, inspecting the results of the analysis of correlation coefficients and effect sizes separately.

Results

Correlation coefficients

The spread of correlation coefficients is indicated in Figure 8.1. The mean overall value was calculated to be $r = 0.69$. This is a very significant average value of r which suggests that, overall, the relationship between peer and teacher marks is strong. Tests for homogeneity of studies indicated that one study lacked homogeneity. However, the distribution of z scores showed no other irregularities that would indicate publication bias.

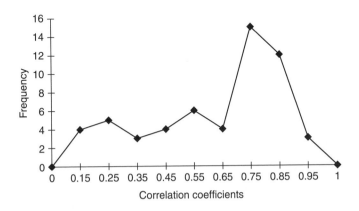

Figure 8.1 Distribution of correlation coefficients

Source: Falchikov and Goldfinch (2000: 305).

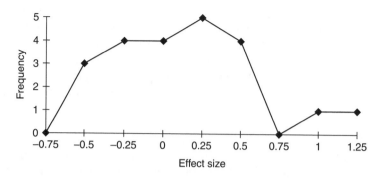

Figure 8.2 Distribution of effect sizes

Effect size subset

The range of effect size values (d) is shown in Figure 8.2. The range of d values, from $d = -4.48$ to $d = 7.34$, indicated that both peer over- and under-marking takes place. A similar problem to the one identified in the correlation coefficients subset was found in the effect size corpus, and an 'outlier' identified. This was a different study from that identified there. However, again, this did not materially affect the results of the study.

Factors which had a significant effect on common metrics

As it was important to investigate not only possible effects of factors in isolation, but also their effects in interaction with each other, weighted multiple regression models were built. These enabled us to identify factors which had a significant effect on common metrics, shown in Table 8.1. The degree of support for hypotheses is also included in the table.

As we saw earlier, analyses of both correlation coefficients (r) and effect sizes (d) identified problematic studies, but p values shown are those including these studies. Any differences due to exclusion of the studies will be identified later. It should be noted that correlation coefficient analysis produced more significant values than that involving effect sizes. However, this is not surprising, given that correlations investigate the rank ordering of scores, while effect sizes relate to absolute values of grades awarded. It can be argued that it is easier to achieve a significant similarity when teachers and students are rank ordering than when they are awarding a specific grade, as a perfect correlation between two rank orders may be achieved even when the marks are very different.

Table 8.1 Factors found to have a significant effect on outcomes

Variable	p value for r	p value for d	Is hypothesis supported/influence of variable clarified?
Subject area	0.34	0.63	Hypothesis 1 not supported. While some correlation coefficients and effect sizes achieved significance, subject area found not to be a significant predictor as a whole
Level	**0.04** (0.49)	0.79	Hypothesis 2 only partially supported by correlational analysis. Overall, assessments in advanced courses more reliable than those in beginner courses. However, exclusion of 'deviant' study resulted in the level of course being rated as a non-significant variable
No. of peers	**0.02**	0.33	Hypothesis 3 not supported. Correlations significantly smaller as number of peers increased. Ratings by singletons do not appear to be less reliable than others
Criteria (student involvement vs teacher supplied)	0.83 (**0.07**)	0.65	When one 'deviant' study omitted, hypothesis 4 supported. Student derived and agreed criteria fairly significantly associated with better teacher–peer agreement than other forms
Quality of study	**0.01**	0.89	Hypothesis 5 supported by correlational analysis. Better-designed and reported studies associated with better agreement between peers and teachers
Dimensions vs global judgement	**0.000**	0.48	Some illumination of variable 6 dilemma. Ratings involving many separate dimensions produced significantly lower mean correlation than global categories. However, overall global judgements which entailed consideration of several dimensions gave rise to slightly better agreement than other categories
Nature of task	**0.001**	0.97	Variable 7 differences supported by correlational analysis. Mean coefficients indicate peer assessments in area of professional practice may be more problematic than those in academic areas

Notes
a Statistically significant values are emboldened.
b Values of calculations omitting 'deviant' studies shown in parentheses.

Table 8.2 Variables which influence agreement between teacher and peer assessments

- PA which requires a global judgement based on well-understood criteria is more valid than assessment which requires marking of several individual dimensions.
- PA of academic products and processes seems to correspond more closely to faculty ratings than PA in context of professional practice.
- Studies that are well designed appear to give rise to better peer–teacher agreements than those with poor experimental designs.
- Student familiarity with, and ownership of, criteria tends to enhance peer assessment validity.

When considering correlation coefficients, only the subject area and type of criteria used appeared not to have any significant effect on the resemblance between teacher and peer marking. However, these, too, reached significance when the problematic study was excluded. Exclusion of this study also resulted in the variable 'level of course' being rated as a non-significant variable.

In the effect size subset, when all studies were included, no variable was found to influence the degree of relationship between teacher and student marks. When the problematic study was excluded, however, the number of peers involved in each grading and the type of grade required (global or involving several dimensions) showed up as having a significant influence. The variables we identified as being influential overall are shown in Table 8. 2.

Other findings

When we considered our hypotheses, we found that, while some had been supported by our analyses, others had not. Overall, we concluded that

- There was no evidence to support the superiority of multiple peer ratings over ratings by singletons. Ratings by very large numbers of peers (20+) appear to lead to poor agreement between teachers and peers.
- In general, peer assessment carried out on advanced level courses is no more valid than that conducted on introductory courses.
- There are no clear differences in validity of peer assessments in terms of the subject area in which they take place.

The lack of support for the superiority of multiple ratings over those by singletons is at odds with conclusions of other researchers (e.g. Magin, 2001a), and, indeed, with my own conclusions on previous occasions. We considered whether diffusion of responsibility, and its consequences such as the 'free-rider' effect (Kerr and Bruun, 1983), which can occur when students work in large groups might be acting to make group marking less thoughtful or careless. Much depends on how group marks were derived. It is also possible that thorough preparation for peer assessment might be acting to minimize differences between assessments derived from different sizes of group. This phenomenon requires further investigation.

We were surprised to find little indication that peer assessment is more valid in upper level courses than in lower ones, given that senior students are likely to have a better chance of understanding the criteria by which they are judged within their discipline than their junior colleagues, and may also have had previous experience of peer assessment. As we argued at the time, the lack of differentiation between students on beginner and advanced courses in the present study may once again indicate that participants in peer assessment studies are generally very well prepared for the task.

While the peer assessment meta-analysis found better teacher–peer correspondence in the assessment of academic products and processes than in the area of professional practice, no discipline differences were found, contrary to our expectations. Again, we turned to the question of preparation, and speculated whether students were being equally well prepared for peer assessment in all areas of study.

Thus, the results we had obtained from the meta-analysis of peer assessment studies seemed to differ in some respects from those we found when looking at self-assessment. As we noted in our paper, these differences might suggest that there the acts of self and peer assessment may differ in some crucial respect. As we argued,

> Self-assessment is usually a private activity which may involve little or no knowledge of the work or performance of others. However, many of the peer assessment studies . . . involve assessment of oral presentations or professional practice in a group context. Thus, the act of assessing takes place within a public domain where comparisons between performances become possible and ranking of peers becomes less difficult for students.
>
> (Falchikov and Goldfinch, 2000: 317)

However, returning to the results of the peer assessment meta-analysis, we concluded that the combination of a high-quality study, an academic task and a global judgement based on consideration of several dimensions or criteria would appear to lead to the highest correlation between peers and faculty.

Table 8.3 Recommendations to practitioners

---

1 Do not use very large numbers of peers per assessment group.
2 Conduct peer assessment studies in traditional academic settings and involve students in peer assessment of academic products and processes.
3 Do not expect student assessors to rate many individual dimensions. It is better to use an overall global mark with well-understood criteria.
4 Involve your students in discussions about criteria.
5 Pay great attention to the design, implementation and reporting of your study.
6 Peer assessment can be successful in any discipline area and at any level.
7 Avoid the use of proportions of agreement between peers and teachers as a measure of validity.

Recommendations to practitioners for implementing peer assessment

If you are concerned to maximize the degree of correspondence between peer and faculty marks, the following recommendations may be made (see Table 8.3).

It is also important to remember that peer assessment has many formative benefits in terms of improving student learning, as we saw in Chapter 4.

Future work in this area

The meta-analysis helped us identify areas where research was lacking. We recommended that future work would be beneficial in a number of areas. Since making those recommendations, some additional work has been carried out. However, much remains to be done. I would, therefore, urge colleagues who are interested in this area, and wishing to embark on some research, to consider the following possibilities:

- Further exploration of interactions between variables should be investigated as soon as new studies are being published each year, thus adding to the corpus which featured in the meta-analysis.
- Although there is a little work being done in this area already (e.g. Jordan, 1999), further investigation of the effects of repeated experience of peer assessment is a key issue to investigate in future work. As we pointed out, the meta-analysis was not able to investigate these effects, as such data as were available were dependent and were combined before entry into the analysis.
- So far, little formal work on gender effects related to peer or self-assessment has been conducted, though there is a growing trickle of information emerging. As we saw in Chapter 2, there seems to be some

evidence of gender differences in cheating behaviour. We shall discuss further gender differences in Chapter 9. This issue deserves more attention from researchers. A study by Falchikov and Magin (1997) provides a methodology to enable investigation of quantitative aspects of gender effects in peer assessments.

- Further investigation of reliability and bias in the context of the single-multiple marker issue is also desirable, particularly given that the multivariate analysis conducted as part of the meta-analysis was able to investigate only the comparison between very large groupings and all others.
- Although there is a growing body of knowledge about the negative effects of friendship on peer assessment, further investigations into friendship (or enemy) effects and their potential for bias might also be conducted. We shall discuss this issue further in Chapter 9.

In the next chapter, we shall look at some of the problems and benefits of conducting self- and peer assessment in the context of group work.

Chapter 9

Assessment of groups by peers

Group project work is widely used in higher education. While it carries many benefits, it can also sometimes be problematic. Webb (1995) discussed theoretical and practical issues that need to be taken into account in the design, use and interpretation of assessments carried out in collaborative small groups. She observed that differing purposes of assessment in the context of groups, sometimes represent competing goals. For example, improving individual achievement may not be consonant with the desire to increase group productivity. She also argued that the group processes involved may be different in the two contexts. 'Behavior that is conducive to producing a high-quality group product may not always be conducive to individual learning and vice versa' (Webb, 1995: 241). Nonetheless, Webb argued that equality of participation and active involvement by all group members is essential for individual learning in the context of collaboration, but that this condition is not always met. She also considered the effects of personality characteristics and status of group members in this context, to which we shall return later.

Gatfield (1999: 365) argued that understanding small group function, dynamics and outputs are 'foundational elements for the anthropologist and the organisational behaviourist'. Helms and Haynes (1990) explored some of the reasons why groups fail. Reasons they suggested to account for group dysfunction were

- divergent individual characteristics of members;
- lack of mutual trust or support;
- possession of incongruent goals or expectations;
- interpersonal conflict;
- manipulation of the group by various personality types for example, the 'Aggressor', 'Blocker', 'Whiner', etc. (Helms and Haynes, 1990: 6).

Effects of group dysfunction may occur either within the group at a social level, or in terms of outcomes. Research by Houldsworth and Mathews (2000) confirmed that 'process loss' was suffered by the majority of groups they studied. They argued that this was due to reactions to the 'sucker effect' (Kerr and Bruun, 1983) by some students who, perceiving that others might be benefiting at the expense of their labour, reduced their effort or withdrew from participation in group work.

Helms and Haynes (1990) suggested strategies to encourage continued group participation. Among these, peer evaluation was seen as an essential element. They argued that it 'provides an outlet for group members to express their possible frustration', and 'a mechanism useful in de-briefing students on their project experience' (Helms and Haynes, 1990: 7).

Peer assessment often takes place in the context of group work, but there is great variation as to the extent of peer involvement and complexity of implementation. Some studies involve simple measurement of group participation which does not influence grades (e.g. Sullivan *et al.*, 1999), while others involve inter- and intra-group peer assessment with student involvement at all stages including the provision of feedback and the summative function of assessment. Although, as we shall see, assessment of group work can be problematic, there seem to be some benefits associated with assessment when it is carried out by groups. In spite of our failure to demonstrate this in the meta-analysis described in the previous chapter, it is widely believed that assessments by multiple raters are more reliable than those of individuals (e.g. Ewers and Searby, 1997; Magin, 2001a). In addition, multiple assessments may be more acceptable to students. For example, Ewers and Searby (1997: 7) reported that having a variety of different opinions not only decreased the likelihood of getting 'a rogue result', but also increased 'the confidence of those being assessed that they are being treated fairly'.

A survey of group peer assessment studies

Group peer assessment studies have been carried out in a variety of contexts, in a variety of ways and with a variety of results.

Studies reporting poor teacher–student correspondence

Freeman (1995) reported the results of a peer assessment exercise in which final-year undergraduate business studies students and their teachers rated the quality of a group presentation, using a checklist provided by the teacher. Content and presentation components were weighted 60 and 40 per cent, respectively. Presentations took place over a ten-week period. Results of an analysis of marks indicated that mean peer marks were lower than staff marks, although no significant difference was found. The correlation between the two was regarded as low (though it was reported to be $r = 0.6$). Freeman noted that the students' ability to peer assess improved in the second half of the semester, which might suggest they were learning the skill. Nonetheless, Freeman (1995: 298) concluded that 'students are not good proxies for staff' and peer marks not reliable enough to be used on their own.

Similarly, Cheng and Warren (1999: 301), whose work was discussed in Chapter 5, concluded that peer assessments are 'not sufficiently reliable to be used to supplement teacher assessments' and that student competencies do not appear to depend on the task being performed.

Studies regarded as successful

Butcher *et al.* (1995) reported results of a self- and peer assessment study conducted as part of a group work project by first-year undergraduate students in the biosciences. They concluded that staff assessment had little advantage over peer assessment. In this study, both inter- and intra-group peer assessments took place, using guidelines and criteria supplied by teachers. Peer assessments were found to provide 'more norm-referenced assessments than corresponding staff-assessments' (Butcher *et al.*, 1995: 165), although assessor variation occurred in both groups. The mean self-mark was found to exceed the mean peer mark, but differences were not found to be statistically significant.

Gatfield (1999) set out to apply peer assessment in group project work, involving a large cohort of students of International Marketing Management from Griffith University. Students were provided with information explaining the rationale behind the peer award assessment principle, together with a worked example illustrating how marks were to be calculated. A sheet with five equally weighted categories, developed by the students earlier in their course, was also provided which was to be used for mark allocation. Students were also awarded a mark by the teacher on completion of the group project. Half of this mark functioned as the 'fixed element' (all group members received it), while the other was 'redistributed by peers in the group' (Gatfield, 1999: 367). Gatfield concluded that the instrument used had content validity and that students were happy using it.

Lopez-Real and Chan (1999) chose to make the group process the focus of peer assessment, and employed an 'additive' model similar to that proposed by Earl (1986). The group product was assessed by the tutor (60 per cent of total), presentations by both tutors and students (15 per cent) and the process by students alone (25 per cent). The researchers wished to implement and evaluate a new method of discriminating between students working together on a group project, using a questionnaire and in-depth interviews. They also hoped to identify any difficulties students may have had when rating each other, and to investigate the reasons for these. Criteria supplied by the teacher were discussed with students so as to achieve a common understanding. Students were asked to rate each presentation using the four criteria on a High, Medium and Low scale. These marks were later converted into percentages, and teacher and peer marks compared. Differences between the two varied from 1 to 11 per cent. No statistical tests seem to have been conducted. Short interviews with half the student body led to modifications to the rating scale, extending the three points to five. Feedback suggested that many students were happy with the presentation part of the scheme, a few less happy and some undecided. A small percentage rated peer assessment as not helpful in terms of their presentations. However, peer assessment of contribution to group work was more positively received.

In recent years, there has been a growing number of web-based group peer assessment studies. For example, the system of web-based peer assessment by Lin *et al.* (2001), 'NetPeas', which we have encountered already, fits into this category. It is described more fully in Chapter 10. Similarly, Sitthiworachart and Joy (2003) described the design and implementation of a web-based peer assessment system, in which students, working in small groups, marked and commented on other student's work. This study is also discussed in greater detail in Chapter 10.

Problems of peer assessment in groups

Many teachers and researchers have encountered some problems associated with peer assessment of group work. Many of these problems are identical with, or very similar to, those already discussed in Chapter 6.

- student reluctance to participate;
- student discomfort during and after participation;
- resentment that weaker students are being carried by the group and receiving inflated grades at the expense of more capable students (e.g. Heathfield, 1999);
- peers deferring to teacher.

Some problems, however, are unique to the group setting. We shall now examine some of these.

Group composition and intra-group communication

Work by Latting and Raffoul (1991) identified some variables that impact on group functioning. Their empirical study investigated *antecedent variables* such as attitude to group work and previous academic attainment, *structural variables* such as group size and construction and *interactional variables* such as 'social loafing', interpersonal conflict and task interdependence. 'Social loafing', sometimes called the 'free riding', has been described as a decrease in individual effort which can happen as a result of being a member of a group (Latané *et al.*, 1979; Kerr and Bruun, 1983). Social presence of others, which leads to a reduction in pressure to work hard, has been identified as the cause of the decrease in effort. Latting and Raffoul's study measured antecedent, structural and interactional variables. Results of an analysis of co-variance (ANCOVA) indicated that

- 'the greater the initial preference to be in a group, the greater the tendency toward social loafing' (Latting and Raffoul, 1991: 54);
- self-selected groups reported lowest levels of interpersonal conflict compared with instructor constructed or mixed groups;
- students who wrote all assignments as a group reported greater amounts of learning from the group than groups who wrote individual assignments;
- the higher the degree of social loafing, the lower the perception of having learned from class-based research.

Thus, Latting and Raffoul suggested that self-selection of group members is desirable in order to minimize dysfunctional intra group conflict.

In contrast, Lejk (1999b) used the Belbin questionnaire in one of his group project study variants to enable group composition to be engineered to some extent. He concluded that, while it was difficult to assess the success of this procedure, use of the questionnaire was an improvement on self-selection of teams, with its attendant problems of diminished objectivity associated with friendship, but probably only as good as random allocation of students. However, Butterfield and Bailey (1996), having used socially engineered groups in order to investigate effects of team composition on group output, concluded that, 'for certain task types, social engineering . . . can be more effective than random assignments or self-selection' (Butterfield and Bailey, 1996: 103).

Houldsworth and Mathews (2000) conducted a study to examine how group composition and processes influence performance. They researched the literature on the subject and identified personality of group members as a factor, but eventually concluded that adjustment was the only trait to have an effect on performance across a range of task types. They also argued that size of group may influence outcomes. They reasoned that groups that are too large may encourage 'social loafing'. They did not quantify 'too large'. Further adverse effects may also be associated with over large groups: behaviour by members to avoid the 'sucker effect' (Kerr and Bruun, 1983). Houldsworth and Mathews (2000) also identified 'withdrawing' by members as another debilitating influence on group functioning. In addition, the setting up of group norms is essential to the smooth and productive running of a group. Groups need to specify 'rules for how group members should behave and thus reflect mutual expectations among group members' (Houldsworth and Mathews, 2000: 43). Conflict between and among individuals may take up time and adversely affect group productivity. Latting and Raffoul (1991) recommended training in group interactional skills and conflict management to help minimize these effects. Jordan (1999) identified a further problem in the context of assessment in groups. Sometimes peer groups avoided engaging in debate and merely endorsed an individual's self-mark. The tactic that Jordan used to encourage group debate was to stress its usefulness in terms of transferable skills, particularly in the workplace.

The potential of group peer assessments to be biased

Lack of reliability associated with variation in marking standards or social interactions is frequently mentioned as a problem of peer assessment in groups, as we saw in Chapter 6 (e.g. Lapham and Webster, 1999; Magin, 2001b). In addition, Reynolds and Trehan (2000) argued that factors such as gender and ethnicity may affect peer group working. Todd (2002) also noted gender bias.

We shall now look at some of these effects.

Friendship effects

I have noticed that students frequently report unease at marking their peers, particularly if they are friends (e.g. Falchikov, 1995a). Similarly, Strachan and Wilcox (1996) reported that, although students rated peer assessment as a very good idea, some preferred written to numeric ratings. 'Ratting on friends' (Strachan and Wilcox, 1996: 350) was disliked, especially when these friends had been made through the group work process. Friendship or loyalty seems to have the capacity to bias peer assessments (e.g. Williams, 1992; Beaman, 1998; Lejk, 1999b). Sitthiworachart and Joy (2003) found that nearly half of their students did not feel comfortable when assigning marks and some reported that it was difficult to avoid 'friendship marking' which resulted in over-marking. Sluijsmans *et al.* (1999) also concluded that friendships can lead to over-marking.

Students themselves are aware of the problem of over-marking, and of its likely causes. For example, as we saw in Chapter 3, Fineman (1981) reported student awareness of overcompensation. Similarly, Cheng and Warren's (1997: 237) students were deemed to doubt their own objectivity, 'claiming that they felt compelled to award a higher score to those with whom they were more friendly'. This is a curious finding, given that, in this case, assessments seem to have been conducted anonymously.

Gender effects

Gender effects have been noted in both academic performance and other related areas. For example, Woodfield and Earl-Novell (2002) conducted a study to investigate Pirie's claim that current levels of female success at all levels of education can best be explained with reference to changes in modes of assessment from traditional examinations to coursework. The authors argued that, if Pirie's views are supported, and if female students prefer coursework to exams, female marks on the coursework element of their social science course would exceed those of their male peers, and the reverse would be true for the examination. Statistical analysis of marks supported the coursework prediction. However, female performance was found to surpass that of their male peers in the examinations as well. This gender gap in performance was found to be statistically significant. However, structured e-mail interviews with 100 final year students indicated that, while some students conformed to the popular stereotype of female 'examophobes' and male 'examophiles' (Woodfield and Earl-Novell, 2002: 3), there were equal numbers who did not. General observations concerning work patterns found gender differences, with males being characterized as more blasé and apathetic and less conscientious than females, and females as more competitive, more committed and less willing to sacrifice work for fun than their male peers.

As we saw in Chapter 6, Adams *et al.* (2000) found gender differences in student views on the purposes of assessment, with males seeing it as a way of measuring achievement and females as a way of receiving feedback. Given that these differences have been found, and given the prevailing view, which I share, that gender differences in attitudes to peer assessment or in peer assessment ability exist, it is surprising that no hard evidence for such differences has come to light. Indeed, working with Doug Magin at the University of New South Wales, I found no evidence of gender bias in peer marking of students' group work (Falchikov and Magin, 1997). Similarly, Gopinath (1999) found no evidence of gender differences in self- and peer assessment. Gatfield (1999) investigated gender effects in satisfaction of students who had taken part in a group peer assessment exercise and found no such differences here either.

However, Irwin (1996) reported research by Newstead which indicated clear inconsistencies between disciplines, as well as gender bias in marking and cheating on the part of students taking examinations (Newstead *et al.*, 1996).

As I have argued elsewhere (Falchikov and Goldfinch, 2000), this is an important area to watch out for.

Age effects

Some age effects have been found in the context of assessment. For example, Hill and Wigfield (1984: 106), in an investigation of *test anxiety*, claimed that in 'our highly competitive educational system and society, this pressure increases with age'. The study of student views on the *purposes of assessment* by Adams *et al.* (2000) also found some age differences. The under 20s group rated giving feedback as their top choice, while the over 30s rated directing students' attention to what matters as theirs. Gatfield (1999), investigating effects of age on *satisfaction* levels of students who had participated in a group peer assessment exercise, found no differences.

However, little is known about any age differences in self- or peer assessment *ability* or *performance*, other than that, in the study by Chatterji and Mukerjee (1983) into the moderating effect of some psychological and biological variables upon accuracy of self-assessment, age and level of qualification appeared to have little effect.

Ability effects

Lejk *et al.* (1999) set out to compare performance of streamed and mixed-ability four-person groups. The job of the group was to carry out a number of tasks, each of which was first attempted individually. Next, students peer reviewed each member's work and arrived at solutions with which all were happy. Agreed group solutions were submitted and marked, though individual solutions were also submitted. Results indicated that high ability students may be disadvantaged by this type of group work, in that these students received lower grades when working in mixed ability groups than in streamed groups. The reverse was observed for lower ability students, who did best when working in mixed ability groups. In addition, lower ability students did better in subsequent examinations after having worked in mixed ability groups than those working in streamed groups. Again, the reverse was found to be true for higher ability students. The authors recommended further work in this area.

Ethnicity effects

Reynolds and Trehan (2000) speculated about the existence of ethnicity effects on peer group working, and Todd (2002) also suggested that unspecified ethnicity effects might exist in the context of assessment. However, once again, there is little evidence on the subject. Gatfield (1999) set out to compare perceptions of Australian students with those of peers from outside Australia on the subject of group projects and peer assessment, and found the latter group to be more satisfied. However, Lin *et al.* (2001) reported research which pointed to a preference in Chinese speaking students for group harmony which worked to prevent critiquing of peers' work.

Effects of prior experience

There is some evidence that practice will both improve peer and self-assessment performance and give rise to improved attitudes. We have already looked at some examples of changes in student attitudes resulting from practice in Chapter 6 (e.g. Cheng and Warren, 1997). As we learned in Chapter 7, Jordan (1999) also investigated this issue, conducting peer and self-assessments twice: halfway through and at the end of a module. She reported that students were more comfortable the second time, and that tutors were required to intervene less than on the first occasion. Jordan (1999: 177) claimed that, by the end of the exercise, students demonstrated maturity in analysing differences in performances and made 'illuminating statements' about the value of self-assessment. Students seemed to appreciate the experience, seeing it as 'a part of learning to learn, and beneficial even when it is problematic' (Jordan, 1999: 178).

However, it does not always follow that practice will lead to improvements. Gatfield (1999) set out to investigate the possible effects of prior work experience on satisfaction levels regarding group work, and found that those without prior work experience were significantly more satisfied with group projects and peer assessment than those with experience.

Collusive or collaborative marking

We encountered this phenomenon in Chapter 6, in the context of peer assessment and feedback. However, it also seems to exist in the context of group work. For example, Sluijsmans *et al.* (1999) identified 'collusive marking' as a problem associated with peer assessment in the group context. The authors noted a lack of differentiation between groups. Earlier, Mathews (1994) had also reported concerns about peer marking in the context of group work. He identified marking patterns that illustrate problems that can arise. We shall discuss these later in the chapter. Pond *et al.* (1995: 320) interpreted low standard deviations of student marking as being indicative of a form of collusive marking, 'the uniform marking of each group member'. They found that collusive marking was strongly associated with high grading. Collaborative mark fixing or collusion can, understandably, lead to divisions within groups (e.g. Lapham and Webster, 1999).

'Decibel marking'

'Decibel marking' was also referred to in Chapter 6 (e.g. Sluijsmans *et al.*, 1999). Pond *et al.* (1995: 321) defined it as occurring when individuals dominate a group and get high marks as a result. They provided an example of this in student feedback in a peer review study which pointed to problems of subgroups being dominated by individuals. In addition, they found further evidence during their inspection of data from previous studies. They claimed that, on average, 'this effect was noticed in almost half of the subgroups' (Pond *et al.*, 1995: 321). However, they also found that high marks associated with collusive marking sometimes obscured the effects of decibel marking. Beaman (1998) also noted problems of students awarding more marks to louder, extraverted students at the expense of quieter ones. She stressed the importance of evidence and criteria, and of collective decision-making. McDowell and Sambell (1999: 78) also reported that bias in favour of 'the confident ones' had been noted as a potential problem in the assessment of oral presentations.

'Parasite' marking: the 'free rider', 'social loafing' or diffusion of responsibility effect

We have already encountered this in Chapter 6, and in our discussion of the effects of group composition (e.g. Webb, 1995; Houldsworth and Mathews, 2000). Parasite marking, the free rider effect or social loafing occur when students fail to contribute but benefit from group work. Webb (1995) attributes the effects to diffusion of responsibility. Webb also described the 'sucker effect' which can result from social loafing, and consequent attempts by group members to avoid this. Pond *et al.* (1995) noted parasite marking in their study of peer review within a small group, as did Sluijsmans *et al.* (1999). McDowell (1995) noted some examples of the negative impact of innovative assessment in studies which involved students in assessment and marking which also included the free rider effect. Similarly, McDowell and Sambell (1999) observed examples of the free rider effect in the context of student involvement in marking a group effort. These difficulties were also noted by students. Social loafing, according to Webb (1995), is always detrimental to individual learning but not to group productivity.

Strategies for designing and marking group assignments

Design strategies

Webb (1995) discussed group assessments in terms of the purposes they aim to serve. She argued that, if the purpose of assessment in group working is to measure individual student learning, then it should be designed to encourage processes that benefit learning. If the purpose is to measure group productivity, students should be informed of which processes benefit this. Students should also be prepared for carrying out group assessments. Webb suggested a number of ways of achieving either end.

Group assessments which aim to improve individual learning should

(1) stress individual accountability in test instructions and focus on this in the test;
(2) require every student to be prepared to summarize and explain the work of the group;
(3) tell students which processes are beneficial for promoting student learning.

On the other hand, *group assessments which aim to measure group productivity* should involve:

(1) practice in collaborative group work;
(2) training in interpersonal, teamwork and communication skills;
(3) equalizing participation and influence of group members.

Webb cited research studies to support her suggestions.

Assessment strategies

A variety of methods have been used to assess group work. Some of these focus on the product, others on the process. Given that group projects typically extend over a period of weeks, emphasis on the process seems particularly appropriate. Some methods result in quantitative scores or measurements, while others are qualitative and primarily used for developmental and evaluative purposes. A few focus on the group as an holistic entity. Boud *et al.* (1999: 421) argued that, 'If students are expected to cooperate and work together, the notion of assessing them in terms of group rather than individual outcomes can appear attractive'. However, the authors concluded that, without sufficient opportunity for developing group planning and group accountability skills, the use of group assessment is 'premature'. They recommended schemes which contain a mix of individual and group assessment for common tasks.

Garvin *et al.* (1995) described the implementation and assessment of small group project work which involved self- and peer assessment of the process, and which also incorporated elements of assessment of the group itself. When the project terminated, students completed a questionnaire which included statements such as, 'Working together on the project has been . . .' This was followed by 16 words or short phrases such as 'difficult', 'not enjoyable', 'stimulating', 'involving' and so on, which students were required to rate on a five-point scale. Other statements related to student perceptions of their personal learning and skills development. Students also rated the working of the group and stated their willingness to work with the same group again in the future. The authors reported positive outcomes in terms of skills development and student satisfaction with the scheme.

Preparing for peer assessment in groups

A number of teachers and researchers have recommended that students receive training in group working and group assessment. We have already encountered Beaman's (1998) useful and inventive suggestions in Chapter 6, where we learned of her 'Egg game', designed to help prepare students for peer assessment. She also devised another game, this time designed to help groups differentiate between members, handle inter-group problems and promote communication. This she called the 'You get a raise!' game. Each group is given a $1000 bonus in paper Monopoly money on completion of the job and asked to divide it among group members according to their contribution to the group effort. One student reported that the play money was easier to handle than marks, and that it made the point very clearly.

Addressing problems of differentiating between group members

A good starting point for any discussion of problems of differentiating between group members jointly engaged in group project work and awarding appropriate marks to each is the work of Mark Lejk (1999a,b) and colleagues (Lejk *et al.*, 1996, 1997, 1999). Before embarking on any experimental work, Lejk *et al.* (1996) surveyed methods of assessment of groups of students, identifying at least eight different ones. We shall use Lejk's survey as the framework for the rest of this section.

1 Multiplication of the group mark by an individual weighting factor

Goldfinch and Raeside (1990: 211) discussed ways of awarding marks to individual members of a group, rejecting the idea of students submitting individual portions of the whole as this 'disrupts the spirit of group work'. They also argued that it is both impractical and potentially disruptive to the functioning of the group for a teacher to sit in on group meetings. They then considered two forms of peer assessment: open discussion of individual contributions by group members and private rating by peers. Their own preference was for students to rate group members privately. In their study, students were required to name those who had contributed in a number of areas and assess the degree of contribution of each member. A numerical peer assessment (PA) score for each student was then calculated, using the following formula:

$$\text{The PA score} = \frac{\text{no. of times named}}{\text{possible no. of mentions}} \times w + \frac{\text{sum recorded}}{\text{highest poss. score}} \times w$$

where w = weighting.

The authors reported that weightings of $\frac{1}{3}$ and $\frac{2}{3}$ were used in practice. Once calculated, PA scores were converted into 'PA factors', using a look-up table prepared by staff. PA factors are a percentage score which can vary from 0 to 140 per cent. Finally, individual marks were calculated as PA factor × group mark.

Goldfinch and Raeside (1990) reported a validation of their technique on a small sample, in which PA scores were compared with those awarded by a teacher observing groups unobtrusively. The agreement between the two was found to be 'quite reassuring' (Goldfinch and Raeside, 1990: 218). The authors argued that the naming of students, the preliminary step in the peer assessment (the nomination method), was found to be 'helpful' and 'reassuring' by students. Students generally reported finding the procedure fair, and preferable to awarding the same mark to all members, though 'many disliked the peer assessment concept' (Goldfinch and Raeside, 1990: 219). To overcome problems of rewarding or penalizing groups twice, a revised PA score was devised which, 'instead of measuring absolute contribution . . . measures students' contributions relative to the rest of their group' (Goldfinch and Raeside, 1990: 220). The group's absolute contribution was measured by the overall mark awarded. A worked example of the calculation using the revised procedure and flow diagram showing steps in the calculation is included in their paper.

This method was modified by Conway *et al.* (1993). They identified a number of drawbacks with Goldfinch and Raeside's formula: there was a poor correlation between mentions and scores ratios, students disliked the nomination method, the 0–4 scale was deemed inadequate and calculations were 'lengthy and tedious' (Conway *et al.*, 1993: 49). In addition, Conway *et al.* were concerned by the apparently arbitrary nature of the weightings applied. However, they felt the scheme had merit, and decided to modify it. In their revised system, students were required to award a mark out of 5 to peers to represent their level of participation in relation to four key tasks. Next, all scores were totalled and an individual weighting factor calculated using the following formula:

$$\text{Individual weighting factor} = \frac{\text{Individual effort rating}}{\text{Average effort rating}}$$

Individual contributions were then calculated by multiplying the group mark by the individual weighting factor.

Later, Goldfinch (1994: 32) herself made a further adjustment to the calculation method which she noted was 'very close to that independently suggested by Conway *et al'*. More recently, Freeman and McKenzie (2001) use Goldfinch's weightings in their online system for self- and peer assessment (SPARK). We shall look at this in a little more detail in Chapter 10.

Rafiq and Fullerton (1996) applied a modified version of Goldfinch and Raeside's original (1990) method to group assessment in civil engineering. They identified a number of problems which included student reluctance to mark each other's work, student bias and participants experiencing difficulty in recalling who did what. The authors were also concerned that it was possible to achieve more than 100 per cent. They proposed to replace the first part of the method altogether in future and replace it with project diaries.

Lopez-Real and Chan (1999) also focused on problems of discriminating amongst individual contributions when the product of group work is to be used for assessment purposes. They described a scheme of peer assessment of a group project in a primary mathematics education course at the University of Hong Kong. While they argued that working co-operatively in a group has intrinsic benefits, they rejected any scheme which involves a weighting factor, arguing that this is contrary to the philosophy of collaboration. All such schemes are really variants on a 'zero sum' game, argued Lopez-Real and Chan, for, as in such games, the total wins and losses at the end must equal zero, and gains for one student imply losses for another. Additionally, Lopez-Real and Chan expressed concern that the weighting factors can give rise to scores which exceed 100 per cent. They also reasoned that, as weightings reflect relative achievement, group composition 'can be a major source of individual differences in final marks' (Lopez-Real and Chan, 1999: 68). Thus, they chose to make the group process the focus of peer assessment, and employed the 'additive' model as described previously.

2 Distribution of a pool of marks

I first encountered this method in Gibbs *et al.* (1986). It has been quoted and re-discovered several times since then. Simply, it involves the splitting of a group mark between group members.

The 'formula' for this method is

Total marks available = Group mark × no. of group members

Individual marks, $M_1 + M_2 + M_3 + \cdots + M_x$ = total marks

For example, four students work together on a group project which receives a mark of 60 per cent. It does not matter how this mark is derived.

It is typically awarded by the teacher, but can as easily involve students. The four students have the task of dividing up the marks to reflect each individual's contribution. First of all, the 60 marks are multiplied by the number of group members, in our case, by 4, making a total of 240 marks. Students then award as many marks as seem appropriate to each group member, provided that they do not exceed the 240 total.

The values of M_1, M_2 and so on may be derived by group consensus or by individuals. In the latter case, individual scores are averaged. Gibbs *et al.* (1986) noted that students may react to this task in three ways:

(1) some groups will agree at the start of the project that all members will receive equal marks;
(2) some groups will not discuss assessment until the time comes to complete the task;
(3) some groups will sit down at the outset and decide which criteria they will use and stick to these when awarding marks.

As Gibbs *et al.* pointed out, the third way is clearly the most satisfactory.

Mathews (1994) described a variant on this method which he used in a peer evaluation study in a management studies group project. The evaluation form was designed to differentiate among group members. Students were allocated a total mark equal to the value of the number in the group times ten and were required to divide up this total between themselves and other group members on a number of dimensions relating to project output, task management and process management.

Mathews reported concerns over some patterns of response:

(1) Equality or same marks for all in every category.
     Mathews rated this as a highly improbable occurrence.
(2) The normal distribution.
     Mathews (1994: 23) commented that, although genuine overall equality of input is unlikely, this pattern of response 'demonstrates give and take within a group and sensible distribution of workload and responsibility'.
(3) The reluctant finger response.
     Mathews argued that people are generally reluctant to 'shop their friends', so that when a consistent level of contribution is recorded this should be taken seriously. It is, he argues, coming from those in 'the best position' to make such judgements (Mathews, 1994: 23).
(4) The stitch them up response.
     Here, collusion between some group members can result in identical patterns of evaluations which point to poor performance by one member.
(5) The out of kilter response.
     Here, perceptions vary between people. Where individuals think they have done more than others in the group, Mathews argued that the

averaged group assessment may give a more consistent evaluation. Almost random responses pose a particularly difficult problem. Unfortunately, Mathews offers no solution.

This type of method is also advocated by the University of Western Australia (2001). Their guidelines suggest that it is helpful to involve students in establishing the criteria or provide criteria for establishing how students are to divide up the marks at the outset of the exercise, thus directing participants to the third option of Gibbs *et al.* However, I have found that, even with explicit criteria discussed and agreed by students, some groups will choose the first option anyway. This may be a way of saving time, avoiding reflection and thought, or side-stepping minor conflict. Where obvious differences in input have occurred, students will use a method of differentiating.

Conway *et al.* (1993) rejected this method, arguing that placing the burden of sharing marks on group members would introduce a final element of competition into what had been a collaborative venture.

3 Group mark +/− a contribution mark

Gibbs *et al.* (1986) proposed that differentiation may also be achieved by awarding a mark for the contribution each individual has made to the final product. This 'contribution mark' is then taken from the group mark. They suggested the use of a simple rating sheet with criteria listed. Students are required to assess whether each person's contribution to the achievement of each is 'major', 'some' or 'little'. Only those rated as making a major contribution receive the group mark. Others incur penalty points. The authors also proposed that the penalty points might reflect the relative importance of the criteria. For example, they suggested deducting one point for 'some' contribution to 'leadership and direction', but three points for the same level of contribution to 'report writing'. Of course, it is also possible for a contribution mark to be added to a group mark (e.g. Earl, 1986). However, Gibbs *et al.* argued that deducting marks would go some way towards combating inflated group marks.

Conway *et al.* (1993: 47) also rejected this method on the grounds that, if the effort marks are high compared with the base marks, 'students who make a greater contribution than their fellows to a project which is skimpy or fatally flawed are likely to end up with a better mark than a lesser contributor to an outstanding project'.

4 Separation of product and process

Keaten and Richardson (1993) described a scheme which used the Peer Assessment Inventory (PAI), an instrument developed to measure the individual contributions to a group project which focussed on the process. The instrument had six dimensions:

(1) out-of-class attendance;
(2) out-of-class participation;
(3) in-class attendance on group days;
(4) in-class attendance;
(5) quality of work;
(6) interest in the project.

Each dimension was assessed using a ten-point scale (1 = extremely poor to 10 = exceptional). Thus, group members assessed participants in terms of the process, and the scheme produced a number at the end to enable differentiation between group members.

Differentiating between product and process is a variant I have used on a number of occasions (e.g. Falchikov, 1988, 1993). I first did this in a study of self- and peer assessment of individual written work (Falchikov, 1986). I formalized the separation and applied it to the assessment of a group project in a study reported in Falchikov (1988). I drew on my experience as a psychologist and turned to one of the most influential schemes for the analysis of group interaction, that devised by Bales (1950). In this, 'task functions' are distinguished from 'maintenance functions'. Task functions referred to roles and actions which moved the group nearer to solving task-centred problems and, thus, achieving its goal, and included 'Information and opinion seeker', 'Summarizer' and 'Evaluator'. Maintenance functions, on the other hand, covered roles and actions designed to ensure smooth running of the group, such as 'Tension reliever', 'Active listener' and 'Encourager of participation'. All functions were discussed thoroughly before the project was started. I also included two open categories, as it seemed likely that some other function would emerge as important. On the completion of the project, students rated each member as having had 'High', 'Medium' or 'Low' participation in each of the categories. Peer ratings were averaged and then used to prepare a profile for each participant. My students found the discussion of their personal profiles an enriching and stimulating experience. I appreciate that this degree of personal attention may no longer be possible given that class sizes are large, even in final years of degree programmes, but it might be feasible to harness the power of technology to assist us here. In a subsequent exercise which also made use of the group process analysis checklist, students were invited to modify the checklist as well as to add their own categories (Falchikov, 1993). This seemed to work well.

Mathews (1994) similarly, differentiated product and process in his peer group evaluation exercise. Students were required to make within group judgements about each team member in three main areas: project output (contribution to the task in terms of time, effort and quality), task management (behaviours which move the task towards completion) and process management (behaviours that determine the quality of relationships between group members). Marks out of 10 were awarded, with 10 representing an equal contribution. 'On the upper side, the maximum rating would be ten times the group size' (Mathews, 1994: 26). Any evaluation of less than six required written justification. On completion of the exercise, Mathews reported his concerns over some styles of response discussed here.

5 Equally shared mark with exceptional tutor intervention

Lejk (1999b) reported that this method is quite widespread (e.g. Mello, 1993), although dealing with individual problems may be time-consuming. The method involves all group members receiving the group grade, unless a situation arises where this would lead to an unfair distribution. For example, the group may experience problems with one member and call in the tutor for help. Lejk reported that each of these situations is dealt with on an individual basis and involves negotiation between the students and tutor.

6 Splitting group tasks and individual tasks

According to Lejk *et al.* (1996), the method of splitting group tasks into smaller individual sub-tasks is also quite widespread. For example, it is recommended by the University of Western Australia (2001). Individual contributions are marked separately by the teacher and the overall group mark is also awarded by teacher. These two marks are then combined. In addition, students may also peer assess the contributions of fellow students. The peer mark may be used to moderate the base group mark for individuals (Gibbs, 1992). I have reservations about this method, as it goes against the spirit and philosophy of collaboration. However, if it is unavoidable, I prefer the peer moderation option for achieving individual marks over the teacher's.

7 Yellow and red cards

This method was devised by Lejk himself (1994; 1999a,b). Lejk (1999a) described four case study examples of group projects carried out at the University of Sunderland in the following areas: design and presentation skills, design and realization, biochemistry and human resource management. All projects involved peer assessment to help assess individuals' contributions to the whole. Small groups of students work on tasks which are independent of each other, but which are of comparable difficulty. After one week, the group members meet, distribute 'solutions' to all tasks and then review peers' solutions. A final agreed set of solutions is submitted for marking. All team members receive the same grade. However, at any time, a group member may be given a red or yellow card. This system was designed to give group members some leverage regarding peers who do not pull their weight. The yellow card serves as a warning to slackers, and, unless subsequently removed by team members, incurs a 20 per cent reduction in mark. The award of a red card excludes a student from the team and attracts a zero grade. Lejk appeared satisfied that this procedure worked.

Deeks (1999) described a system of self- and peer assessment of an information systems group project which also used Lejk's yellow and red cards. Peer assessments were used to arrive at individual weightings for 80 per cent of the assessment. Teams were supplied with a feedback pack which included a standard comments list, spreadsheet printouts explaining the marks distribution and all scribbled comments made by assessors. Peer assessment results were scrutinized by Deeks (1999: 135) 'to ensure fairness in teams'. Near miss students were given a formal viva. Students appeared to be satisfied with the system (about 1 per cent queried their mark).

8 Deviation from the norm

This method was also devised at the University of Sunderland, by Thompson in the School of Computing, Engineering and Technology. It is based upon an agreed percentage contribution to the final product by each member of the group. Lejk (1999b) quotes the formula for calculating an individual mark as

Individual mark = GM + GM$((A - N)/100)$

where
GM = group mark
$\quad$ A = allocated per cent contribution
$\quad$ N = 'normal' contribution (i.e. 25 per cent for a group of 4, 33.33 per cent for a group of 3, etc.)

Thus, it seems there are methods to suit most situations, and more being developed all the time.

Summary: recommendations for overcoming problems associated with peer assessment in groups

In this chapter, we looked at a selection of group peer assessment studies and identified some of the key problems encountered. Some problems and solutions are summarized in Table 9.1.

Table 9.1 Some problems of group work and their solution

Problems of peer assessment in groups	Strategies and solutions
Student reluctance to participate: • due to traditional expectations • due to lack of experience	Reluctance, for whatever reason, resembles that found in non-group situations. See Chapter 6 for suggestions on handling it. Preparation and practice is always useful.
Student discomfort during and after participation	Preparation and training.
Peers deferring to teacher	Structure activities so as to prevent any opportunity for this to occur.
Group composition and intra-group communication	Have strategies for dealing with conflict before it escalates. Make sure students are aware of procedures. Keep abreast of research in this area. Conduct experiments of your own. Publish the results!
Bias: friendship effects	Consider using peer assessment for formative purposes only. Require students to justify ratings. Consider scaling marks, if the overall standard is high compared with the teacher's.
Bias: • gender effects • age effects • ability effects	Discuss potential sources of bias openly. Require students to justify ratings. Keep abreast of research in this area. Conduct experiments of your own. Publish the results!
Bias: ethnicity effects	Make cultural expectations and practices explicit. Discuss these. Ensure that all understand, and are happy with, what is required of them.
Collusive or collaborative marking and 'decibel marking'	Require students to justify their ratings and explicitly link criteria with judgements.
'Parasite' marking	Peer assessment should reduce this tendency, rather than give rise to it.

The chapter will end with some further recommendations for helping to overcome some of the problems of peer assessment in groups. First of all, advice given by many proponents of co-operative learning (e.g. Johnson and Johnson, 1985; Slavin, 1985) is relevant here. As Adams and

Hamm (1996) have pointed out, co-operative learning works best when the following conditions are present:

- positive interdependence;
- face-to-face interaction;
- individual accountability;
- frequent practice with small-group interpersonal skills;
- regular group processing and reflection.

Positive interdependence may be said to be present within a group when individuals realize that they can achieve their own personal learning goals only when everyone in the group reaches theirs. When all individuals take on the responsibility for doing a fair share of work and for moving the group closer towards its goals, individual accountability has been achieved. These two features may be said to differentiate between a group of individuals working in the close juxtaposition of a group and true co-operation.

Lejk (1999b: 194–6) has made a number of useful suggestions. First of all, he stressed that tutors need to be interested in group work and be prepared to be involved in the process. He reiterated advice often encountered in the literature, but well worth repeating, that the assessment task should be well-structured and have clear deadlines. He also addressed some issues associated with the conflict between true co-operative working and its assessment which tends to pull in the opposite direction and undermine the co-operative tendency. When co-operative learning is desired, he argued, 'serious attention needs to be given to the balance between group assessment and individual assessment of the learning achieved' (Lejk, 1999b: 196). He recommends that practitioners carry out the following actions:

(1) Embed group assessment into the curriculum and be seen to value it.
(2) Control the amount of group assessment included.
(3) Prepare students for group working, project management, peer and self-assessment.
(4) Allow sufficient time for group members to get to know each other.
(5) Avoid undermining co-operative learning by thinking carefully about the balance between individual and group assessment elements.
(6) Use an holistic rather than category-based approach in quantitative peer assessment. Holistic peer assessment mechanisms appear to support group project objectives better than category-based mechanisms.
(7) Avoid including self-assessment in quantitative group assessment.
(8) Enable quantitative peer assessments to be made in private, to encourage greater honesty.

The question of whether or not to 'engineer' group composition seems still open. Lejk (1999b) advocates it. His experiments suggested that streaming groups increases the correlation between individual marks and marks for group assessments compared with self-selected groups. His results also indicated that there are significant learning benefits when students of all abilities work with high-ability students. However, as we have seen earlier, other researchers (e.g. Latting and Raffoul, 1991; Butterfield and Bailey, 1996) have pointed to the advantages of self-selection.

What, perhaps, has not been sufficiently stressed so far is that great benefits are to be derived from peer assessment in the context of group work. The advantages and benefits associated with peer assessment have been discussed in Chapter 4, but group working itself, particularly if it is co-operative, may also be hugely beneficial. It is worth giving some time to the solution of potential problems.

Chapter 10

Computer Assisted Assessment (CAA) and student involvement

This chapter is concerned with student involvement in Computer Assisted Assessment (CAA). Before embarking on an investigation of this, it is useful to trace the development of CAA as a method of assessment and determine what, exactly, computer assessed assessment is. It is defined by the Computer Assisted Assessment Centre (CAA Centre, 2003), simply, as the use of computers in assessment. 'The term encompasses the use of computers to deliver, mark and analyse assignments or examinations. It also includes the collation and analysis of data gathered from optical mark readers (OMRs)' (CAA Centre, 2003).

The CAA Centre website contains answers to a number of frequently asked questions. These, together with a brief summary of the answers suggested are contained in Table 10.1.

What can be achieved by the use of CAA?

A relatively few years ago, multiple choice testing represented the full extent of how computers could play a part in assessment. Many educators were concerned that such assessment, although more reliable than many alternatives, failed to test 'real' learning. For example, Mooney et al. (1998) argued that multiple-choice questions (MCQs) assess only recall and recognition, and promote a surface approach to studying. Similarly, Davies (2000b: 348) argued that conventional CAA systems, often objective-based multiple choice, 'suffer the criticism of merely assessing facts not knowledge and understanding'. Mooney et al. also argued that even knowledge recalled at the time may be lost as a result of the surface

Table 10.1 The CAA Centre's answers to frequently asked questions regarding computer assisted assessment

Question	Answer
What is the difference between CAA and CAL?	'CAL stands for Computer Aided Learning and refers to teaching and learning content material delivered by computers. CAA refers specifically to assessment, but elements of CAA may be included within CAL packages.'
How is CAA used?	CAA is used for • Diagnostic assessment • Self-assessment • Formative assessment (often takes form of objective questions with feedback to students during/ immediately after assessment) • Summative assessment
What are some of the advantages of CAA?	*Pedagogic advantages*: • Lecturers can monitor student progress regularly. • Students can monitor own progress and self-assessment can be promoted. • Detailed, specific feedback available to students during and immediately after a test. • A wide range of topics within a body of knowledge can be tested very quickly. • Students acquire information technology (IT) skills (CBA only). • Potential to introduce graphics and multimedia allows for inclusion of questions not possible with paper assessments (CBA only). • Quality can be monitored by looking at the facility and discrimination of questions and tests. • Formative assessments can be repeated as frequently as desired to aid student learning. • Adaptive testing can be used to match the test to the student's ability. • Students can be provided with clues and marked accordingly. *Administrative advantages*: • Marking is not prone to human error. • Computerized marking of tests saves staff time. • Large groups can be assessed quickly. • Diagnostic reports and analyses can be generated. • Aids with the transmission and administration of marks (automatic entering into information management systems and student records databases). • Can reduce cheating through the randomization of questions. • Eliminates need for double marking.

(Table 10.1 continued)

Table 10.1 Continued

Question	Answer
What are some of the limitations of CAA?	• Construction of good objective tests requires skill and practice and so is initially time-consuming. • Because of the above, testing of higher order skills is difficult. • Implementation of a CAA system can be costly and time-consuming. • Hardware and software must be carefully monitored to avoid failure during examinations. • Students require adequate IT skills and experience of the assessment type. • Assessors and invigilators need training in assessment design, IT skills and examinations management. • A high level of organization is required across all parties involved in assessment (academics, support staff, computer services, quality assurance unit, administrators).
What subjects are suitable for CAA?	The 1999 CAA Centre survey showed that nearly every academic discipline registered some CAA activity. Subject areas with the highest numbers of CAA tests were • computing/IT, • biomedical science, • geological science, • mathematics, • engineering, • other sciences (chemistry, physics), • modern languages, • business and accountancy. There is also increasing use of CAA in other disciplines e.g. recent CAA work in humanities: • *Poetica* is a project which delivers CAA to students taking a first year poetry module at the University of Sunderland. • 'Web + *Qmark* + *Humanities*' a case study detailing the introduction of CAA into a first year module called 'Modernity and Modernization' offered by the Cultural Studies department at Sheffield Hallam University.

Note
This information (and more) may be found at http://www.caacentre.ac.uk/resources/faqs/index.shtml (accessed 13. 02. 04).

approach taken. However, the CAA Centre (2003) asserted that the belief that objective testing carried out by CAA is limited to MCQs, while common, is erroneous.

Tsai *et al.* (2001) noted that computer aided instruction (CAI) has been given a boost by the increasing popularity of the World Wide Web (WWW), and that it has received considerable attention within the field of education. The various forms of CAA currently in use appear to vary from the simple and relatively quick to more complex and lengthy applications. Thus, although many computer packages still provide MCQs for self-assessment, some dramatic advances are being made. For example, Michaelson (1999) claimed that the Internet and existing web software may be tailored to support group-based learning, and that the use of an integrated system for group learning can improve student motivation and support new forms of assessment. MacDonald (2003) saw opportunities for the use of computers in the assessment of online collaboration. In fact, she argued that the assessment of online collaborative work has 'a conspicuous advantage' over assessment of face to face collaboration, 'because the medium provides a written record of the interactions between students' (MacDonald, 2003: 378). She described a case study of assessing online collaborative learning conducted at the UK's Open University, the findings of which she believed underlined the importance of assessment in ensuring online participation.

The CAA Centre have argued that a further common, but erroneous, assumption is that CAA is suitable for testing only lower order skills, at the first three levels of Bloom's taxonomy (knowledge, comprehension or manipulation and application) (Bloom, 1965).

Let us explore some of these assertions more closely.

CAA and assessment of higher order skills

The GLOW (Graduate Learning On the Web) system is described in some detail on the CAA Centre website, and made available for readers to experiment with. The system is designed to help academics use the web to support postgraduate science and engineering courses. The CAA Centre website notes that a central focus of GLOW is the development of tools to deliver self-assessment materials online. The system illustrates the 'logical level-by-level progression from the assessment of lower order skills through to higher order skills', using MCQs where possible 'in order to keep the explanation as simple as possible and to show how higher order learning can be assessed in this way' (CAA Centre, 2003). A brief description of skills to be assessed and question words often used to test those skills are also given.

An example at the level of analysis, an 'assertion–reason question type', is shown in Box 10.1. This is considered a difficult question, which will

Box 10.1 An example of a question representing Bloom's level of analysis

---

Read carefully through the paragraph below, and decide which of the options (1)–(4) is correct.

> The basic premise of pragmatism is that questions posed by speculative metaphysical propositions can often be answered by determining what the practical consequences of the acceptance of a particular metaphysical proposition are in this life. Practical consequences are taken as the criterion for assessing the relevance of all statements or ideas about truth, norm and hope.

(1) The word 'acceptance' should be replaced by 'rejection'.
(2) The word 'often' should be replaced by 'only'.
(3) The word 'speculative' should be replaced by 'hypothetical'.
(4) The word 'criterion' should be replaced by 'measure'.

Explanation
This question requires prior knowledge of, and understanding about, the concept of pragmatism. The paragraph, seen in this light, contains one word that vitiates its validity, and the student is tested on his/her ability to analyse it to see whether it fits with the accepted definition of pragmatism. With this in mind, (2) is correct. Option (1) would degrade the paragraph further, while (3) and (4) would simply result in changing to acceptable synonyms. Note that this question does not address Level 6 (Evaluation), as the student is not asked to pass a value judgement on the text.

---

require a high level of reading. Should you choose to use this type of question, it is as well to bear in mind that there will be a significant time factor involved.

Box 10.2 shows the example included to illustrate the level of evaluation. The CAA Centre supplies links to further examples of questions at all levels of Bloom's taxonomy and to examples of more complex types of CAA questions, extending beyond the use of MCQs.

The Tripartite Interactive Assessment Delivery System (TRIADS), the University of Glasgow's assessment engine, claims to provide 'flexibility of interactivity and feedback'. It is intended to be 'capable of delivering a wide variety of question styles in a wide variety of modes to facilitate the testing of higher order learning skills'. There are facilities to enable randomization of question delivery and it claims to be able to support a wide range of marking systems. TRIADS was developed and is currently

Box 10.2 An example of a question representing Bloom's level of evaluation

A student was asked the following question: 'Briefly list and explain the various stages of the creative process'.

As an answer, this student wrote the following:

> The creative process is believed to take place in five stages, in the following order: ORIENTATION, when the problem must be identified and defined, PREPARATION, when all the possible information about the problem is collected, INCUBATION, when there is a period where no solution seems in sight and the person is often busy with other tasks, ILLUMINATION, when the person experiences a general idea of how to arrive at a solution to the problem, and finally VERIFICATION, when the person determines whether the solution is the right one for the problem.

How would you judge this student's answer?

(1) EXCELLENT (All stages correct, in the right order with clear and correct explanations.)
(2) GOOD (All stages correct, in the right order, but the explanations are not as clear as they should be.)
(3) MEDIOCRE (One or two stages are missing OR the stages are in the wrong order, OR the explanations are not clear OR the explanations are irrelevant.)
(4) UNACCEPTABLE (More than two stages are missing AND the order is incorrect AND the explanations are not clear AND/OR they are irrelevant.)

Explanation
In the above question, one is expected to make value judgement on the content of the given text (knowledge of the subject is required), the meaning of the terminology used (comprehension), and structure (analysis) of the answer for the right order of events. The correct answer here is 1, but appropriate modification could provide a small bank of questions with other correct answers.

maintained by the Centre for Interactive Assessment Development (CIAD, 2004) at the University of Derby, UK.

Further examples of CAA which support the development or assessment of higher order skills are discussed later.

Davies (2003b) noted that the use of computerized peer assessment of essays is spreading within the higher education sector in spite of some continuing 'negativity' on the part of both tutors and students. Tutor hostility may be fuelled by results of poorly implemented schemes or those introduced merely to reduce staff time rather than to enhance student learning. Students, too, need to be made aware of the potential benefits to them of engaging in peer assessment. This use of CAA, too, will be discussed in a later section.

Functions of CAA

Computer Assisted Assessment now appears to fulfil a number of functions. We shall look at each function in turn. It should be noted that some examples of CAA may fit into more than one category.

Supporting the assessment process

Foubister *et al.* (1997) described the *CEILIDH* system (2003), an interactive environment which supports computer programming course organization, practical work and assessment. The system was developed at the University of Nottingham and extended by Heriot-Watt University, Edinburgh. Ceilidh enables students to compare their outputs' on a fixed repertoire of inputs' (Foubister *et al.*, 1997: 102) with those from a model solution. When students are satisfied with their answer, they submit it to the system. Teachers can monitor student progress and marks are recorded automatically. Two of the aims of using the system are to provide students with timely feedback while saving staff marking time. The system was evaluated to determine its impact on subsequent exam performance, which was found not to differ for two groups of students, a Ceilidh using group and a hand-marked group. Students of all abilities seemed to benefit equally from the system. The authors reported a saving of 'a significant component of lecturer time' over each term. Students liked the swift feedback and some felt the system helped build confidence in programming skills. The scheme was perceived as fair.

Foxley *et al.* (2001) claimed that copies of Ceilidh have been taken up by in excess of 300 institutions around the world, and that at least a third of these were using the software. They also described a development of the Ceilidh system, the *CourseMaster*,[1] which they claimed has better functionality and is easier to support. Further improvements are planned, including online delivery and use of email, which they claim will improve the learning experience of students, though it is not clear how these practical changes will achieve this end.

Another example of a computer application used to support the assessment process itself is provided by Ney (1991). This application involves a specially written computer program which records comments and grades derived from peer assessment. Ney's (1991) model of collaborative learning combines elements from peer teaching and co-operative learning, but also includes some peer assessment, in that students grade each other's daily quizzes. All comments and grades are recorded electronically in a computer program written for that purpose. The program also adjusts the total score of each student and provides a daily report on each student's standing in the class. Attitudinal surveys showed that students had positive perceptions of the model as a whole. Attendance was noted to be 'almost perfect' for the duration of the class and an 'adequate level' of mastery was noted (Ney, 1991: 153).

Computer-based clinical simulations

The assessment process may be supported in other ways. For example, Swanson *et al.* (1995) described the use of computer-based clinical simulations for use in performance-based assessment of health professionals. These are developments of the traditional clinical simulations which were described in Chapter 1. Swanson *et al.* (1995: 6) reported that the simulations have been converted to electronic format and now include 'high-fidelity models of the patient care environment, requiring examinees, in an uncued fashion, to select from the full range of diagnostic and therapeutic modalities available in clinical settings'. Computer simulated patients respond to the 'therapeutic efforts' of examinees. Simulations take from 15 to 60 minutes, with 30 minutes being a typical duration. The authors do not include an evaluation of these simulations in their paper, but report that they are not currently in widespread use in 'high-stakes testing' (Swanson *et al.*, 1995: 6).

Bull and McKenna (2004) described a further example of the use of simulations to support assessment in a medical setting. Online exercises are used to develop and assess medical students' knowledge and skills at the MCP Hahnemann School of Medicine at Drexel University in the US. The exercises use a variety of different media, depending on the computing and networking capabilities of users. Simulated 'patients' respond to text-based questions posed by students.

Web-based testing

Chou's (2000) web-based Computer-Assisted Testing and Evaluation System (CATES) is designed to test student achievement and evaluate courseware in web-based learning environments. This system was developed at the National Chaio Tung University (NCTU) in Taiwan. Chou described the design, progress-to-date and evaluation of CATES. Test situations in which CATES was used varied from entrance, course and final examinations, through mid-term and distance education testing to self-assessment and practice. The author noted the difficulty of designing test systems for self-assessments and practice compared with examinations. The CATES system consists of a test-item bank containing multiple choice, matching, short answer and essay questions. Analysis of online questionnaire responses indicated that 70 per cent of users liked the system, 67 per cent rated web-testing as more efficient than paper and pencil testing and 50 per cent said they would choose web-testing over pencil and paper. However, nearly a third felt that web-testing increased their anxieties. The sound of typing was mentioned as a source of anxiety, as was the possibility of disconnection or breakdown. The author supports Web-based testing as a major testing alternative, particularly if safe and reliable systems are available.

Computer-based self- and peer assessment

Some developments of CAA are directly designed to facilitate self- and peer assessment. Three examples are included in this section, and further examples in the section which follows.

MUCH system (Rushton *et al.*, 1993)

An early example of a computer-based peer assessment tool is described by Rushton *et al.* (1993). The authors examined the use of MUCH, a multiple user hypermedia tool which supports collaborative authoring, in the Department of Computer Science at the University of Liverpool. In addition to the conventional facilities supplied by any word processing package, MUCH also allows students to read each other's work and to comment on it. Rushton *et al.* conducted a peer assessment exercise in which a student's mark was based, curiously, on the number of times it was selected for comment and on the nature of the comments recorded. The authors soon amended this system to prevent what they termed as 'abuse of the selection system' (Rushton *et al.*, 1993: 77). Later, five criteria were added to 'better facilitate peer assessment' and students were required to award up to ten points for each. Totals were doubled to give a percentage mark. The authors reported that, contrary to expectations, peer marks awarded were 'remarkably similar' to those awarded by the tutors. Student attitude measurement indicated that the majority were very sceptical about peer assessment, even though they believed that the exercise of peer marking had 'enhanced the educational process by reinforcing what they had learned while producing their own work' (Rushton *et al.*, 1993: 79).

'Peers' system of computerized peer assessment (Ngu *et al.*, 1995)

Ngu *et al.* (1995) described another early computer assisted peer assessment system, 'Peers', used in marking postgraduate assignments within a master of Information Science course at the University of New South Wales. The system consists of three parts. In part 1, assessment criteria are developed. The lecturer enters an initial set of criteria and weightings. These are inspected by the students who are at liberty to suggest new criteria or new weights for existing criteria. Part 2, the lecturers' component, consists of six major frames which allow lecturers to

- view and/or modify criteria;
- set up administrative details;
- check peer marking;
- scrutinize individual student's assignments and marking specifications and enter assessment comments;
- monitor the process;
- define the formula for calculating the final mark.

Part 3, the students' component, has four frames which allow them to

- access administrative details;
- submit assignments (essays);
- view a completed assignment and marking specifications and entered marks and comments;
- collect assessed assignments online.

Thus feedback is automatic and delivered instantly.

Ngu *et al.* (1995: 585) described a small study of 'Peers' in use. Seventeen students participated, though five students were not included in the final calculation, two having not participated fully and three having been rated as 'bad samples' due to their marking being too much at odds with that of the lecturer. Peer marks were compared with teacher marks, and a correlation coefficient of 0.67 calculated.

Feedback suggested that 80 per cent of the sample wanted peer assessment to remain part of the course, though most stated a preference for lecturer marking due to lack of confidence in peer marking. Most said the experience had helped them learn some more about the subject. The major advantage to the lecturer was the time saved in the administration of assessment, though other benefits were also identified: asynchronous marking, lack of paper copies, scope for automatic analysis of assessment information.

SPARK online system for self- and peer assessment (Freeman and McKenzie, 2001)

Freeman and McKenzie's Self and Peer Assessment Resource Kit (SPARK), in use at the University of Technology, Sydney, enables students to rate their own and each other's contributions to team working. Such ratings are used to produce self- and peer assessment marks which are used to moderate the team mark for individuals. The weightings used are based on the work of Goldfinch (1994) which we encountered in Chapter 9. The authors claim that SPARK can also be used for formative feedback prior to completion of an assignment. Students were reported to have appreciated aspects of the system that ensure that free riders are penalized and seen the link between assessment and learning objectives. Complaints about team working were reported to have diminished substantially. Lecturer satisfaction was reported as a benefit. In addition, use of SPARK is less time-consuming than previously used paper-based methods. The authors believe the system can encourage effective peer learning.

CAA systems focussed on feedback and discussion

Davies (2003b) noted arguments which suggest that teacher feedback is not always readily understood by students and that feedback provided by student peers may be more accessible and relevant. Examples of CAA practices which facilitate this are described next.

Denton's use of freely available software to generate feedback

An example of CAA designed to provide students with feedback is reported in research by Denton (2001a,b). Denton (2001b) pointed out that software for generating feedback is available on the Internet and described the use of a Microsoft Office-based report writing system of electronic feedback, involving e-mail and MS Excel and Word. The system has been used by tutors at Liverpool John Moores University to aid 'traditional' marking of essays and laboratory reports. Feedback is created and e-mailed to individual students. Denton also described another example of such software, from the Department of Information Science at the University of Loughborough. In this, feedback statements are divided into four categories:

(a) grade comments which depend on the overall mark awarded;
(b) general comments directed to the class as a whole;
(c) personal comments to individuals;
(d) standard comments, 'statements that experience shows are most likely to be required when marking student work'. Each comment is numbered to enable rapid allocation to students.

Two modes of operation are described: normal and criterion modes. In the former, standard comments are 'stand-alone', while in the second, statements relate to criteria by which the work is being judged. Denton reported that both tutors and students have responded positively to the use of the software. Further details of the evaluation are to be found in Denton (2001a).

Denton also noted that, despite the availability of software capable of generating feedback, such programs were not used widely by UK academics.

'NetPeas' system (Lin *et al.*, 2001)

Research by Lin *et al.* (2001) explored more complex issues in the evaluation of their web-based peer assessment system, 'NetPeas'. The aim of the study, as we saw in previous chapters, was to investigate attitudes to peer assessment and to inspect the relationship between achievement and attitude. Feedback was also a key feature.

The system involved seven steps:

(1) Students are instructed to write a survey paper by the teacher.
(2) Students design a home page and select their topics.
(3) Once completed, the project is made available to peers through NetPeas.
(4) Students review and grade the work of six peers, and provide feedback to each. Six criteria are provided by the teacher. A ten-point Likert scale (1 = poor, 10 = satisfactory) is used to rate performance on each criterion.
(5) The system 'organizes' grades and feedback, and informs both authors and teacher.
(6) Students revise their work in line with feedback supplied.
(7) Steps 4 to 6 are then repeated.

Correlation coefficients relating scores awarded by the teacher and a teaching assistant were found to be high. Similarly, inter-rater reliabilities were calculated for grading reviewers' comments and feedback and also found to be high. As we learned in the previous chapter, results indicated that 65 per cent of the computer science students using the system held a positive attitude towards peer assessment.

System to enable students provide and critique feedback (Sitthiworachart and Joy, 2003)

Sitthiworachart and Joy's (2003) web-based peer assessment system involves computer science students in marking and providing feedback on other students' work. The authors believe students to be capable of this task as they are provided with guidance, automatic test scores and results, a marking scheme and 'well explained criteria' (Sitthiworachart and Joy, 2003: 1).

Their process involves three steps:

(1) Students do the assignment in their own time and submit it via the online system. Ten automatic tests are then run on submitted programs to ensure that they function correctly.
(2) Students are organized into mixed ability groups of three. No organizational details are supplied. Each group is assigned three programs to mark during a lab class. Marking consists of completing an on-screen matrix which lists criteria and gives three boxes to indicate the extent to which each criterion has been achieved. A link is provided to explanations of marking criteria. Students work individually at first, awarding marks and giving feedback. Peer marking is then discussed with group members. This activity contributes 30 per cent to the final mark.
(3) In their own time, students then mark the quality of the three markers' marking. In order to do this, answers to three questions are required. Questions relate to the relevance and usefulness of feedback and to the quality of explanations given. This process contributes 20 per cent to the mark. Students are then able to see their own marks (peer marks for both the program and the quality of assessment) along with feedback and comments.

Students are able to revise their marks right up to the marking deadline. Peer marks are the average of three individual peer grades. A final 'monitor marking' page with all marks is available to tutors only.

The results of an analysis of data derived from an online questionnaire, to which we referred briefly in the previous chapter, indicated to Sitthiworachart and Joy that most students agreed that seeing a variety of programs written by others helped them learn programming. Two-thirds of the group agreed that the act of marking helped them see mistakes in their own work and develop their understanding of computer programming. However, nearly half did not feel comfortable when assigning marks, and some over-marking was reported. A few students did not understand the criteria.

Davies's use of the Computerized Assessment by Peers (CAP) system to provide feedback

Davies (2003b) described how his Computerized Assessment by Peers (CAP) system, a development of his earlier Computerized Assessment with Plagiarism system (confusingly also known as CAP), might be used to facilitate student generation of feedback and analyse output. The plagiarism system is described in some detail in Chapter 2. The 2003b assessment study, which functioned in a similar way, focussed on the *quality of feedback* supplied by students to each other. Participants were postgraduate students studying computer technology. In developing the system, feedback given by peer markers was analysed manually. Ten common categories were noted:

(1) readability;
(2) aimed at correct level;
(3) personal conclusions;
(4) referencing;
(5) research and use of the web;
(6) content and explanations;
(7) examples and case studies;
(8) overall report quality;
(9) introduction and definitions;
(10) report presentation and structure.

Davies (2003b) noted that both positive and negative comments were found within each category. Next, a database of categories and comments was built up and a marking tool created. This is illustrated in Figure 10.1.

Comments relating to each criterion are made available. Both positive and negative comments are included. For example, 'referencing', may be described positively, using 'Good use of quotations' or 'Excellent referencing throughout', and negatively, as 'Poorly referenced' or 'Inconsistent referencing throughout'. In addition, the window at the right-hand side of the screen allows free text to be added.

Davies (2003b) used this process to quantify feedback, calculating a 'feedback index', using numbers of positive and negative comments found. This aspect of the process is, at the time of writing, still under development (Davies, 2003a). However, Davies (2003b) argued that, if there a significant correlation between the final peer mark and the feedback index, then it may be possible to evaluate the quality of work by inspecting the quality of feedback.

Analysis of feedback indicated that some categories tended to attract negative rather than positive comments (e.g. content and explanations, examples and case studies, research and use of the web), while the reverse was true for other categories (e.g. readability, overall report quality, introduction and definitions). Essays rated as falling within the second highest quartile attracted some under-marking, while the reverse was true of essays in all other quartiles. Davies (2003b) suggested that better students are more willing or able to criticize their peers than the weaker students. However, given that the calculation of the index is still under development, any conclusions based on current calculations should be seen as very tentative.

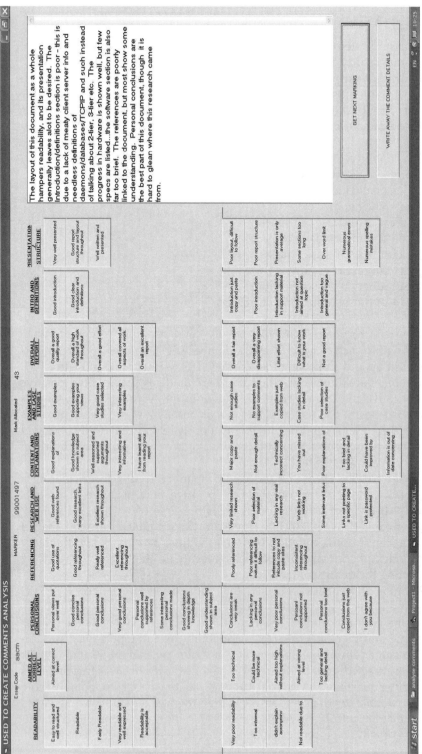

Figure 10.1 Marking tool for creating feedback comments

Source: Davies (2003b): reproduced with permission of the author.

Davies (2003b) debated whether it might be useful to structure and automate the peer marking process further by using comments or categories derived from previous cohorts. He argued that both receiving and creating feedback may be considered as positive learning experiences and that over-structuring might act to limit these experiences. He concluded that a mix of pre-selected comments accessible from a pull down menu might be used in conjunction with some free text responses.

Students receive a *mark for marking* which constitutes half the available marks. Davies (2003a: 8) reported that marks are awarded for

- consistency in marking;
- original comments (constructive input, 'supported suggestions' and demonstration of analytical skills);
- marker responses to author requests for re-marking/clarification.

At present, it is the tutor who provides this mark, but, with suitable adjustments and preparation, this process might be used as another peer assessment exercise.

Results of an analysis of study data indicated that 70 per cent of peer markings were agreed on the first pass of feedback which increased to 80 per cent after re-marking. A clear majority of students rated the whole CAP system positively, and 'few negative comments of any significance' (Davies, 2003b: 11) were recorded. The time-consuming nature of the exercise was noted (40 minutes per essay), however. Students felt they had benefited from reading their peers' comments and that using the system had aided their learning. The marking process was thought to have facilitated personal reflection. Reactions to the discussion and remarking procedure were also positive, though some negative responses were also noted.

Davies (2003a) also described how the CAP system had been used to support anonymous *computer-mediated discussions* between peer markers and authors.

Supporting learning and assignment preparation

Boud and Knights (1994) claimed that some computer-based dialogue can contribute to reflection. For example, computer conferencing has been used to *support collaborative learning* and stimulate reflection (see also later). Lea (2001) described a system of computer conferencing used by students at the UK's Open University. She investigated the relationship between students' use of computer conferencing and their assessed written work, and concluded that the technology enabled reflexivity in student learning and provided the opportunity to learn collaboratively.

Other reports of CAA implementations are designed to *ensure that learners engage in higher-level cognitive activities*. For example, computer-based assessment technique, by Mooney *et al.* (1998), required students to analyse, associate ideas, synthesize and evaluate. These authors also claimed that their implementation promotes the generation of ideas, goal setting and reflection in learners. They also argued that such computer-based assessment techniques, commonly used in medical education, provide a valuable resource to help students evaluate their levels of knowledge and progress, and provide them with instant personalized feedback.

The authors described a classification system which illustrates a wide variety of interactions that computer-based self-assessment can offer. The following levels of interaction are now deemed possible:

- exploration based (involving analysis and association);
- puzzle based (both high and low level forms are available, low-level puzzles promote recall, recognition, location and linking, while high level versions stimulate analysis, synthesis and evaluation);
- case based (promotes generation of ideas, goal setting, reflection and pattern recognition).

The web-based peer review strategy of Lui *et al.* (2001) also involves students in providing feedback to, and receiving feedback from, peers, revising work in line with feedback received and grading the final product. This strategy is derived from constructivist theory and makes use of the authors' web-based peer review system. Third year computer science undergraduates involved in the study were asked to act as 'true researchers' (Lui *et al.*, 2001: 247). Initially, they worked independently and submitted their homework in HTML format. Six randomly assigned student reviewers then rated and commented on each piece of work. Next, student authors were required to make revisions in line with the feedback received. This process was completed a total of four times, after which the work was submitted to the teacher for grading. The grade awarded by the teacher was based on the six reviewers' grades. Teachers also graded the quality of the reviewers' comments. Over 60 per cent of students perceived they had benefited from reading others' work and comparing it with their own. Three-quarters preferred peer review to traditional assessment procedures, but 9 per cent questioned the fairness of the system. The authors reported that peer review students appeared to display *high-level thinking skills*.

A similar system is in use at the National Chiao Tung University in Taiwan where Tsai *et al.* (2001) have implemented a networked peer assessment system, also based on constructivist principles, which emphasizes *learner participation* and *knowledge construction*. The system uses a 'Vee graph', an heuristic strategy which 'allows learners to view the interaction between "scientific theories" (thinking) and the "practices of science" (doing)' (Tsai *et al.*, 2001: 220). The authors argued that the Vee heuristic can easily display all related ideas of a science activity. In practice, this translates into the use of a template with hot links to aid the design of science activities (the assignment task). The template is based on the shape of the letter 'V', with 'Thinking' and three associated buttons (theory, principles and concepts) making up the left-hand stroke and 'Doing' (this time with four buttons: value claims, knowledge claims, transformation and record) the right. At the top of the screen is the button 'Focus question', and at the bottom, joining the two strands, 'Events/ objects'. Twenty-four pre-service student teachers enrolled on a science education course took part in the exercise. They connected with the website in the usual way, through their web browsers. Tsai *et al.* reported that the WWW system carries all of the tasks, starting with assigning the homework to recording the peers' grades and comments. Students are able to organize their science activities through the Vee heuristic as described here. The networked peer assessment model entailed nine steps in all:

(1) homework assignment (design of a science activity for secondary school students) discussed by teacher and students;
(2) each student's activity design entered into the system;
(3) peer reviewer assigned randomly (specialization matched);
(4) reviewers grade the work and comment on it;
(5) teacher grades the work and looks at peer comments;
(6) system notifies students of their grades and comments;
(7) original work modified, taking comments into account;
(8) steps 2 to 7 repeated once or twice more;
(9) final assessment carried out by teacher.

Data were analysed, and the relationship between teacher and student grades generally found to be positive.

However, in a later report (Tsai *et al.*, 2002: 241), the authors reported that peer evaluations were 'not highly consistent with experts' (e.g. university professors) grades'. The relationship between the two sets of grades may have been positive, but it was found to be not significant in seven out of nine outcome variables. Tsai *et al.* (2002: 249) suggested that complex interactions among background knowledge, preferences and 'interrelations of others' may have reduced the validity of using peer assessment. Student comments took the form of 'corrective, reinforcing, didactic and suggestive feedback' (Tsai *et al.*, 2001: 228). The later study also reported that students who offered detailed and constructive comments to peers appeared to benefit in terms of *improvements to their own work*, particularly in the beginning stages. Student ratings of the system were generally positive.

Computers are also able to simulate conditions to which students normally do not have access. Bull and McKenna (2004) cite the example of the University of Glasgow Veterinary School's virtual horse which allows students to *practice their skills* before trying them out on live animals. Interested readers might wish to refer to Bull and McKenna (2004). Their chapter 8 is particularly useful.

Aiding portfolio building

Chang (2001: 144) described a web-based learning portfolio (WBLP) system designed as an alternative to traditional pencil and paper assessments which was characterized as 'authentic assessment'. The WBLP interface is designed to help students produce their personal learning portfolios quickly and easily. Users are able to complete setting of goals and acquire coursework information. In addition, the system allows them to carry out 'reflection and self-assessment record writing' (Chang, 2001: 146). Students are provided with a guide to portfolio creation and helped with selection of contents. Assessment criteria are agreed by teachers and students together. The WBLP system includes a portfolio discussion board which allows for asynchronous discussions. Evaluation of the system suggested that most students considered it to be helpful in 'improving quality, enhancing the learning process, understanding the authentic learning process and outcome, and providing chances for displaying and improving works' (Chang, 2001: 154).

An assessment working group in the Faculty of Medicine at the University of New South Wales is presently specifying a software system for managing and guiding assessment. Hughes (2003), a team member, informed me that portfolio assessment, including a reflective essay supported by evidence, is a major strand in the whole programme. Students are to be encouraged to present self- and peer assessments of team work and presentations as additional evidence for the team work and communication capabilities.

Given the current popularity of portfolios and the difficulties of assessing them (see Chapter 1) this area seems one likely to develop rapidly in future years.

CAA as a reflective tool

Bull and McKenna (2004) reviewed examples of CAA used to facilitate reflection. An early example they described is THESYS, an expert system developed at Nottingham Trent University. This system guides students through self-assessments of their projects. It poses 38 generic questions grouped into sections relating to understanding, time management, quality of work, originality and effort. Students rank themselves against opposing statements and are given 'feedback' on their strengths and weaknesses, as they have identified them. In other words, the system appears to summarize the students' own ratings. However, Bull and McKenna reported that when tutors also used the package, there was no significant variation between tutor and student assessments.

Helping detect plagiarism

Davies's (2000b) Computerized Assessment with Plagiarism (CAP) system, used by students to detect plagiarism of materials from the WWW, was discussed in Chapter 2.

Investigating the processes of CAA itself

Investigations of the processes of CAA can vary widely in their focus. At their simplest, they investigate reliability, while more complex systems provide information about individual differences of users. In an example of the first type, Shermis *et al.* (2001) reported a study which examined the feasibility of using Project Essay Grade (PEG) software to evaluate web-based essays at a Mid-Western university. Research hypotheses were

(1) Computer ratings will be more accurate than those of human judges.
(2) Grading will be accomplished more rapidly using PEG.
(3) Machine-readable essays will be graded more economically than the usual procedure.

Unlike other computer assessment systems which evaluate content correctness, PEG was designed to assess general writing. Essays written by university and high school students were used to create a statistical model for PEG. Students were asked to evaluate their answers and explain any changes they would make, given more time. This information, however, does not appear to have been used in the study reported. Writing was analysed in terms of 'trins' and 'proxes'. Shermis *et al.* (2001: 251) explained that 'trins' are 'in*trins*ic variables of interest such as fluency or grammar', while 'proxes' (ap*prox*imations) are observed variables such as length of essay or average word length. Grading by human judges was compared with that of the PEG software. Inter-rater correlation was $r = 0.62$ for human raters and $r = 0.71$ for the computer. Although all three research hypotheses were supported, it is not clear how useful this system is more widely, given its narrow focus.

Summary: advice to practitioners

Advice to practitioners which summarizes information contained in the chapter is to be found in Table 10.2. CAA is a rapidly growing area. It is

Table 10.2 Advice to practitioners: summary of the functions of CAA

Function of CAA	What may be achieved	Illustrative studies
Supporting the process of assessment	Automatic recording of marks, responses and feedback	Ney (1991); Foubister et al. (1997)
	Computer-based clinical simulations	Swanston et al. (1995)
	Monitoring of progress	Foubister et al. (1997)
	Provision of report on student's standing	Ney (1991)
	Provision of timely feedback	Foubister et al. (1997)
	Saving staff time	Foubister et al. (1997)
	Support of course organization	Foubister et al. (1997)
Web-based testing	Evaluation and attitude measurement online	Chou (2000)
	Evaluation of courseware	Chou (2000)
	Testing student achievement	Chou (2000)
Computer-based self- and peer assessment	Asynchronous marking	Ngu et al. (1995)
	Automatic analysis of assessment data	Ngu et al. (1995)
	Computer-based criteria development	Ngu et al. (1995)
	Support of collaborative authoring	Rushton et al. (1993)
	Support of self and/or peer assessment	Rushton et al. (1993); Ngu et al. (1995); Freeman and McKenzie (2001)
Supporting learning and assignment preparation	Improvements to work/opportunities for revisions/modifications subsequent to receipt of feedback	Lui et al. (2001); Tsai et al. (2001); Tsai et al. (2002)
	Instant personalized feedback	Mooney et al. (1998); Tsai et al. (2001)
	Knowledge construction	Tsai et al. (2001); Tsai et al. (2002)
	Peer feedback	Mooney et al. (1998); Lui et al. (2001); Tsai et al. (2001); Tsai et al. (2002)
	Promotion of higher level cognitive activities/thinking skills	Mooney et al. (1998); Lui et al. (2001)
	Promotion of idea generation	Mooney et al. (1998)
	Promotion of goal-setting	Mooney et al. (1998)
	Self-evaluation of knowledge and progress	Mooney et al. (1998)
	Support for collaborative learning	Boud and Knights (1994); Lea (2001)
	Stimulation of reflection	Boud and Knights (1994); Lea (2001)

Category	Description	References
CAA systems focussed on feedback and discussion	Awarding a 'mark for marking' to encourage care	Davies (2002)
	Creation of feedback	Denton (2001b); Freeman and McKenzie (2001)
	Critiquing feedback	Sitthiworachart and Joy (2003)
	Develop understanding of computer programming	Sitthiworachart and Joy (2003)
	Development of higher order cognitive skills	Davies (2002)
	E-mailing of feedback to students	Denton (2001a,b)
	Generation of electronic feedback by system	Denton (2001b)
	Help students identify mistakes in own work	Sitthiworachart and Joy (2003)
	Investigate relationship between achievement and attitude	Lin et al. (2001)
	Measure student attitudes to peer assessment	Lin et al. (2001)
	'Monitor marking' page for tutors only	Sitthiworachart and Joy (2003)
	Motivating students	Sitthiworachart and Joy (2003)
	Peer assessment and feedback	Davies (2002, 2003b); Sitthiworachart and Joy (2003)
	'Reflective self-assessment' (based on feedback)	Davies (2002)
	Relate quality of feedback to attitude	Lin et al. (2001)
	Self-assessment (with decisions justified)	Davies (2002)
	Supply of feedback from system databank to students	Denton (2001b)
Plagiarism detection (in context of peer assessment)	Address some concerns about quality of assessment	Davies (2000b)
	Help save staff time in locating possible sources of web plagiarism	Davies (2000b)
	Peer assessment (anonymous)	Davies (2000b)
Aiding portfolio building	Help students produce personal learning portfolios by	Chang (2001)
	• supplying coursework information through the web interface;	
	• structuring setting of goals;	
	• prompting selection of contents;	
	• involving students in agreeing criteria;	
	• encouraging use of discussion board.	
CAA as a reflective tool	Guidance through SA of projects	Bull and McKenna (2004)
Investigating processes of CAA	Analysis of writing	Shermis et al. (2001)
	Evaluation of web-based essay marking	Shermis et al. (2001)

clear that computers, e-mail and the WWW are being used in a variety of ways to support the assessment process. Future developments may become more and more useful to those of us who wish to involve our students as active participants in their assessment and learning. However, we may have to wait a while longer until we are able to choose from a variety of software packages to help us carry out the assessment of higher-level cognitive functions. Similarly, student involvement in CAA is often at a relatively low level, frequently being limited to formative self-assessment. However useful it is for students, it is to be hoped that they will soon be able to participate in assessment activities that give them a greater degree of power and control over decision making. There are some encouraging developments in the realm of peer assessment, however, as we have seen.

Note

1 Note that the Ceilidh web page (CEILIDH, 2003) claims that Ceilidh was replaced in 1998 by *Coursemarker* (http://cs.nott.ac.uk/coursemarker) rather than *CourseMaster*.

Chapter 11

Past, present and futures

In this short final chapter, I shall review what has gone before, chapter by chapter, and attempt to identify important issues raised. I shall then suggest directions for future research.

Chapter 1: The seven pillars of assessment

The title of Chapter 1, 'The seven pillars of assessment', is clearly derived from T.E. Lawrence's famous account of his life in the desert (Lawrence, 1939). This does not imply that I perceive work on assessment to be a desert – far from it. Nor is the ground scattered with skeletons: there are several well fleshed out bodies of knowledge in evidence. Of course, many researchers have preceded me, whom I am pleased to acknowledge. Where this book does resemble T.E. Lawrence, however, is in its focus on the fight for an ideal. Nonetheless, where Lawrence spoke of fighting for 'the ideal', I am too much a realist and seek only something better. He spoke of the fight becoming a possession, then a faith. I, too, have fought for a more egalitarian relationship between teachers and learners for the greater part of my professional life. I strongly believe in involving students in assessment. However, where Lawrence spoke of unquestioning possession, I speak of evidence. Lawrence claimed to provide no lessons for the world. I hope I have, through the 'whirling campaigns' of these pages, provided something useful for readers.

Of the seven questions I posed in the first chapter, I see the 'How well do we assess?' as key. Traditional assessment does not seem to be doing a very good job of providing reliable or valid assessment, as we elaborated in Chapter 2. Student involvement in assessment entails many benefits, but before colleagues may be persuaded to try it, they need to be convinced that students are capable of carrying out the tasks of assessment. Thus, we need to be able to provide some evidence on this. Evidence requires numbers, statistics even, and I have used both to assure myself that students are to be trusted, and to provide colleagues with information based on research findings.

Chapter 2: What's wrong with traditional assessment?

Traditional assessment has been found wanting. It contains inherent biases, it reinforces the power imbalance between teachers and learners, and is driven by the needs of the teacher rather than needs of learners. It has adverse side effects; its rewards are too often extrinsic, and it relies on competition and discourages co-operation. Traditional assessment seems to produce passive consumers, which is particularly dangerous at a time when some self-funding students are only too ready to assert their mistaken beliefs that money pays for a degree rather than the opportunity to earn one. Traditional assessment has been linked to stress in students. It also gives rise to intense stress in teachers, who are often required to complete marking of traditional essays and examinations in time scales more suited to making a cup of coffee. In addition, it has been argued that traditional assessment practices cannot adequately test for independent critical thinking or creativity, and that this inadequacy is particularly marked in time limited examinations (e.g. Elton, in Elton and Johnson, 2002).

However, people tend not to question the validity of traditional assessments. We have been engaged in them for so long and we may take them for granted, losing sight of why we are using them and what we wish to achieve. Validity of new assessments such as portfolios or competence assessments is far more often questioned. In fact, Birenbaum (1996: 12) argued that, 'on the available criteria alternative assessment seems to compare unfavorably with standardized tests'. Maybe different validity criteria are required. For example, in the context of competency assessment, van der Vleuten *et al.* (2000) argued that definition of constituent attributes has been found to be problematic, as individual competencies are not independent of each other. They recommended that greater validity may be achieved by the use of diversity, and recommended use of a variety of different test methods.

Alternative assessments are also not immune from bias. Miller and Parlett (1974) noted the relationship between the complexity of a task and difficulty of marking it. The high complexity that often characterizes alternative assessments is associated with subjectivity, whereas the low task complexity of much traditional assessment increases reliability. More recently, Birenbaum (1996) noted that portfolios, and alternative assessments generally, compare unfavourably with traditional assessment, particularly when considering inter-rater reliability. However, non-traditional assignments can be very challenging.

Traditional assessment has recently been linked with academic dishonesty. Of course, cheating is not limited to traditional settings, given sufficient motivation. It can, and does, occur just about anywhere. I would argue that competition, scarce resources and work overload, which very often characterize higher education today, provide such motivation. Alternative assessments, too, can be subject to cheating, particularly where the Internet is concerned. Is there any difference in the degree of dishonesty associated with traditional as compared with newer forms of assessment? Again, I turned to research to find an answer. A comparison of evidence relating to both types found more opportunities for dishonest behaviour associated with traditional contexts. However, we need to acknowledge the limitations of all assessment, including the innovative. Improvement does not take place if we turn away from the problem.

Chapter 3: Changing definitions of assessment

The concept of assessment has undergone change over the past half century. Pearson *et al.* (2001) provided a useful framework within which to view these changes. While it is tempting to simply dismiss earlier conceptualizations, such as assessment as measurement or procedure, this would be unwise, and, in my case, hypocritical, given my penchant for statistical evidence. However, it is one thing to see measurement as the raison-d'être of assessment, and quite another to use measurement to achieve other ends while espousing a more modern conceptualization such as assessment as enquiry. In other words, all stages have their strengths and weaknesses, and all are products of their time. Assessment as measurement is grounded in positivism. It is based on a behaviouristic theory of learning and it assumes that learners are empty vessels waiting to be filled with knowledge. It employs psychometric methods in its service. It is fascinated by work on intelligence. These were the cutting edge technologies of the middle of the last century. Such features do not sit well with more recent conceptions which stress constructivism and social interactionism, and embrace cognitive theories of learning. If we consider intelligence at all now, it is seen as a multi-dimensional entity and subject to cultural or gender bias. What interests me are the triggers to change. My knowledge of social history is inadequate to the task of a rigorous analysis, but the move to learner-centred education seems a likely candidate for such a trigger to the third phase. The reasons researchers gave for involving students in assessment, which were the subject of Chapter 4, pointed to this change occurring sometime during the 1970s.

I proposed that we acknowledge a fourth phase, 'assessment as quality control', based on current calls for standardized testing and the growing acceptance of external influence, which encompasses the hyperaccountability of Pearson *et al.* This model takes account of the recent increase in accountability and the move to standardized testing in higher education, in the UK, at least. As we have seen, UK teachers are now subject to guidance and coercion from external bodies such as the Quality Assurance Agency for Higher Education (QAA). If such organizations stimulate debate about quality, which helps us put our academic houses in order by addressing questions of bias and lack of reliability of teacher marking, we can only welcome them. However, this does not seem to be the only consequence of external accountability. It has been argued that when examination results are increasingly being used as measures of teaching quality and as performance indicators for teachers, they can exert undue pressure, particularly on those teachers with a vested interest in maximizing their own pass rates. Patterns of degree class results have been under scrutiny in the UK, and subject to fierce debate in the educational press. As we learned in Chapter 2, O'Donovan *et al.* (2000) reported growing concern over reliability and standards. They noted and questioned the recent rise in the proportion of 'good' degree results at a time of rapid expansion of student numbers and severe cuts in the unit of resource in higher education. Similarly, Newstead (in Irwin, 1996) pointed out the increase of 50 per cent in the number of first class degrees awarded in the UK since 1980, and differing proportions of good results across universities which were not explicable in terms of the characteristics of student intakes.

At least two phases now co-exist, assessment as enquiry and as quality control. Teachers need to juggle to fulfil the needs of both. How do concerns about quality impact on student involvement? Central to many arguments against greater involvement of students is the fear that standards may be compromised. Throughout this book, it has been argued that nothing could be further from the truth, and that, rather, involving students has the power to redress many of the negative aspects of traditional teacher assessment. I would argue that student involvement can present a means of improving the quality of assessment, rather than act as a barrier to it. However, challenging tradition is hard and unpopular. Few of us like change, even when it is change for the better. However, some of us may begin to consider changing to more effective practices if we are provided with good reason to do so. It is our challenge to persuade less adventurous colleagues to consider modifying their practice. Bringing about change is most effective if it is based on concrete evidence. I hope I have provided some ammunition for use by 'the good guys'.

Chapter 4: Why do teachers involve students in assessment?

Reasons for involving students in assessment have changed over the decades, in tune with the changes in definitions of assessment which featured in Chapter 3. In the 1950s the emphasis was firmly on measurement and testing. By the 1960s, other reasons were being put forward and researchers were making tentative attempts to understand the processes of student involvement. Measurement continued as a rationale, however. Studies conducted in the 1970s provided four main categories of reasons: 'Measurement', 'Investigating the process', 'Addressing problems' and 'Benefits'. In addition there are early indications of two categories that achieve greater prominence in later decades: 'Pressure' and 'Teachers beginning to question their power'. By the end of the 1980s, the number of reasons had again increased, but the original 'Measurement' persisted. To this was added 'Benefits', 'Assessing and developing professional and communication skills', 'Addressing problems of assessment', 'Investigating the process', 'Transferring power' and 'Pressure'. The 1990s were characterized by benefits and pressures, but, in total, nine different categories of reason were identified. With the arrival of the new millennium came the use of technology to support student involvement. This was accompanied by a return to some earlier patterns of reasons for involving students. Measurement once again has become a major feature in CAA studies involving students.

However, the overriding reason teachers give for involving students, particularly in recent years, is the benefit the experience brings to learners. Sometimes evidence to support claims of beneficial outcomes is provided, on other occasions it is absent. Much evidence comes from self-report or questionnaire data. While this may not satisfy those who are concerned with strict objective measures, it may be the best that can be achieved without subverting our attempts to empower students.

Chapter 5: How may students be involved in assessment?

The main ways in which students may be involved in assessment are peer assessment, self- and collaborative assessment. Students are also increasingly involved in providing feedback to their peers. However, the degree of involvement varies, from the near trivial to complete. In recent years, studies of student involvement are characterized by a move towards more openness and transparency.

My own preferred way of involving students is through peer assessment, although my first venture into this territory was stimulated by John Cowan's self-assessment experiments. Why do I now prefer peer assessment? I have grown to appreciate the value of learning together. Two heads really are better than one, even if the second head is not as talented as one's own. Co-operation brings benefits to learning, as many psychologists and educators will affirm. Discussing and explaining are invaluable ways of increasing one's own understanding and of glimpsing another's point of view. Cognitive conflict is recognized as a means of stimulating critical awareness and reflection, and structured academic controversy is a recognized form of peer tutoring, as I have argued elsewhere (Falchikov, 2001).

Students may be granted less or more power by teachers. Their level of involvement can vary from activities that require them to check knowledge, performance or skill to involvement with an emancipatory component in which they have greater decision-making power and are required to reflect on criteria. At an intermediate level, students and teachers discuss and negotiate criteria. It may be tempting to argue that we should cede all power to students – and, indeed, some have taken this stance. While my own work has tended towards the emancipatory, I am not happy to give up all decision-making to my students. This is not due to any desire to retain total control, but because I feel that we, as teachers, have something to contribute to student learning beyond giving them freedom to develop. I feel that we owe it to students to use our expertise and experience to structure their learning environment so as to guide them and maximize their learning and development. However, as I argued in Chapter 5, sometimes teachers find themselves in conflict over the needs and rights of students and the demands of the system. It is a fine juggling act we are expected to perform.

Chapter 6: Practical peer assessment and feedback – problems and solutions

This chapter focused on problems of, and hindrances to, involving students in peer assessment. In the early part of the chapter, I discussed a number of questions that have been asked, or might be asked, by colleagues who are sceptical about innovation in general, and peer assessment in particular. I suggested some responses, though I know how difficult it is to persuade someone when they are adamant that their way is right. Given that, for all of us, time is a limited and valuable commodity, we may do well to concentrate our efforts where they are most likely to be fruitful. My experience tells me that induction programmes for new teachers, and courses in learning and teaching for new and other interested teachers may be good places for us to make a start. With the increasing professionalization of higher education, in the UK at least, we are being presented with more and more opportunities to spread the word and disseminate good educational practice.

In practical terms, peer assessment works best when all parties are well prepared for it. Guidelines are essential, and without thorough preparation most ventures are doomed to failure or very limited success. Even when we take time and expend effort in preparing ourselves and our students, total success cannot be guaranteed on a first run through. However, most students quickly come to see the benefits of peer assessment, as they grow in confidence and competence. The use of research-based evidence is, if not essential, very desirable at all stages.

Some colleagues have been tempted, after conducting a successful peer assessment exercise, to base all future practice on it, and to re-use materials prepared for the first cohort on subsequent occasions. I strongly advise against this practice, although I can fully see why it might be a tempting strategy. It is essential that each new cohort of students coming to peer assessment take ownership of their own criteria and of any materials developed from them. Although what each cohort ends up with is very likely to resemble its predecessor's, it is the process of getting to that point that is important. As I have said before, reinvent the wheel on a regular basis.

Chapters 7 and 8: 'How well are students able to judge their own work?' and 'How reliable or valid are student peer assessments?'

I have chosen to discuss Chapters 7 and 8 together as there are many issues held in common. These chapters are about reliability and validity. Unfortunately, both these statistical concepts require a standard against which to measure performance, which, in the case of self- or peer assessment, is teacher marking. Whatever one's view on involving students in assessment, the evidence about reliability of teacher marking itself makes some of us very uneasy about its use as the gold standard against which to judge student assessments. However, as it is teachers whom we wish to persuade to try to involve students, it is perhaps opportunistic to use their assessment outputs to attempt to standardize student outputs. Given the lack of reliability of much teacher assessment, it is surprising that many formal comparisons indicate close resemblance between teacher and student marking. Perhaps something else might be at work here. Good self- or peer assessment requires transparency and openness, which, as we noted earlier, seem to characterize many recent studies. It seems that the need to be explicit helps teachers as well as students.

To return to the questions posed by the chapter titles, a quick, and somewhat flippant answer to both might be, 'Quite well (or quite reliable) mostly, if they are taught how to'. Both integrative studies discussed in the two chapters found that well-conceived and well-conducted studies were associated with better teacher–student agreement than those poorly conceived and conducted.

Most research on the topic of self- or peer assessment is conducted by practising teachers, and is, thus, a form of action research. Action research has been defined in many ways, but Cohen *et al.* (2000: 226) quoted a well-used one. Action research is '. . . the combination of action and research (which) renders that action a form of disciplined inquiry, in which a personal attempt is made to understand, improve and reform practice'. Thus, action research requires that we formulate and carry out our regular activities more carefully than we might usually. We need to be more rigorous and, at the same time, more reflective. Action research has the explicit aim to improve practice and is designed to bridge the gap between research and practice. According to Cohen *et al.*, it combines diagnosis with reflection. Uzzell (2000) sees action research as having its origins in the work of Kurt Lewin (1935) who believed that, in order to gain insight into a process, it is necessary to create change and then observe its effects. A friend put this in a different, more literary way. He advocated that we stand back and observe with Bettelheim's (1970) 'informed heart' or Lessing's (1974) 'small personal voice'.

Chapter 9: Assessment of groups by peers

Much of what has been said about peer assessment conducted by individuals also applies to peer assessment in groups. In groups, students can be reluctant to participate and they may experience discomfort prior to, during and after participation. The jury still out on best practice for group selection. Opinions differ. Some advocate social engineering (e.g. Butterfield and Bailey, 1996; Felder and Brent, 2001), while others prefer self-selection (e.g. Latting and Raffoul, 1991). Yet others try one but end up advocating another (e.g. Lejk, 1999b). I ended up taking a pragmatic approach – allowing some choice within real constraints. Students choosing to work together had to be on the same programme, available at enough times in common, and located on the same campus during the daytime. They had to be willing to make some details available about how they might be contacted. There is little point in constructing perfectly balanced groups of students who never meet out of class, or, indeed, in large classes, in class. Worse still, group members who are located in widely separated geographical locations of the university at all times, except when they meet for a class, are unlikely to make good progress with the group task.

Peer assessment in groups may be subject to bias due to friendship, gender, age, ability, ethnicity or prior experience. Students may be advantaged or disadvantaged by collusion, 'decibel' marking or 'parasite' marking which involves 'social loafing' (Latané *et al.*, 1979). It is important to be aware of all these possibilities and to plan implementations in such a way as to minimize the likelihood of their occurring. As in most situations, prepare yourself and your students well and keep procedures transparent. Require all participants to be responsible and give group members enough power to enable them to deal fairly with defaulters.

Chapter 10: Computer Assisted Assessment and student involvement

As we saw in Chapter 4, there has been an increase in studies which use technology to help involve students in assessment. A few years ago, I would have found these observations grounds for despondency, given the primitive level of development of what technology had to offer at the time. While I am not claiming that the future is, or must be computerized, there are, as we have seen in Chapter 10, some interesting developments which use technology to allow students to be involved actively in assessment. At the same time, many of these initiatives provide a structure to help teachers administer the modules or courses in which student assessment is taking place. While many CAA implementations are in early stages of development, the future seems promising. At last, the tail does not seem to be wagging the dog. We are now using the technology, rather than being slaves to it.

How does the information we have gained about what works and what doesn't in face to face self- or peer assessment relate to CAA studies? As criteria selection is an important issue in non-technological student involvement, we should look at what happens in CAA. All CAA studies seem to involve the use of explicit criteria, some of which are agreed between students and teachers. Students in the study by Ngu *et al.* (1995), for example, are able to add new criteria to those supplied by the teacher via the system, or to suggest new weights for existing criteria. Discipline or subject differences have been investigated in face to face situations, but such differences have not yet been explored in the area of CAA. This is not very surprising, as the vast majority of CAA studies so far have been conducted within computing science departments. Similarly, there are still too few studies for a systematic investigation of course or student level effects.

At present, CAA does not seem to be able to handle assessment of free text. Bull and McKenna's book (2004) has no full chapter devoted to this topic, although there is one page about automated marking of essays. They claim that the area is still small but growing. I attended a seminar on the subject in 2003, and came away underwhelmed by what I heard. Given the difficulties the artificial intelligence community has experienced over the past twenty years, this is, perhaps hardly surprising. The semantics of natural language present a vast challenge.

So far, CAA does not seem to have moved too far away from paper-based versions of self- or peer assessment. However, the automatic administration of assessment, and capturing of both assignments and assessment details, represent a major advantage to both students and lecturers. Other benefits have also been identified, such as asynchronous marking. In addition, there is a hint that CAA enables students to carry out more assessments than non-technological equivalents, thus giving them increased opportunity to see how their peers approach tasks. For example, Sitthiworachart and Joy's (2003) system requires students to assess three pieces of work, as does that of Tsai *et al.* (2001). Lin *et al.*'s (2001) system, on the other hand, requires six assessments per student. This does not seem to happen in non-technological equivalent studies.

Is student experience of CAA as rich or effective as that of students involved in non-CAA assessment? The little evidence we have suggests that it is. Many students have reported experiencing benefits from participating in assessment exercises.

Futures?

What is there on the horizon in terms of involving students in assessment? What do I hope to see there? These may be simple questions, but they cannot be given simple answers. As a realist, what I hope for depends, inevitably, on the starting point of what we have now. Looking back over the material covered by this book, I see both richness and ignorance. I see enthusiasm and suspicion. I have encountered good and not so good practice. I have observed conflict and tension between key influences on initiatives that involve students in assessment, between quality, accountability and economy. While accountability and quality may be seen to be working together to ensure and enhance both the student experience and educational outcomes, economy seems too often to be pulling in the opposite direction. The tension between these forces must be regarded as a necessary feature of any future scenario and we shall need to employ all our creativity to ensure that the quality of student learning is safeguarded.

A first step toward a bright new future would be to bring at least a modicum of light where there is now darkness. Although some have already made a start on this journey, we know too little about many key aspects of student involvement in assessment. For example, we have little understanding of how important personal and societal variables might impact on student involvement and its outcomes. A co-ordinated cross-cultural research programme to investigate student involvement in assessment is highly desirable. Only then may we fully understand the effects of friendship and hostility, gender, ethnicity, age, ability and prior experience, across a variety of settings and cultures. Such a large-scale venture requires support at all levels within higher education and beyond. We need all users of assessment – policymakers, administrators teachers and students – to work together.

I would argue that the expansion of Computer Aided Assessment (CAA) is inevitable, particularly given the need for higher education to be seen to be exercising financial restraint while supporting great numbers of students. What are desirable ways of students using technology to help them assess? I welcome attempts to continue the development of software that enables testing of higher order cognitive skills. The CAA Centre website examples in Chapter 10 provide possible templates for future question preparation. We learned that the best of CAA can already support self- and peer assessment, and help students with assignment preparation and portfolio building. CAA has also been identified as able to stimulate reflection in students. However, a necessary development for CAA to become part of mainstream assessment practice, as I believe it can, is for those with sufficient expertise and enthusiasm to carry out 'missionary work' and attempt to embed CAA systems in other disciplinary areas.

With or without technology, students will continue to be involved in assessment. We know that studies implemented with care can benefit all concerned. We also appreciate that student involvement helps improve the process of assessment itself. Let us attempt a giant leap together to co-ordinate and extend the body of knowledge and experience that exists. The next step, unlike the truth, *is* out there!

References

AAHE Assessment Forum (1997) *Learning Through Assessment: A Resource Guide for Higher Education*, L.F. Gardiner, C. Anderson and B.L. Cambridge (Eds), Washington, DC: American Association for Higher Education.

AAHE (2001a) Program models Alverno College, Series on service-learning in the disciplines, *Teacher Education Volume*.

AAHE (2001b) American Association for Higher Education Assessment Forum: *9 Principles of Good Practice when Assessing Students* (Authors: A.W. Astin; T.W. Banta; P. Cross; E. El-Khawas; P.T. Ewell; P. Hutchings; T.J. Marchese; K.M. McClenney; M. Mentowski; M.A. Miller; T. Moran; B.D. Wright).

Adams, D. and Hamm, M. with the collaboration of Drobnak, M. and Lazar, A. (1996) *Cooperative Learning. Critical Thinking and Collaboration across the Curriculum* (2nd Edition), Springfield, IL: Charles Thomas Publishers.

Adams, C. and King, K. (1994) Towards a framework for student self-assessment, *Innovations in Education and Training International*, 32, 4: 336–43.

Adams, C., Thomas, R. and King, K. (2000) Business students' ranking of reasons for assessment: gender differences, *Innovations in Education and Training International*, 37, 3: 234–43.

Akister, J., Brannon, A. and Mullender-Lock, H. (2000) Poster presentations in social work education assessment: a case study, *Innovations in Education and Training International*, 37, 3: 229–33.

Allal, L. and Ducrey, G.P. (2000) Assessment of – or in – the zone of proximal development, *Learning and Instruction*, 10: 137–52.

Allen, G. (1998) Risk and uncertainty in assessment: exploring the contribution of economics to identifying and analysing the social dynamic in grading, *Assessment and Evaluation in Higher Education*, 23, 3: 241–58.

Alschuler, A.S. and Blimling, G.S. (1995) Curbing epidemic cheating through systemic change, *College Teaching*, 43, 4: 123–6.

Alverno College (2001) Quick facts for educators, Milwaukee, WI: Alverno College.

Alverno College (2003) http://www.alverno.edu/about_alverno/about_index.html (accessed 1.10.03).

Anderson, J.B. and Freiberg, H.J. (1995) Using self-assessment as a reflective tool to enhance the student teaching experience, *Teacher Education Quarterly*, Winter, 22: 77–91.

Angelo, T.A. (1999) Doing assessment as if learning matters most, *AAHE Bulletin*, accessed via the WWW, http:www.aahe.org/Bulletin/angelomay99.htm (accessed September 13, 2001).

Angelo, T.A. and Cross, K.P. (1993) *Classroom Assessment Techniques: A Handbook for College Teachers* (2nd Edition), San Francisco: Jossey-Bass Publishers.

Archer, J. and Lamnin, A. (1985) An investigation of personal and academic stressors on college campuses, *Journal of College Students Personnel*, 26, 3: 210–15.

Armstrong, M. and Boud, D.J. (1983) Assessing class participation: an exploration of the issues, *Studies in Higher Education*, 8, 1: 33–44.

Arter, J.A. and Spandel, V. (1992) Using portfolios of student work in instruction and assessment, *Educational Measurement: Issues and Practice*, 11, 1: 36–44.

Ashcroft, K. and Foreman-Peck, L. (1994) *Managing Teaching and Learning in Further and Higher Education*, London and Washington, DC: The Falmer Press.

Ashworth, P., Bannister, P. and Thorne, P. (1997) Guilty in whose eyes? University students' perceptions of cheating and plagiarism in academic work and assessment, *Studies in Higher Education*, 22, 2: 187–203.

Askham, P. (1997) An instrumental response to the instrumental student: assessment for learning, *Studies in Educational Evaluation*, 23, 4: 299–317.

Bales, R.F. (1950) *Interaction Process Analysis: A Method for the Study of Small Groups*, Cambridge, MA: Addison Wesley.

Bangert, A.W. (1995) Peer assessment: an instructional strategy for effectively implementing performance-based assessments, Doctor of Education dissertation, The University of South Dakota.

Bangert-Drowns, R.L., Wells-Parker, E. and Chevillard, I. (1997) Assessing the methodological quality of research in narrative reviews and meta-analyses, in K.J. Bryant, M. Windle and S.G. West (Eds) *The Science of Prevention. Methodological Advances from Alcohol and Substance Abuse*, Washington, DC: American Psychological Association.

Beaman, R. (1998) The unquiet . . . even loud, andragogy! Alternative assessments for adult learners, *Innovative Higher Education*, 23, 1: 47–59.

Ben-David, M.F. (1999) AMEE Guide no. 14: outcome-based education: part 3 – assessment in outcome-based education, *Medical Teacher*, 21, 1: 23–5.

Ben-David, M.F. (2000) The role of assessment in expanding professional horizons, *Medical Teacher*, 22, 5: 472–7.

Bergee, M.J. (1993) A comparison of faculty, peer, and self-evaluation of applied brass jury performances, *Journal of Research in Music Education*, 41, 1: 19–27.

Bettelheim, B. (1970) *The Informed Heart*, London: Paladin.

Biggs, J. (1999) *Teaching for Quality Learning at University: What the Student Does*, Buckingham: Society for Research into Higher Education and Open University Press.

Billington, H.L. (1997) Poster presentations and peer assessment: novel forms of evaluation and assessment, *Journal of Biological Education*, 31, 3: 218–20.

Birenbaum, M. (1996) Assessment 2000: towards a pluralistic approach to assessment, in M. Birenbaum and F.J.R.C. Dochy (Eds) (1996) *Alternatives in Assessment of Achievements, Learning Processes and Prior Knowledge*, Boston, Dordrecht and London: Kluwer Academic Publishers.

Birenbaum, M. and Dochy, F.J.R.C. (Eds) (1996) *Alternatives in Assessment of Achievements, Learning Processes and Prior Knowledge*, Boston, Dordrecht and London: Kluwer Academic Publishers.

Black, P. and Wiliam, D. (1998) Inside the black box: raising standards through classroom assessment, *Phi Delta Kappan*, 80, 2: 139–48.

Bloom, B.S. (1965) A *Taxonomy of Educational Objectives Handbook 1: Cognitive Domain* (2nd Edn), New York: McKay.

Boud, D. (1989) The role of self-assessment in student grading, *Assessment and Evaluation in Higher Education*, 14, 1: 20–30.

Boud, D. (1990) Assessment and the promotion of academic values, *Studies in Higher Education*, 15, 1: 101–11.

Boud, D. (1995a) *Enhancing Learning through Self-assessment*, London and Philadelphia: Kogan Page.

Boud, D. (1995b) Assessment and learning: contradictory or complimentary?, in P. Knight (Ed.) *Assessment for Learning in Higher Education*, London: Kogan Page in association with the Staff and Educational Development Association.

Boud, D. (2000) Sustainable assessment: rethinking assessment for the learning society, *Studies in Continuing Education*, 22, 2: 151–67.

Boud, D. (2002) Personal communication, 28.10.02.

Boud, D. and Falchikov, N. (1989) Quantitative studies of student self-assessment in higher education: a critical analysis of findings, *Higher Education*, 18, 5: 529–49.

Boud, D.J. and Holmes, W.H. (1981) Self and peer marking in an undergraduate engineering course, *IEEE Transactions on Education*, E-24, 4: 267–74.

Boud, D. and Knights, S. (1994) Designing courses to promote reflective learning, *Research and Development in Higher Education*, 16: 229–34.

Boud, D.J. and Tyree, A.L. (1979) Self and peer assessment in professional education: a preliminary study in law, *Journal of the Society of Public Teachers of Law*, 15, 1: 65–74.

Boud, D., Cohen, R. and Sampson, J. (1999) Peer learning and assessment, *Assessment and Evaluation in Higher Education*, 24, 4: 413–26.

Boud, D., Cohen, R. and Sampson, J. (Eds) (2001) *Peer Learning in Higher Education: Learning With and From Each Other*, London: Kogan Page.

Breakwell, G.M. and Wood, P. (2000) Diary techniques, in G.M. Breakwell, S. Hammond and C. Fife-Schaw (Eds) *Research Methods in Psychology* (2nd Edn), London, Thousand Oaks, CA and New Delhi: Sage Publications.

Brehm, T.W. (1974) Peer evaluation of fixed partial dentures in a preclinical course, *Journal of Dental Education*, 36, 2: 54–5.

Brew, A. (1999) Toward autonomous assessment: using self-assessment and peer assessment, in S. Brown and A. Glasner (Eds) *Assessment Matters in Higher Education: Choosing and Using Diverse Approaches*, Buckingham and Philadelphia, PA: The Society for Research into Higher Education and Open University Press (Chapter 13, 159–71).

Broadfoot, P. (1979) Communication in the classroom: a study of the role of assessment in motivation, *Educational Review*, 31, 1: 3–10.

Broadfoot, P. (Ed.) (1986) *Profiles and Records of Achievement: A Review of Issues and Practice*, London: Holt, Rinehart and Winston.

Broadfoot, P. (1995) Performance assessment in perspective: international trends and current experience, in H. Torrance (Ed.) *Evaluating Authentic Assessment: Problems and Possibilities in New Approaches to Assessment*, Buckingham and Philadelphia: Open University Press.

Broadfoot, P. (1999) Editorial: 'testing: friend or foe?' *Assessment in Education*, 6, 2: 173–5.

Brown, G. with Bull, J. and Pendlebury, M. (1997) *Assessing Student Learning in Higher Education*, London and New York: Routledge.

Brown, S. and Glasner, A. (Eds) (1999) *Assessment Matters in Higher Education: Choosing and Using Diverse Approaches*, Buckingham and Philadelphia, PA: The Society for Research into Higher Education and Open University Press.

Bruffee, K.A. (1978) The Brooklyn Plan: Attaining Intellectual Growth through Peer-Group Tutoring, *Liberal Education*, 64, 4: 447–68.

Bucklow, C. (1993) Comparing chalk and cheese – quality in assessing work-based learning, Ch. 23 in M. Shaw and E. Roper (Eds) *Aspects of Educational and Training Technology, volume XXVI Quality in education and training*, 140–3.

Bull, J. and McKenna, C. (2004) *Blueprint for Computer-assisted Assessment*, London and New York: RoutledgeFalmer.

Burke, R.J. (1969) Some preliminary data on the use of self-evaluations and peer-ratings in assigning university course grades, *Journal of Educational Research*, 62, 10: 444–8.

Burnett, W. and Cavaye, G. (1980) Peer assessment by fifth year students of surgery, *Assessment in Higher Education*, 5, 3: 273–8.

Butcher, A.C., Stefani, L.A.J. and Tariq, V.N. (1995) Analysis of peer-, self- and staff-assessment in group project work, *Assessment in Education*, 2, 2: 165–85.

Butler, S.A. and Hodge, S.R. (2001) Enhancing student trust through peer assessment in physical education, *Physical Educator*, 58, 1: 30 (accessed electronically 23.01.02).

Butterfield, J. and Bailey, J.J. (1996) Socially engineered groups in business curricula: an investigation of the effects of team composition on group output, *Journal of Education for Business* 76, 2: 103–6.

Byrne, C. (1980) Tutor marked assignments at the Open University: a question of reliability, *Assessment in Higher Education*, 5(2), 150–66.

CAA Centre web site (2003) http://www.caacentre.ac.uk/ (accessed 30.1.4). See also Active Learning (1994) Issue 1 devoted to CAA, http://www.caacentre.ac.uk/

CAID (2004) http://www.derby.ac.uk/assess/talk/quicdemo.html (accessed 13.02.04).

Capano, K.M. (1991) Stopping students from cheating: halting the activities of term-paper mills and enforcing disciplinary sanctions against students who purchase term papers, *Journal of College and University Law*, 18, 2: 277–97.

CAREI (2003) Center for Applied Research and Educational Improvement, University of Minnesota, 'Observation of a group' guidelines, http://education.umn.edu/CAREI/Programs/pedagogy/tasks/Sociology/observation.html

Carnevale, D. (1999) How to proctor from a distance, *Chronicle of Higher Education*, 46, 12: A47–A48.

Carter, R. and Neal, B. (1995) Assessing competence in engineering project management, in A. Edwards and P. Knight (Eds) (1995) *Assessing Competence in Higher Education*, London: Kogan Page in association with the Staff and Educational Development Association.

Caruana, A., Ramaseshan, B. and Ewing, M.T. (2000) The effect of anomie on academic dishonesty among university students, *The International Journal of Educational Management*, 14, 1: 23–30.

Catterall, M. (1995) Peer learning research in marketing, in *Enhancing Student Learning through Peer Tutoring in Higher Education*, Jordanstown: University of Ulster, Educational Development Unit (pp. 54–62).

CEILIDH (2003) http://www.cs.nott.ac.uk/%7Eceilidh/papers.html

Challis, M. (1999) AMEE Medical education guide no. 11 (revised): portfolio-based learning and assessment in medical education, *Medical Teacher*, 21, 4: 370–86.

Chang, C.-C. (2001) Construction and evaluation of a web-based learning portfolio system: an electronic assessment tool, *Innovations in Education and Teaching International*, 38, 2: 144–55.

Chatterji, S. and Mukerjee, M. (1983) Accuracy of self-assessment and its relation with some psychological and biographical factors, *New Zealand Journal of Psychology*, 12: 28–35.

Cheng, W. and Warren, M. (1997) Having second thoughts: student perceptions before and after a peer assessment exercise, *Studies in Higher Education*, 22, 2: 233–9.

Cheng, W. and Warren, M. (1999) Peer and teacher assessment of the oral and written tasks of a group project, *Assessment and Evaluation in Higher Education*, 24, 3: 301–14.

Chou, C. (2000) Constructing a computer-assisted testing and evaluation system on the World Wide Web – the CATES experience, *IEEE Transactions on Education*, 43, 3: 266–72.

Clandinin, D.J. and Connelly, F.M. (1994) Personal experience methods, in N.K. Denzin and Y.S. Lincoln (Eds) *Handbook of Qualitative Research*, Thousand Oaks, CA, London and New Delhi: Sage Publications.

Clarke, D. and Stephens, M. (1996) The ripple effect: the institutional impact of the systematic introduction of performance assessment in mathematics, in M. Birenbaum and F.J.R.C. Dochy (Eds) *Alternatives in Assessment of Achievements, Learning Processes and Prior Knowledge*, Boston, Dordrecht and London: Kluwer Academic Publishers.

Cohen, L., Manion, L. and Morrison, K. (2000) *Research Methods in Education* (5th Edition), London and New York: RoutledgeFalmer.

Cole, S. and McCabe, D.L. (1996) Issues in academic integrity, *New Directions for Student Services*, 73, 67–77.

Columbia College Student Council (2002) Proposal for and Academic Judicial System, http://www.columbia.edu/cu/ccsc/pdfs/proposalAcademicJudicial.pdf

Concise Oxford Dictionary (1976) (6th Edition), Oxford: Oxford University Press.

Conway, R., Kember, D., Sivan, A. and May, W. (1993) Peer assessment of an individual's contribution to a group project, *Assessment and Evaluation in Higher Education*, 18, 1: 2–36.

Cooper, H. (1998) *Synthesizing Research, A Guide for Literature Reviews* (3rd Edition), Thousand Oaks, CA: Sage Publications.

Cowan, J. (1988) Struggling with student self-assessment, in D. Boud (Ed.) *Developing Student Autonomy in Learning* (2nd Edition), London: Kogan Page.

Cowan, J. (2001) Plus/minus marking – a method of assessment worth considering? ILTHE Members' Resources (accessed 15.05.01).

Cox, R. (1967) Examinations and higher education: a survey of the literature, *University Quarterly*, 292–340.

Crooks, T.J., Kane, M.T. and Cohen, A.S. (1996) Threats to the valid use of assessments, *Assessment in Education*, 3, 3: 265–85.

Cumming, J.J. and Maxwell, G.S. (1999) Contextualising authentic assessment, *Assessment in Education*, 6, 2: 177–94.

Curtis, S.J. (1968) *History of Education in Great Britain* (7th Edition), London: University Tutorial Press.

D'Aoust, C. (1992) Portfolios: process for students and teachers, in K. Blake Yancey (Ed.) *Portfolios in the Writing Classroom*, Urbana, IL: National Council of teachers of English.

D'Augelli, A.R. (1973) The assessment of interpersonal skills: a comparison of observer, peer and self ratings, *Journal of Community Psychology*, 1: 177–9.

Davies, P. (2000a) Computerised self/peer support, learning and assessment of final year undergraduates? Paper delivered at the 7th International ALT-C Conference on Integrating Learning Technology, Policy, Practice & Partnership, 11–13th September, UMIST, Manchester.

Davies, P. (2000b) Computerized peer assessment, *Innovations in Education and Training International*, 37, 4: 346–55 (accessed online 24.09.01).

Davies, P. (2002) Using student reflective self-assessment for awarding degree classifications, *Innovations in Education and Teaching International*, 39, 4: 307–19.

Davies, P. (2003a) Closing the communications loop on the computerized peer-assessment of essays, *ALT-J*, 11: 1.

Davies, P. (2003b) Evaluating the quality of computerized peer-feedback compared with computerized peer-marking, paper delivered at the 10th International ALT-C Conference: Communities of practice, Sheffield, 8–10 Sept.

Davis, A. and Rose, D. (2000) The experimental method in psychology, in G.M. Breakwell, S. Hammond and C. Fife-Shaw (Eds) *Research Methods in Psychology* (2nd Edition), London: Sage Publications.

Davis, S.F. (1992) Your cheatin' heart, *Psychology Today*, 25, 6: 9–18 (accessed electronically 28.09.01).

Deeks, D. (1999) The Information Systems group project, in M. Taras (Ed.) *Innovations in Learning and Teaching: Teaching Fellowships at the University of Sunderland*, Sunderland: University of Sunderland Press (pp. 127–58).

Deckert, G.D. (1993) Perspectives on plagiarism from ESL students in Hong Kong, *Journal of Second Language Writing*, 2, 2: 131–48.

Denton, P. (2001a) Generating coursework feedback for large groups of students using MS Excel and MS Word, *University Chemistry Education*, 5: 1–8.

Denton, P. (2001b) Microsoft Office software for returning feedback to students via email, ILT members' resources, November.

Desruisseaux, P. (1999) Cheating is reaching epidemic proportions worldwide, researchers say, *The Chronicle of Higher Education*, April 30, 45, 34: A45.

Dfes (2003) Department for education and skills, National Record of Achievement web site, http://www.dfes.gov.uk/nra/

Denehy, G.E. and Fuller, J.L. (1974) Student peer evaluation: an adjunct to pre-clinical laboratory evaluation, *Journal of Dental Education*, 38, 4: 200–3.

Dickinson, L. (1988) Collaborative assessment: an interim report, in H. Holec (Ed.) Project no. 12, Learning and teaching modern languages for communication, *Autonomy and Self-Directed Learning: Present Fields of Application*, Strasbourg: Council for Cultural Co-operation, Council of Europe (pp. 121–8).

Diekhoff, G.M., LaBeff, E.E., Shinohara, K. and Yasukawa, H. (1999) College Cheating in Japan and the United States, *Research in Higher Education*, 40, 3: 343–53.

Dierick, S. and Dochy, F. (2001) New lines in edumetrics: new forms of assessment lead to new assessment criteria, *Studies in Educational Evaluation*, 27: 307–30.

Dietel, R.J., Herman, J.L. and Knuth, R.A. (1991) *What Does Research Say about Assessment?* Oak Brook: North Central Regional Laboratory.

Dochy, F. (2001) A new assessment era: different needs, new challenges, *Research Dialogue in Learning and Instruction*, 2: 11–20.

Dochy, F., Segers, M. and Sluijsmans, D. (1999) The use of self-, peer and co-assessment in higher education: a review, *Studies in Higher Education*, 24, 3: 331–49.

Dochy, F.J.R.C. and McDowell, L. (1997) Assessment as a tool for learning, *Studies in Educational Evaluation*, 23, 4: 279–98.

Earl, S. (1986) Staff and peer assessment – measuring an individual's contribution to group performance, *Assessment and Evaluation in Higher Education*, Spring, 11, 1: 60–9.

Earl, S., Westwood, J. and Percival, F. (2003) Postgraduate certificate in teaching and learning in higher education, Module 4: independent professional study, Edinburgh: Educational Development, Napier University.

Edwards, A. and Knight, P. (1995) The assessment of competence in higher education, in A. Edwards and P. Knight (Eds) *Assessing Competence in Higher Education*, London: Kogan Page in association with the Staff and Educational Development Association.

Edwards, E. and Sutton, A. (1991) A practical approach to student-centred learning, *British Journal of Educational Technology*, 23, 1: 4–20.

Eisenberg, T. (1965) Are doctoral comprehensive examinations necessary? *American Psychologist*, XX: 168–9.

Elias, M.J. (1989) Schools as a source of stress to children: an analysis of causal and ameliorative influences, *Journal of School Psychology*, 27, 4: 393–407.

Ellington, H., Percival, F. and Race, P. (1993) *Handbook of Educational Technology* (3rd Edn), London: Kogan Page.

Elton, L. and Johnson, B. (2002) *Assessment in Universities: A Critical Review of Research*, LTSN Generic Centre (accessed through the Internet, 25.02.03).

Ewers, T. and Searby, M. (1997) Peer assessment in music, *The New Academic*, 6, 2: 5–7.

Falchikov, N. (1986) Product comparisons and process benefits of collaborative self and peer group assessments, *Assessment and Evaluation in Higher Education*, 11, 2: 146–66.

Falchikov, N. (1988) Self and peer assessment of a group project designed to promote the skills of capability, *Programmed Learning and Educational Technology*, 25, 4: 327–39.

Falchikov, N. (1993) Group process analysis: self and peer assessment of working together in a group, *Educational Technology and Training International*, 30, 3: 275–84.

Falchikov, N. (1994) Learning from peer feedback marking: student and teacher perspectives, in H.C. Foot, C.J. Howe, A. Anderson, A.K. Tolmie and D.A. Warden (Eds) *Group and Interactive Learning*, Southampton and Boston, Computational Mechanics Publications.

Falchikov, N. (1995a) Peer feedback marking: developing peer assessment, *Innovations in Education and Training International*, 32, 2: 175–87.

Falchikov, N. (1995b) Improving feedback to and from students, in P. Knight (Ed.) *Assessment for Learning in Higher Education*, London: Kogan Page.

Falchikov, N. (1996a) Improving learning through critical peer feedback and reflection, *Higher Education Research and Development*, 19, 214–18.

Falchikov, N. (1996b) Involving students in feedback and assessment. Paper presented at the Assessment Strategies in Scottish Higher Education Conference, Stirling.

Falchikov, N. (2001) *Learning Together. Peer Tutoring in Higher Education*, London and New York: RoutledgeFalmer.

Falchikov, N. (2004) Involving students in assessment, *Psychology Learning and Teaching*, 3, 2: 102–8.

Falchikov, N. and Boud, D. (1989) Student self-assessment in higher education: a meta-analysis, *Review of Educational Research*, 59, 4: 395–430.

Falchikov, N. and Goldfinch, J. (2000) Student peer assessment in higher education: a meta-analysis comparing peer and teacher marks, *Review of Educational Research*, 70, 3: 287–322.

Falchikov, N. and MacLeod, L. (1996) Using psychology in the community: developing transferable skills, *Psychology Teaching Review*, 5, 2: 63–74.

Falchikov, N. and Magin, D. (1997) Detecting gender bias in peer marking of students' group process work, *Assessment and Evaluation in Higher Education*, 22, 4: 393–404.

Felder, R.M. and Brent, R. (2001) Issues relating to group composition, in N. Falchikov (Ed.) *Learning Together. Peer Tutoring in Higher Education*, London and New York: RoutledgeFalmer.

Festinger, L. (1957) *A Theory of Cognitive Dissonance*, Stanford, CA: Stanford University Press.

Fineman, S. (1981) Reflections on peer teaching and peer assessment – an undergraduate experience, *Assessment and Evaluation in Higher Education*, 6, 1: 82–93.

Foubister, S.P., Michaelson, G.J. and Tomes, N. (1997) Automatic assessment of elementary Standard ML programs using Ceilidh, *Journal of Computer Assisted Learning*, 13: 99–108.

Foxley, E., Higgins, C., Symeonidis, P. and Tsintsifas, A. (2001) The CourseMaster Automated Assessment System – a next generation Ceilidh, paper delivered at the Conference on Computer Assisted Assessment to support the ICS disciplines, University of Warwick, April 5th–6th.

Freeman, M. (1995) Peer assessment by groups of group work, *Assessment and Evaluation in Higher Education*, 20, 3: 289–300.

Freeman, M. and McKenzie, J. (2001) Aligning peer assessment with peer learning for large classes: the case for an online self and peer assessment system, in D. Boud, R. Cohen and J. Sampson (Eds) *Peer Learning in Higher Education: Learning With and From Each Other*, London: Kogan Page.

Freeman, R. and Lewis, R. (1998) *Planning and Implementing Assessment*, London: Kogan Page.

Frey, C. (2001) Computer aided cheating, downloaded from http://www.latimes.com (accessed 9.01, no longer freely available).

Friesen, D.D. and Dunning, G.B. (1973) Peer evaluation and practicum supervision, *Counselor Education and Supervision*, 12: 229–35.

Fry, S.A. (1990) Implementation and evaluation of peer marking in higher education, *Assessment and Evaluation in Higher Education*, 15, 3: 177–89.

Fuqua, D.R., Johnson, A.W., Newman, J.L., Anderson, M.W. and Gade, E.M. (1984) Variability across sources of performance ratings, *Journal of Counselling Psychology*, 31, 2: 249–52.

Gaberson, K.B. (1997) Academic dishonesty among nursing students, *Nursing Forum*, 32, 3: 14 (7pp.) (accessed through the Internet, 4.10.01).

Garvin, J.W., Butcher, A.C., Stefani, L.A.J., Tariq, V.N., Lewis, M.H.R., Blumsom, N.L., Govier, R.N. and Hill, J.A. (1995) Group projects for first-year university students: an evaluation, *Assessment and Evaluation in Higher Education*, 20, 3: 273–88.

Gatfield, T. (1999) Examining student satisfaction with group projects and peer assessment, *Assessment and Evaluation in Higher Education*, 24, 4: 365–77.

George, J. and Cowan, J. (1999) *A Handbook of Techniques for Formative Assessment. Mapping the Student's Learning Experience*, London and Sterling, VA: Kogan Page.

Gibbs, G. (1995) *Assessing Student-centred Courses*, Oxford: Oxford Centre for Staff Development.

Gibbs, G. (1999) Using assessment strategically to change the way students learn, in S. Brown and A. Glasner (Eds) (1999) *Assessment Matters in Higher Education: Choosing and Using Diverse Approaches*, Buckingham and Philadelphia, PA: The Society for Research into Higher Education and Open University Press (Chapter 4, 41–53).

Gibbs, G., Habeshaw, S. and Habeshaw, T. (1986) 53 interesting ways to assess your students, Bristol: Technical and Educational Services.

Gibelman, M., Gelman, S.R. and Fast, J. (1999) The downside of cyberspace: cheating made easy, *Journal of Social Work Education*, 35, 3: 367 (accessed electronically, 13.08.01).

Gipps, C. (1995) Reliability, validity and manageability in large-scale performance assessment, in H. Torrance (Ed.) *Evaluating Authentic Assessment: Problems and Possibilities in New Approaches to Assessment*, Buckingham and Philadelphia: Open University Press.

Glass, G.V., McGaw, B. and Smith, M.L. (1981) *Meta-analysis in Social Research*, Beverly Hills, CA: Sage Publications.

Glick, S.M. (2001) Cheating at medical school, *British Medical Journal*, 3 February, 322: 250–1.

Goldfinch, J. (1994) Further developments in peer assessment of group projects, *Assessment and Evaluation in Higher Education*, 19, 1: 29–36.

Goldfinch, J. and Raeside, R. (1990) Development of a peer assessment technique for obtaining individual marks on a group project, *Assessment and Evaluation in Higher Education*, 15, 3: 210–25.

Goldfinch, J., Laybourn, P., MacLeod, L. and Stewart, S. (1999) Improving group-working skills in undergraduates through employer involvement, *Assessment and Evaluation in Higher Education*, 24, 1: 41–51.

Goode, S. (1999) Students get A+ for easy cheating, *Insight on the News*, Sept. 20, 15, 35: 18.

Gopinath, C. (1999) Alternatives to instructor assessment of class participation, *Journal of Education for Business*, 75, 1: 10–14.

Gosling, D. (2000) Using Habermas to evaluate two approaches to negotiated assessment, *Assessment and Evaluation in Higher Education*, 25, 3: 293–304.

Gough, H.G., Hall, W.B. and Harris, R.E. (1964) Evaluation of performance in medical training, *Journal of Medical Education*, 39: 679–92.

Gray, T.G.F. (1987) An exercise in improving the potential of exams for learning, *European Journal of Engineering Education*, 12, 4: 311–23.

Greenan, K., Humphreys, P. and McIlveen, H. (1997) Developing transferable personal skills: part of the graduate toolkit, *Education + Training*, 39, 2: 71–8.

Greer, L. (2001) Does changing the method of assessment of a module improve the performance of a student? *Assessment and Evaluation in Higher Education*, 26, 2: 127–38.

Guilford, J.D. (1965) *Fundamental Statistics in Psychology and Education* (4th Edition), New York: McGraw Hill.

Habermas, J. (1987) *Knowledge and Human Interests*, trans. J. Shapiro, London: Polity Press.

Hahlo, K. (1997) An exercise in student self-assessment, *The New Academic*, 6, 2: 8–9.

Hall, D. (1992) Professional development portfolios for teachers and lecturers, *British Journal of In Service Education*, 18: 81–6.

Hall, K. (1995) Co-assessment: participation of students with staff in the assessment process, paper presented at the European Association for Research on Learning and Instruction (EARLI) electronic conference (accessed through EARLI-AE discussion list).

Halsall, R. (1995) Assessing competence in teacher education, in A. Edwards and P. Knight (Eds) (1995) *Assessing Competence in Higher Education*, London: Kogan Page in association with the Staff and Educational Development Association (Chapter 6, pp. 98–111).

Hamilton, T.M. (2000) Chemistry and writing, *College Teaching*, 48, i4, 136- (electronic version, 12.09.01).

Hammond, K.R. and Kern, F. Jr. with Crow, W.J., Githers, J.H., Groesbeck, B., Gyr, J.W. and Saunders, L.H. (1959) *Teaching Comprehensive Medical Care*, Cambridge, MA: Harvard University Press.

Hammond, S. (2000) Using psychometric tests, in G.M. Breakwell, S. Hammond and C. Fife-Schaw (Eds) (2000) *Research Methods in Psychology* (2nd Edition), London, Thousand Oaks, CA and New Delhi: Sage Publications.

Hardin, C. and Bader, C. (1999) Your cheatin' heart: dishonest or misinformed? *Journal of Educational Psychology*, 88: 229–41 (accessed electronically, 29.01.03).

Harpp, D.N. and Hogan, J.J. (1998) The case of the ultimate identical twin, *Journal of Chemical Education*, 75, 4: 482–3.

Harris, M.M. and Schaubroeck, J. (1988) A meta-analysis of self-supervisor, self-peer and peer-supervisor ratings, *Personnel Psychology*, 41: 43–62.

Hartog, P. and Rhodes, E.C. (1936) *The Marks of Examiners*, London: Macmillan.

Hassmén, P., Sams, M.R. and Hunt, D.P. (1996) Self-assessment responding and testing method: effects on performers and observers, *Perceptual and Motor Skills*, 83, 1091–104.

Heathfield, M. (1999) Group-based assessment: an evaluation of the use of assessed tasks as a method of fostering higher quality learning, in S. Brown and A. Glasner (Eds) *Assessment Matters in Higher Education: Choosing and Using Diverse Approaches*, Buckingham and Philadelphia, PA: The Society for Research into Higher Education and Open University Press (Chapter 11, pp. 132–45).

Heider, F. (1958) *The Psychology of Interpersonal Relations*, New York: Wiley.

Helms, M. and Haynes, P.J. (1990) When bad groups are good: an appraisal of learning from groups, *Journal of Education for Business*, 66, 1: 5–8.

Hill, K.T. and Wigfield, A. (1984) Test anxiety: a major educational problem and what can be done about it, *The Elementary School Journal*, 85, 1: 105–26.

Hill, R.W., Zrull, M.C. and McIntire, K. (1998) Differences between self- and peer ratings of interpersonal problems, *Assessment*, 5, 1: 67–83.

Holt, M.E., Rees, F., Swenson, J.D. and Kleiber, P.B. (1998) Evolution of evaluations for critical, reflective and deliberative discourse: national issues forums on-line, paper delivered at the 5th European Electronic Conference on Assessment and Evaluation, March 30–April 3 (accessed through EARLI-AE discussion list, 7.03.02).

Horgan, D.D. (1997) An examination of the interrelationships among self, peer, and instructor assessments, paper presented at the 7th European Association for Research on Learning and Instruction conference, Athens.

Houldsworth, C. and Mathews, B.P. (2000) Group composition, performance and educational attainment, *Education + Training*, 42, 3: 40–53.

Hounsell, D. (2003) No comment? Feedback, learning and development, in M. Slowey and D. Watson (Eds) *Higher Education and the Lifecourse*, Buckingham: SRHE and Open University.

Hounsell, D., McCulloch, M.L. and Scott, M. (Eds) (1996) *The ASSHE Inventory: Changing Assessment Practices in Scottish Higher Education*, Edinburgh, Centre for Teaching Learning and Assessment, The University of Edinburgh and Napier University, Edinburgh, in association with the Universities and Colleges Staff Development Agency.

Housego, S. and Freeman, M. (2000) Case studies – integrating the use of web based learning systems into student learning, *Australian Journal of Educational Technology*, 16, 3: 258–82. http://cleo.murdoch.edu.au/ajet/ajet16/housego.html

Hudson, L. (1967) *Contrary Imaginations. A Psychological Study of the English Schoolboy*, Harmondsworth: Pelican/Penguin Books.

Hughes, C. (2003) Personal Communication, c.hughes@unsw.edu.au

Hughes, I.E. and Large, B.J. (1993) Staff and peer-group assessment of oral communication skills, *Studies in Higher Education*, 18, 3: 379–85.

Hunt, D.P. (1982) Effects of human self-assessment responding on learning, *Journal of Applied Psychology*, 67, 1: 75–82.

Hunter, D. and Russ, M. (1996) Peer assessment in performance studies, *British Journal of Music Education*, 13: 67–78.

Irwin, A. (1996) How cheats prosper in exams, *The Times Higher Education Supplement*, 12 April (accessed electronically 17.09.02).

Jacobs, A. (1974) The use of feedback in groups, in A. Jacobs and W.W. Spradlin (Eds) *The Group as Agent of Change*, New York: Behavioral Publication.

Jacobs, R.M., Briggs, D.H. and Whitney, D.R. (1975) Continuous-progress education: III. Student self-evaluation and peer evaluation, *Journal of Dental Education*, 39, 8: 535–41.

JISC (2002) Joint Information Systems Committee electronic plagiarism detection project report, http://www.jisc.ac.uk/plagiarism/start.html (accessed 23.08.02).

Johnson, D.W. and Johnson, R.T. (1985) The internal dynamics of cooperative learning groups, in R. Slavin, S. Sharan, S. Kagan, R. Herz-Lazarowitz, C. Webb and R. Schmuck (Eds) *Learning to Cooperate, Cooperating to Learn*, New York and London: Plenum Press.

Jordan, S. (1999) Self-assessment and peer assessment, in S. Brown and A. Glasner (Eds) (1999) *Assessment Matters in Higher Education: Choosing and Using Diverse Approaches*, Buckingham and Philadelphia, PA: The Society for Research into Higher Education and Open University Press (Chapter 14, pp. 172–82).

Joy, M. and Luck, M. (1999) Plagiarism in programming assignments, *IEEE Transactions on Education*, 42, 2: 129–33.

Kang, D.-H., Coe, C.L. and McCarthy, D.O. (1996) Academic examinations significantly impact immune responses, but not lung function, in healthy and well-managed asthmatic adolescents, *Brain, Behavior and Immunity*, 10, 2: 164–81.

Keaten, J.A. and Richardson, M.E. (1993) A field investigation of peer assessment as part of the student group grading process, paper presented at the Annual Meeting of the Western Speech Communication Association convention, Albuquerque, NM, February 12–16.

Kegel-Flom, P. (1975) Predicting supervisor, peer, and self-ratings of intern performance, *Journal of Medical Education*, 50: 812–15.

Keith, S.Z. (1996) Self-assessment materials for use in portfolios, *Primus*, VI, 2: 178–92.

Kelmar, J. (1992) Peer assessment: a study of graduate students, paper presented at the 'Forum on Higher Education Teaching and Learning – the Challenge' conference, The Teaching and Learning Group, Curtin University of Technology, Perth, WA, 12–13 February.

Kember, D. (2003) To control or not to control: the question of whether experimental designs are appropriate for evaluating innovations in higher education, *Assessment and Evaluation in Higher Education*, 28, 1: 89–101.

Kennedy, K., Nowak, S., Raghuraman, R., Thomas, J. and Davis, S.F. (2000) Academic dishonesty and distance learning: student and faculty views, *College Student Journal*, 34, 2: 309 (accessed electronically, 4.10.01).

Kerkvliet, J. and Sigmund, C.L. (1999) Can we control cheating in the classroom? *Research in Economic Education*, Fall, 331–43.

Kerr, N.L. and Bruun, S.E. (1983) Dispensability of member effort and group motivation losses: free-rider effects, *Journal of Personality and Social Psychology*, 44, 1: 78–94.

Kibler, W.L. (1993) Academic dishonesty: a student development dilemma, *NASPA Journal*, 30, 4: 252–67.

Kimbrough, W.M. (1995) Self-assessment, participation and value of leadership skills, activities and experiences for Black students relative to their membership in historically Black fraternities and sororities, *Journal of Negro Education*, 64, 1, 63–74.

Klenowski, V. (1995) Student self-evaluation processes: empowering students in learner-centred contexts, paper presented at the American Educational Research Association Annual Meeting, San Francisco, CA.

Kloss, R.J. (1996) Writing things down vs. writing things up: are research papers valid? *College Teaching*, 44, 1: 3–7.

Kniveton, B.H. (1996) Student perceptions of assessment methods, *Assessment and Evaluation in Higher Education*, 21, 3: 229–37.

Korman, M. and Stubblefield, R.L. (1971) Medical school evaluation and internship performance, *Journal of Medical Education*, 46: 670–3.

Kubany, A.J. (1957) Use of sociometric peer nominations in medical education research, *Journal of Applied Psychology*, 41: 389–94. Kang, D.-H., Coe, C.L. and McCarthy, D.O. (1996) Academic examinations significantly impact immune responses, but not lung function, in healthy and well-managed asthmatic adolescents, *Brain, Behavior and Immunity*, 10, 2: 164–81.

Kwan, K.-P. and Leung, R. (1996) Tutor versus peer group assessment of student performance in a simulation training exercise, *Assessment and Evaluation in Higher Education*, 21, 3: 205–14.

Laming, D. (1990) The reliability of a certain university examination compared with the precision of absolute judgements, *The Quarterly Journal of Experimental Psychology*, 42A, 2: 239–54.

Lapham, A. and Webster, R. (1999) Peer assessment of undergraduate seminar presentations: motivations, reflection and future directions, in S. Brown and A. Glasner (Eds) (1999) *Assessment Matters in Higher Education: Choosing and Using Diverse Approaches*, Buckingham and Philadelphia, PA: The Society for Research into Higher Education and Open University Press (Chapter 15, pp. 183–90).

Latané, B., Williams, K. and Harkins, S. (1979) Many hands make light the work: the causes and consequences of social loafing, *Journal of Personality and Social Psychology* 37, 6: 822–32.

Latting, J.K. and Raffoul, P.R. (1991) Designing students work groups for increased learning: an empirical investigation, *Journal of Social Work Education* 27, 1: 48–59.

Lawrence, G. and Branch, J. (1974) *Guidelines for Developing a Competency-based Inservice Teacher Education Program*, State of Florida, Department of Education.

Lawrence, G. and Branch, J. (1978) Peer managed assessment of competencies, *Educational Technology*, 18 (August): 12–14.

Lawrence, T.E. (1939) *Seven Pillars of Wisdom*, volumes I and II, London: The Reprint Society by arrangement with Jonathan Cape Ltd.

Laybourn, P., Goldfinch, J., Graham, J., MacLeod, L. and Stewart, S. (2001) Measuring changes in groupworking skills in undergraduate students after employer involvement in group skill development, *Assessment and Evaluation in Higher Education*, 26, 4: 367–80.

Lea, M. (2001) Computer conferencing and assessment: new ways of writing in higher education, *Studies in Higher Education*, 26, 2: 163–81.

Leach, L., Neutze, G. and Zepke, N. (2001) Assessment and empowerment: some critical questions, *Assessment and Evaluation in Higher Education*, 26, 4: 293–305.

Leavitt, F.J. (1995) Cheating in medical school, *British Medical Journal*, 310, 6985: 1014–15.

LeBold, W.K., Budny, D.D. and Ward, S.K. (1998) Understanding of mathematics and science: efficient models for student assessments, *IEEE Transactions on Education*, 41, 1: 8–16.

Lejk, M. (1994) Team assessment, win or lose, *The New Academic*, 3, 3: 10–11.

Lejk, M. (1999a) Successful group assessment case studies, in M. Taras (Ed.) *Innovations in Learning and Teaching: Teaching Fellowships at the University of Sunderland*, Sunderland: University of Sunderland Press (pp. 45–60).

Lejk, M. (1999b) Group assessment on undergraduate computing courses in higher education in the UK, PhD thesis, University of Sunderland.

Lejk, M., Wyvill, M. and Farrow, S. (1996) A survey of methods of deriving individual grades from group assessments, *Assessment and Evaluation in Higher Education*, 21, 3: 267–80.

Lejk, M., Wyvill, M. and Farrow, S. (1997) Group learning and group assessment on undergraduate computing courses in higher education in the UK: results of a survey, *Assessment and Evaluation in Higher Education*, 21,1: 81–91.

Lejk, M., Wyvill, M. and Farrow, S. (1999) Group assessments in systems analysis and design: a comparison of the performance of streamed and mixed-ability groups, *Assessment and Evaluation in Higher Education*, 24, 1: 5–14.

Lennon, S. (1995) Correlations between tutor, peer and self assessments of second year physiotherapy students in movement studies, in *Enhancing Student Learning Through Peer Tutoring in Higher Education*, Jordanstown: University of Ulster, Educational Development Unit (pp. 66–71).

Leon, P. (2001) Working students focus on marks, *The Times Higher*, December 7, p. 4.

Lessing, D.M. (1974) *A small Personal Voice*, in P. Schlueter (Ed.) New York: Knopf.

Lewin, K. (1935) *A Dynamic Theory of Personality*, New York: McGraw Hill.

Lin, S.S.-J., Liu, E.Z.-F. and Yuan, S.-M. (2001) Web based peer assessment: attitude and achievement, *IEEE Transactions on Education*, 44, 2 (accessed electronically 01.05.04).

Linn, B.S., Arostegui, M. and Zeppa, R. (1975) Performance rating scale for peer and self assessments, *British Journal of Medical Education*, 9: 98–101.

Longhurst, N. and Norton, L.S. (1997) Self-assessment in coursework essays, *Studies in Educational Evaluation*, 23, 4: 319–30.

Lopez-Real, F. and Chan, Y.-P.R. (1999) Peer assessment of a group project in a primary mathematics education course, *Assessment and Evaluation in Higher Education*, 24, 1: 67–79.

Lui, E.Z.-F., Lin, S.S.J. and Yuan, S.-M. (2001) Web-based peer review: the learner as both adapter and reviewer, *IEEE Transactions on Education*, August, 44, 3, 246–51.

Lupton, R.A., Chapman, K.J. and Weiss, J.E. (2000) A cross-national exploration of business students' attitudes, perceptions, and tendencies toward academic dishonesty, *Journal of Education for Business*, 75, 4: 231–5.

Lynch, D.H. and Golen, S. (1992) Peer evaluation of writing in business communication classes, *Journal of Education for Business*, 68, 1, 44–8.

Lyons, P.R. (1989) Assessing classroom participation, *College Teaching*, 37: 36–8.

MacAlpine, J.M.K. (1999) Improving and encouraging peer assessment of student presentations, *Assessment and Evaluation in Higher Education*, 24, 1: 15–25.

MacDonald, J. (2000) Innovative assessment for networked communities, in *Improving Students Learning Strategically*, Proceedings of the 8th ISL Conference, UMIST, September (pp. 9–17).

MacDonald, J. (2001) Exploiting online interactivity to enhance assignment development and feedback in distance education, *Open Learning*, 16, 2: 179–89.

MacDonald, J. (2003) Assessing online collaborative learning: process and product, *Computers and Education*, 40: 377–91.

MacDonald, J., Mason, R. and Heap, N. (1999) Refining assessment for resource based learning, *Assessment and Evaluation in Higher Education*, 24, 3: 345–54.

McDowell, L. (1995) The impact of innovative assessment on student learning, *Innovations in Education and Training International*, 32, 4, 302–13.

McDowell, L. and Brown, S. (2001) Assessing students: cheating and plagiarism, ILTHE Members' Resource area, 9 pp. (accessed 26.07.01).

McDowell, L. and Sambell, K. (1999) The experience of innovative assessment: student perspectives, in S. Brown and A. Glasner (Eds) *Assessment Matters in*

Higher Education: Choosing and Using Diverse Approaches, Buckingham and Philadelphia, PA: The Society for Research into Higher Education and Open University Press (Chapter 6, pp. 71–82).

McLaughlin, J. (2001) A cheap device for a weak premise, *WebNet Journal*, January–March, 58, 27.

MacLeod, L. and Falchikov, N. (1997) Student development through structured voluntary work in the community, paper presented at the Conference on the student experience in the 1990s, Napier University, Edinburgh.

McMartin, F., McKenna, A. and Youssefi, K. (2000) Scenario assignments as assessment tools for undergraduate engineering education, *IEEE Transactions on Education*, 43, 2: 111–19.

McNamara, M.J. and Deane, D. (1995) Self-assessment activities: toward language autonomy in language learning, *TESOL Journal*, 5, 1: 17–21.

Magin, D. (1993) Should student peer ratings be used as part of summative assessment? *Higher Education Research and Development*, 16: 537–42.

Magin, D. (2001a) A novel technique for comparing the reliability of multiple peer assessments with that of single teacher assessments of group process work, *Assessment and Evaluation in Higher Education*, 26, 2: 139–52.

Magin, D. (2001b) Reciprocity as a source of bias in multiple peer assessment of group work, *Studies in Higher Education*, 26, 1: 53–63.

Magin, D.J. and Helmore, P. (1999) The skills that matter: criteria used by teaching staff in assessing engineering students' oral presentations, Engineering Faculty, University of New South Wales.

Magin, D.J. and Helmore, P. (2001) Providing written feedback on students' oral presentations: an analysis, Proceedings 12th Australasian Conference on Engineering Education (AAEE), Queensland University of Technology, Brisbane (pp. 409–14).

Magin, D.J. and Reizes, J.A. (1995) Assessing oral communication skills in large engineering classes: an investigation of peer assessment techniques, paper presented at the International UNESCO Conference of Engineering Education. International UNESCO Conference of Engineering Education, Moscow.

Magin, D., Helmore, P. and Baker, J. (2001) Assessing students' oral communication skills – which skills? Proceedings of the 4th UICEE Annual Conference on Engineering Education, Bangkok, 7–10 February (pp. 237–42).

Manning, B.H. and Payne, B.D. (1984) Student teacher personality as a variable in teacher education, *Teacher Educator*, 20.

Mansell, J. (1986) Records of achievement and profiles in further education, in P. Broadfoot (Ed.) *Profiles and Records of Achievement. A Review of Issues and Practice*, London and New York: Holt, Rinehart and Winston.

Marcoulides, G.A. and Simkin, M.G. (1997) Evaluating Student Papers, *Journal of Education for Business*, 67: 80–3.

Maricopa Center for Learning and Instruction, Faculty in Progress Program (Maricopa FIPP, 2003–04) http://www.mcli.dist.maricopa.edu/fipp/contract.php (accessed 14.10.03).

Marshall, I. and Mill, M. (1993) Using learning contracts to enhance the quality of work-based learning, Ch. 24 in M. Shaw and E. Roper (Eds) *Aspects of Educational and Training Technology, volume XXVI Quality in education and training*, pp. 144–8.

Mathews, B.P. (1994) Assessing individual contributions: experience of peer evaluation in major group projects, *British Journal of Educational Technology*, 25, 1: 19–28.

Mathews, C.O. (1999) The honor system, *Journal of Higher Education*, 70, 5: 504 (accessed electronically 04.10.01).

Megarry, J. (1978) Retrospect and prospect, in R. McAleese (Ed.) *Perspectives on Academic Gaming and Simulation 3: Training and Professional Education*, London: Kogan Page.

Mello, J.A. (1993) Improving individual member accountability in small work group settings, *Journal of Management Education*, 17, 2: 253–9.

Melvin, K.B. and Lord, A.T. (1995) The Prof/Peer method of evaluating class participation: interdisciplinary generality, *College Student Journal*, 29: 258–63.

Mentkowski, M. and associates (2000) *Learning that Lasts. Integrating Learning, Development and Performance in College and Beyond*, San Francisco: Jossey-Bass Publishers.

Michaelson, R. (1999) Web-based tools for group learning, Proceedings of the 10th Annual CTI- Accounting Finance and Management Conference, Brighton, August, East Anglia: CTI-AFM Publications (pp. 58–64).

Miller, B. (1992) Peer and self assessment, in G. Brown and M. Pendlebury (Eds) *Assessing Active Learning, Part 2: Illustrative Examples of Core Materials*, Sheffield: CVCP Universities' Staff Development and Training Unit.

Miller, C.M.L. and Parlett, M. (1974) *Up to the Mark: A Study of the Examination Game*, London: Society for Research into Higher Education.

Miller, G.E. (1990) The assessment of clinical skills, competence/performance, *Academic Medicine*, pp. 565–9.

Miller, P.J. (2003) The effect of scoring criteria specificity on peer and self-assessment, *Assessment and Evaluation in Higher Education*, 28, 4: 383–94.

Milligan, C. (2003) TALISMAN project, Heriot-Watt University, http://www.icbl. hw.ac.uk/ltdi/cookbook/checklists/index.html#endhead (accessed 12.06.03).

Mogey, N., (2003) Coordinator, LTDI, Heriot-Watt University, http://www.icbl. hw.ac.uk/ltdi/cookbook/info_likert_scale/ (accessed 12.06.03).

Montgomery, B.M. (1986) An interactionist analysis of small group peer assessment, *Small Group Behavior*, 17, 1: 19–37.

Mooney, G.A., Bligh, J.G. and Leinster, S.J. (1998) Some techniques for computer-based assessment in medical education, *Medical Teacher*, 20, 6: 560–6.

Moreland, R., Miller, J. and Laucka, F. (1981) Academic achievement and self-evaluation of academic performance, *Journal of Educational Psychology* 73, 3: 335–44.

Morgan, C. and O'Reilly, M. (1999) *Assessing Open and Distance Learners*, London and Sterling, VA: Kogan Page.

Morton, J.B. and Macbeth, W.A.A.G. (1977) Correlations between staff, peer, and self assessments of fourth-year students in surgery, *Medical Education*, 11, 3: 167–70.

Moss, P. A. (1994) Can there be validity without reliability? *Educational Researcher*, 23, 2: 5–12.

Mowl, G. and Pain, R. (1995) Using self and peer assessment to improve students' essay writing: a case study from geography, *IETI*, 32, 4: 324–35.

Muir, S.P. and Tracy, D.M. (1999) Collaborative essay testing, *College Teaching*, 47, 1: 33 (accessed through the Internet, 04.10.01).

Mwamwenda, T.S. and Monyooe, L.A. (2000) Cheating among University of Transkei students, *Psychological Reports*, 87, 1: 148–50.

Newkirk, T. (1984) Direction and misdirection in peer response, *College Composition and Communication*, 35, 3: 301–11.

Newmann, F.M. and Archbald, D.A. (1992) The nature of authentic academic achievement, in H. Berlak, F.M. Newmann, E. Adams, D.A. Archibald, T. Burgess, J. Raven and T.A. Romberg (Eds) *Toward a New Science of Educational Testing and Assessment*, Albany, NY: State University of New York Press.

Newstead, S.E. and Dennis, I. (1990) Blind marking and sex bias in student assessment, *Assessment and Evaluation in Higher Education*, 15: 132–9.

Newstead, S.E. and Dennis, I. (1994) Examiners examined: the reliability of exam marking in psychology, *The Psychologist*, 7, 5: 216–19.

Newstead, S.E., Franklyn-Stokes, A. and Armstead, P. (1996) Individual differences in student cheating, *Journal of Educational Psychology*, 87, 2: 229–41.

Nevo, D. (1995) *School-based Evaluation: a Dialogue for School Improvement*, Oxford, New York and Tokyo: Pergamon and Elsevier Science Ltd.

Ney, J.W. (1991) Collaborative learning in university grammar classes, *Innovative Higher Education*, 15, 2: 153–65.

Ngu, A.H.H., Shepherd, J. and Magin, D. (1995) Engineering the 'Peers' system: the development of a computer-assisted approach to peer assessment, *Research and Development in Higher Education*, 18: 582–7.

Norton, L.S. and Brunas-Wagstaff, J. (2000) Students' perceptions of the fairness of assessment, paper given at The Institute for Learning and Teaching in Higher Education Annual 2000, College of Ripon and York St John, 27–9 June.

Norton, L.S. and Norton, J.C.W. (2001) *Essay Feedback: How Can it Help Students Improve their Academic Writing?* 1st International Conference of the European Association for the Teaching of Academic Writing across Europe (EATAW), Groningen, 18–20 June.

Norton, L.S., Dickins, T.E. and McLaughlin Cook, N. (1996) 'Rules of the game' in essay writing, *Psychology Teaching Review*, 5, 1: 1–13.

Norton, L.S., Brunas-Wagstaff, J. and Lockley, S. (1999) Learning outcomes in the traditional coursework essay: do students and tutors agree?, Chapter 21 in C. Rust (Ed.) *Improving Student Learning: Improving Students Learning Outcomes*, Proceedings of the 1998 6th International Symposium, Oxford: The Oxford Centre for Staff and Learning Development, pp. 240–8.

Norton, L.S., Tilley, A.J., Newstead, S.E. and Franklyn-Stokes, A. (2001) The pressures of assessment in undergraduate courses and their effect on student behaviours, *Assessment and Evaluation in Higher Education*, 26, 3: 269–84.

NTU (2003) Northern Territory University Faculty of Education, Health and Science, School of Education, Australia, Guidelines http://www.ntu.edu.au/faculties/site/schools/education/practicum/Attachments/Assessment.pdf (accessed 29.10.03).

Obah, T.Y. (1993) Learning from others in the ESL writing class, *English Quarterly*, 25, 1: 8–13.

O'Donovan, B., Price, M. and Rust, C. (2000) The student experience of criterion-referenced assessment (through the introduction of a common criteria assessment grid), *Innovations in Education and Training International*, 38, 1: 74–85.

Oldfield, K.A. and MacAlpine, M.K. (1995) Peer and self-assessment at tertiary level – an experimental report, *Assessment and Evaluation in Higher Education*, 20, 1: 125–31.

Oliver, R. and Omari, A. (1999) Using online technologies to support problem based learning: learners' responses and perceptions, *Australian Journal of Educational Technology*, 15, 1, 14pp. (accessed electronically, 31.07.01).

Oltmanns, T.F., Turkheimer, E. and Strauss, M.E. (1998) Peer assessment of personality traits and pathology in female college students, *Assessment*, 5, 1: 53–65.

Orpen, C. (1982) Student versus lecturer assessment of learning: a research note. *Higher Education*, 11: 576–2.

Orsmond, P., Merry, S. and Reiling, K. (1996) The importance of marking criteria in the use of peer assessment, *Assessment and Evaluation in Higher Education*, 21, 3: 239–50.

Orsmond, P., Merry, S. and Reiling, K. (2000) The use of student derived marking criteria in peer and self-assessment, *Assessment and Evaluation in Higher Education*, 25, 1: 23–38.

Pain, H., Bull, S. and Brna, P. (1996) A student model 'for its own sake', Proceedings of the European Conference on Artificial Intelligence in Education, pp. 191–8, Lisbon: Edicoes Colibri. http://cbl.leeds.ac.uk/~paul/ (accessed 17.06.03).

Pain, R. and Mowl, G. (1996) Improving geography essay writing using innovative assessment, *Journal of Geography in Higher Education*, 20, 1: 19–31.

Pangaro, L.N. (2000) Investing in descriptive evaluation: a vision for the future of assessment, *Medical Teacher*, 22, 5: 468–81.

Pearson, P.D., Vyas, S., Sensale, L.M. and Kim, Y. (2001) Making our way through the assessment and accountability maze. Where do we go now? *The Clearing House*, 74, 4: 175–82.

Pease, D. (1975) Comparing faculty and school supervisor ratings for educational students, *College Student Journal*, 9, 1: 91–4.

Pemberton, M.A. (1992) Threshold of desperation: winning the fight against term paper mills, *Writing Instructor*, 11, 3: 143–52.

Penny, A.J. and Grover, C. (1996) An analysis of student grade expectations and marker consistency, *Assessment and Evaluation in Higher Education*, 21, 2: 173–83.

Percival, F. (1978) Evaluation procedures for simulating gaming exercises, in R. McAleese (Ed.) *Perspectives on Academic Gaming and Simulation 3: Training and Professional Education*, London: Kogan Page.

Poltorak, Y. (1995) Cheating behavior among students of four Moscow Universities, *Higher Education*, 30, 2: 225–46.

Pond, K., Ul-Haq, R. and Wade, W. (1995) Peer review: a precursor to peer assessment, *Innovations in Education and Training International*, 32, 4: 314–23.

Powell, B.J., Rice, B.H. and Leonard, L.A. (1987) The use of videotapes in treatment plan presentation seminars, *Journal of Dental Education*, 51, 12: 720–22.

Prestwich, M. (2001) Days of judgement set the course of years, http://www.dur.ac.uk/Alumni/pubs/d1/df13/rae.htm

PREVENTION (2003) (Extract from *Indiana University's Writing Tutorial Services*, accessed 05.03.03) http://www.indiana.edu/~wts/wts/plagiarism.html

Price, J. and Cutler, H. (1995) The development of skills through peer-assessment, in A. Edwards and P. Knight, (Eds) *Assessing Competence in Higher Education*,

London: Kogan Page in association with the Staff and Educational Development Association (Chapter 10, pp. 150–9).

Pullen, R., Ortloff, V., Casey, S. and Payne, J.B. (2000) Analysis of academic misconduct using unobtrusive research: a study of discarded cheat sheets, *College Student Journal*, 34, Dec: 616–25.

Purcell, J. (2001) National Vocational Qualifications and competence-based assessments for technicians – from sound principles to dogma, *Education + Training*, 43, 1: 30–9.

Purchase, H.C. (2000) Learning about interface design through peer assessment, *Assessment and Evaluation in Higher Education*, 25, 4: 341–52.

Quality Assurance Agency for Higher Education (QAA) (2000) Code of practice for the assurance of academic quality and standards in higher education, Section 6: assessment of students.

Race, P. (2002) Why fix assessment? ILTHE discussion list (accessed 15.03.02).

Radnor, H. and Shaw, K. (1995) Developing a collaborative approach to moderation, in H. Torrance, *Evaluating Authentic Assessment*, Buckingham and Philadelphia: Open University Press.

Rafiq, Y. and Fullerton, H. (1996) Peer assessment of group projects in civil engineering, *Assessment and Evaluation in Higher Education*, 21.1: 69–81.

Ramaprasad, A. (1983) On the definition of feedback, *Behavioral Science*, 28: 4–13.

Ramsden, P. (1997) The context of learning in academic departments, in F. Marton, D. Hounsell and N. Entwistle (Eds) *The Experience of Learning*, Edinburgh: Scottish Academic Press.

Reynolds, M. and Trehan, K. (2000) Assessment: a critical perspective, *Studies in Higher Education*, 25, 3: 267–78.

Rezler, A.G. (1989) Self-assessment in problem-based groups, *Medical Teacher*, 11, 2: 151–6.

Ritter, L. (1997) An educreational approach to the teaching of history in an Australian College of Advanced Education, in P. Ritter (Ed.) *Educreation and Feedback: Education for Creation, Growth and Change* (pp. 391–410) (Ed.) Oxford: Pergamon Press.

Roach, P. (1999) Using peer assessment and self-assessment for the first time, in S. Brown and A. Glasner (Eds) *Assessment Matters in Higher Education: Choosing and Using Diverse Approaches*, Buckingham and Philadelphia, PA: The Society for Research into Higher Education and Open University Press (Chapter 16, pp. 191–201).

Rogers, C.R. (1969) *Freedom to Learn*, Columbus, OH: Charles E Merrill Publishing Company.

Roig, M. (1999) When college students' attempts at paraphrasing become instances of potential plagiarism, *Psychological Reports*, 84, 3: 973.

Roig, M. and Bellow, C. (1994) Attitudes toward cheating of self and others by college students and professors, *The Psychological Record*, 44, 1: 3–13.

Rorty, R. (1989) *Contingency, Irony and Solidarity*, Cambridge: Cambridge University Press.

Rosbottom, J. and Topp, R. (1993/94) Peer assessment of programming skills, *Monitor*, 4, 124–9.

Rowntree, D. (1987) *Assessing Students: How Shall we Know Them?* (2nd edition), London: Kogan Page.

Rushton, C., Ramsey, P. and Rada, R. (1993) Peer assessment in a collaborative hypermedia environment: a case study, *Journal of Computer-Based Instruction*, 20, 3: 73–80.

Safoutin, M.J., Atman, C.J., Adams, R., Rutar, T., Kramlich, J.C. and Fridley, J.L. (2000) A design attribute framework for course planning and learning assessment, *IEEE Transactions on Education*, 43, 2: 188–99.

Sambell, K. and McDowell, L. (1998) The construction of the hidden curriculum: messages and meanings in the assessment of student learning, *Assessment and Evaluation in Higher Education*, 23, 4: 391–402.

Saphe (Self-Assessment in Professional and Higher Education) web site (1999, accessed 11.6.03) http://www.ukcle.ac.uk/directions/issue1/saphe.html

Sarros, J.C. and Densten, I.L. (1989) Undergraduate student stress and coping strategies, *Higher Education Research and Development*, 8, 1: 47–57.

Scott, J.B. and Watson, A.P. (1992) Towards practical peer marking in undergraduate engineering assessment, Proceeding Australasian Association for Engineering Education 4th annual conference Brisbane (pp. 512–16).

Scouller, K.M. (1998) The influence of assessment method on student's learning approaches: multiple choice question examination versus assignment essay, *Higher Education*, 35: 453–72.

Segers, M.S.R. (1996) Assessment in a problem-based economics course, in M. Birenbaum and F.J.R.C. Dochy (Eds) *Alternatives in Assessment of Achievements, Learning Processes and Prior Knowledge*, Boston, Dordrecht and London: Kluwer Academic Publishers (pp. 201–24).

Serafini, F. (2000) Three paradigms of assessment: measurement, procedure, and enquiry, *The Reading Teacher*, Dec., 54, i4, 384- (accessed electronically, 11.09.01).

Sensi, S., Pace-Palitti, V., Merlitti, D. and Guagnano, M.T. (2000) Impact of different scoring methods on the clinical skills assessment of internal medicine students, *Medical Teacher*, 22, 6: 601–3.

Shaw, M. and Roper, E. (Eds) (1993) *Aspects of Educational and Training Technology, Volume XXVI, Quality in Education and Training*, London and New Jersey: Kogan Page and Nichols Publishing Company.

Shermis, M.D., Mzumara, H.R., Olson, J. and Harrington, S. (2001) On-line grading of student essays: PEG goes on the World Wide Web, *Assessment and Evaluation in Higher Education*, 26, 3: 247–59.

Shortt, K. (2002) The benefits of negotiating student versus staff control over learning, *Psychology Teaching Review*, 10, 1: 61–7.

Siders, J.A. (1983) Instructor, self and peer review: a formative evaluation triad, *College Student Journal*, 17, 2: 141–4.

Simpson, M. and Tuson, J. (1995) *Using Observations in Small-Scale Research*, Edinburgh: Scottish Council for Research in Education.

Sitthiworachart, J. and Joy, M. (2003) Web-based peer assessment in learning computer programming, Department of Computer Science, University of Warwick, e-mail: jirarat@dcs.warwick.ac.uk

Sivan, A. (2000) The implementation of peer assessment: an action research approach, *Assessment in Education*, 7, 2: 193–213.

Slavin, R.E. (1985) An introduction to cooperative learning research, in R. Slavin, S. Sharan, S. Kagan, R. Herz-Lazarowitz, C. Webb, and R. Schmuck (Eds) *Learning to Cooperate, Cooperating to Learn*, New York and London: Plenum Press.

Sluijsmans, D., Dochy, F.J.R.C. and Moerkerke, G. (1999) Creating a learning environment by using self-, peer- and co-assessment, *Learning Environments Research*, 1: 293–319.

Sluijsmans, D.M.A., Moerkerke, G., van Merriënboer, J.G. and Dochy, F.J.R.C. (2001) Peer assessment in problem based learning, *Studies in Educational Evaluation*, 27: 153–73.

Snyder, B.R. (1971) *The Hidden Curriculum*, Cambridge, MA: MIT Press.

Srole, L. (1956) Social integration and certain corollaries: an exploratory study, *American Social Review*, December, 21: 709–16.

Stanier, L. (1997) Peer assessment and group work as vehicles for student empowerment: a module evaluation, *Journal of Geography in Higher Education*, 21, 1: 95–8.

Stefani, L.A.J. (1992) Comparison of collaborative, self, peer and tutor assessment in a biochemical practical, *Biochemical Education*, 20, 3: 148–51.

Stefani, L.A.J. (1994) Peer, self and tutor assessment: relative reliabilities, *Studies in Higher Education*, 19, 1: 69–75.

Stefani, L.A.J. (1998) Assessment in partnership with learners, *Assessment and Evaluation in Higher Education*, 23, 4: 339–50.

Stefani, L.A.J., Tariq, V.-N., Heylings, D.J.A. and Butcher, A.C. (1997) A comparison of tutor and student conceptions of undergraduate research project work, *Assessment and Evaluation in Higher Education*, 22, 3: 271–88.

Stiggins, R.J. (1987) Design and development of performance assessments, *Educational Measurement: Issues and Practice*, 6, 3: 33–42.

Storch, E.A. and Storch, J.B. (2001) Organisational, nonorganisational, and intrinsic religiosity and academic dishonesty, *Psychological Reports*, 88, 2: 548–52.

Storch, E.A. and Storch, J.B. (2002) Fraternities, sororities, and academic dishonesty, *College Student Journal*, June, 36, 4 pp (accessed through FindArticles.com, located at http://www.findarticles.com).

Strachan, I.B. and Wilcox, S. (1996) Peer and self assessment of group work: developing an effective response to increased enrolment in a third-year course in microclimatology, *Journal of Geography in Higher Education*, 20, 3: 343–53.

Straw, J. (2000) Keep your eyes off the screen: online cheating and what can we do about it, *Academic Exchange*, Fall, 21–5.

Sullivan, M.E., Hitchcoch, M.A. and Dunnington, G.L. (1999) Peer and self-assessment during problem-based tutorials, *The American Journal of Surgery*, 177: 266–9.

Surtees, P. *et al.* (2000) Student mental health, use of services and academic attainment: a report to the Review Committee of the University of Cambridge Counselling Service, March. through http://www.brookes.ac.uk/student/services/osmhn/researchers/review.html (accessed 05.03.03).

Swanson, D., Case, S. and van der Vleuten, C. (1991) Strategies for student assessment, in D. Boud and G. Feletti (Eds) *The Challenge of Problem Based Learning*, London: Kogan Page.

Swanson, D.B., Norman, G.R. and Linn, R.L. (1995) Performance-based assessment: lesson from the health professionals, *Educational Researcher*, 24, 5: 5–11.

Syder, C.A. and Shore, B.M. (2001) Science fairs: what are the sources of help for students and how prevalent is cheating? *School Science and Mathematics*, 101, 4: 206–20.

Tait, H. and Godfrey, H. (1998) Defining and assessing competence in generic skills, paper delivered at the 3rd Northumberland Assessment Conference, University of Northumbria, 2–4 September.

Tait, J. and Knight, P. (1994) Assessment and continuous quality improvement: a North American case study, *Innovations in Education and Training International*, 32, 4: 356–61.

Tamir, P. (1996) Science assessment, in M. Birenbaum and F.J.R.C. Dochy (Eds) *Alternatives in Assessment of Achievements, Learning Processes and Prior Knowledge*, Boston, Dordrecht and London: Kluwer Academic Publishers (pp. 93–129).

Tankersley, K.C. (1997) Academic integrity from a student's perspective, *Journal of Dental Education*, 61, 8: 692–3.

Taras, M. (1999) Student self-assessment as a means of promoting students autonomy and independence, in M. Taras (Ed.) *Innovations in learning and teaching: Teaching Fellowships at the University of Sunderland*, Sunderland: University of Sunderland Press (pp. 61–83).

Tariq, V.N., Stefani, L.A.J., Butcher, A.C. and Heylings, D.J.A. (1998) Developing a new approach to the assessment of project work, *Assessment and Evaluation in Higher Education*, 23, 3: 221–40.

ten Cate, Th.J. and De Haes, J.C.J.M. (2000) Summative assessment of medical students in the affective domain, *Medical Teacher*, 22, 1: 40–3.

Todd, Z. (2002) 'Nice legs – shame about the teaching', *The Times Higher*, February 1: 21.

Topping, K.J. (1998) Peer assessment between students in colleges and universities, *Review of Educational Research*, 68, 3: 249–76.

Topping, K.J., Smith, E.F., Swanson, I. and Elliot, A. (2000) Formative peer assessment of academic writing between postgraduate students, *Assessment and Evaluation in Higher Education*, 25, 2: 149–66.

Torrance, H. (Ed.) (1995a) *Evaluating Authentic Assessment: Problems and Possibilities in New Approaches to Assessment*, Buckingham and Philadelphia: Open University Press.

Torrance, H. (1995b) Teacher involvement in new approaches to assessment, in H. Torrance (Ed.) *Evaluating Authentic Assessment: Problems and Possibilities in New Approaches to Assessment*, Buckingham and Philadelphia: Open University Press.

Trevitt, C. and Pettigrove, M. (1995) Towards autonomous criterion-referenced assessment and self-assessment: a case study, paper presented at the European Association for Research on Learning and Instruction (EARLI) electronic conference (accessed through EARLI-AE discussion list).

Tsai, C.-C., Lin, S.S.J. and Yuan, S.-M. (2002) Developing science activities through a networked peer assessment system, *Computers and Education*, 38, 241–52.

Tsai, C.-C., Lui, E.Z.-F., Lin, S.S.J. and Yuan, S.-M. (2001) A networked peer assessment system based on a Vee heuristic, *Innovations in Education and Teaching International*, 38, 3: 220–30.

University of Dundee (2003) Guidelines to the use of automatic self peer assessment program, Centre for Learning and Teaching, http://www.srip.dundee.ac.uk/learning/leu/ilt/self_instruct.htm (accessed 01.05.03).

University of Western Australia (2001) Issues of teaching and learning. Assessing group assignments http://www.csd.uwa,edu.au/newsletter/issue0398/group_assignments.html

Uzzell, D. (2000) Ethnographic and action research, in G.M. Breakwell, S. Hammond and C. Fife-Schaw (Eds) *Research Methods in Psychology* (2nd Edition), London, Thousand Oaks, CA and New Delhi: Sage Publications.

van Daalen, M. (1999) Test usefulness in alternative assessment, *Dialog on Language Instruction*, 13, 1&2: 1–26.

van der Vleuten, C.P.M., Scherpbier, A.J.J.A., Dolmans, D.H.J.M., Schuwirth, L.W.T., Verwijnen, G.M. and Wolfhagen, H.A.P. (2000) Clerkship assessment assessed, *Medical Teacher*, 22, 6: 592–600.

van Duzer, E. and McMartin, F. (2000) Methods to improve validity and sensitivity of a self/peer assessment instrument, *IEEE Transactions on Education*, 43, 2: 153–8.

Walker, J. (1998) Student plagiarism in universities: what are we doing about it? *Higher Education Research and Development*, 17, 1: 89–106.

Weaver, R.L. and Cotrell, H.W. (1986) Peer evaluation: a case study, *Innovative Higher Education* 11, 1: 25–39.

Webb, N.M. (1995) Group collaboration in assessment: multiple objectives, processes, and outcomes, *Educational Evaluation and Policy Analysis*, 17, 2: 239–61.

Webb, W.B. (1955) Self-evaluations, group evaluations and objective measures, *Journal of Consulting Psychology*, 19, 3: 210–12.

Wilhoit, S. (1994) Helping students avoid plagiarism, *College Teaching*, 42, 4: 161–4.

Wiliam, D. and Black, P. (1996) Meanings and consequences: a basis for distinguishing formative and summative functions of assessment? *British Educational Research Journal*, 22, 5: 527–48.

Williams, E. (1992) Student attitudes towards approaches to learning and assessment, *Assessment and Evaluation in Higher Education*, 17, 1: 45–58.

Williams, J. (1995) Using peer assessment to enhance professional capability, in M. Yorke (Ed.) *Assessing Capability in Degree and Diploma Programmes*, Vol. 1, Liverpool: Centre for Higher Education Development, Liverpool: John Moores University.

Winter, R. (1995) The assessment of professional competencies: the importance of general criteria', in A. Edwards and P. Knight, (Eds) *Assessing competence in higher education*, London: Kogan Page in association with the Staff and Educational Development Association.

Wolf, A. (1995) Authentic assessments in a competitive sector: institutional prerequisites and cautionary tales, in H. Torrance (Ed.) *Evaluating Authentic Assessment: Problems and Possibilities in New Approaches to Assessment*, Buckingham and Philadelphia: Open University Press.

Wolf, D., Bixby, J., Glenn, J. III and Gardner, H. (1991) To use their minds well: investigating new forms of student assessment, *Review of Research in Education*, 17, 31–73.

Woodfield, R. and Earl-Novell, S. (2002) Gender and performance in HE: the impact of mode of assessment, ILT members' resources, February.

Woodward, H. (1998) Reflective journals and portfolios: learning through assessment, *Assessment and Evaluation in Higher Education*, 23, 4: 415–23.

Young, G. (1999) Using portfolios for assessment in teacher preparation and health sciences in S. Brown and A. Glasner (Eds) *Assessment Matters in Higher Education: Choosing and Using Diverse approaches*, Buckingham and Philadelphia,

PA: The Society for Research into Higher Education and Open University Press (Chapter 10, pp. 121–31).

Zakrzewski, S. and Bull, J. (1998) The mass implementation and evaluation of computer-based assessments, *Assessment and Evaluation in Higher Education*, 23, 2: 141–52.

Zoller, U. and Ben-Chaim, D. (1997) Student self-assessment in HOCS science examinations: is it compatible with that of teachers? paper presented at the 7th European Association for Research on Learning and Instruction (EARLI) conference, Athens.

Author index

Subject index

ability effects 207
academic dishonesty 247; fraternity and sorority membership 47; and individual differences 50
academic products 193
accountability 62; external 63; 'hyperaccountability' 63
Accreditation and Support for Specified Expertise and Training (ASSET) 74
action research 7, 251–2
age effects 207; on satisfaction levels 207; on test anxiety 207; on views about purposes of assessment 207
alienation 37
alternative assessment 63; activities 81; characteristics 82
Alverno College 15, 62, 69, 79
American Association for Higher Education (AAHE) 24, 69; principles of good practice 69
Anglia Polytechnic 74
anxiety 161
assessment *see also* evaluation, grading; academic products 139–40; changing definitions 59; collaborative 125, 126; of competency 147; continuous 7, 22; convergent 7; criterion referenced 6; divergent 7; external 7; foci 8, 23; formative 3, 4, 83; idiographic 7; idiosyncratic strategies 159; internal 7; modes 4; nomothetic 7; obtrusive 8; performance in academic settings 140; power relations in 35; of process 6; of product 6; of

professional practice 140–1; purposes 1–5, 200; qualitative 4, 6; quantitative 4, 6; rating scales 141; sources 27; summative 3, 4, 83, 124; terminal 7, 22; timing of 22; traditional 32; unobtrusive 8; users/stakeholders 4
assessment and accountability 62
assessment as enquiry 59, 62, 66; activities 81; variants 68
assessment involving students 83, 88, 108–11; benefits 84, 85, 88, 102, 105, 112, 114–16; feedback 94, 101, 107; investigating the process 94, 100, 102, 103; pressures 85, 92, 105, 107; problems 94, 100; skills acquisition and development 91, 96, 100, 102, 105; transferring power 94, 100, 106, 107
assessment as learning, key features 69
assessment as measurement 32, 59, 60, 65; characteristics 61; limitations of 32
assessment paradigms 59; characteristics 65; problems 67
assessment, peer 151–76; cultural differences 159; *see also* peer assessment
assessment as procedure 59, 60, 65
assessment as quality control 60, 63, 66, 68
Assessment Strategies in Scottish Higher Education (ASSHE) 117, 139
Association of Accounting Technicians (AAT) 75